Antiquity and Social Reform

Antiquity and Social Reform:
Religious Experience in the Unification
Church, Feminist Wicca and Nation of Yahweh

By

Dawn L. Hutchinson

CAMBRIDGE
SCHOLARS
P U B L I S H I N G

Antiquity and Social Reform:
Religious Experience in the Unification Church, Feminist Wicca and Nation of Yahweh,
by Dawn L. Hutchinson

This book first published 2010

Cambridge Scholars Publishing

12 Back Chapman Street, Newcastle upon Tyne, NE6 2XX, UK

British Library Cataloguing in Publication Data
A catalogue record for this book is available from the British Library

ISBN (10): 1-4438-2287-6, ISBN (13): 978-1-4438-2287-9

This manuscript is dedicated to my husband Jesse
and daughter Piper.

TABLE OF CONTENTS

ACKNOWLEDGEMENTS

This project began as a dissertation for the Department of Religion at the Florida State University. Thus, I would like to acknowledge the guidance of my dissertation committee: John Corrigan, Amy Koehlinger, Amanda Porterfield, and Irene Padavic. Without John Corrigan's careful tutelage, I would not have been able to complete this project. Likewise, the faculty of the Department of Religion at Florida State University prepared me for this task. In addition, James Strange and Dell deChant at the University of South Florida influenced the way that I approach primary texts and religious people as subjects. I would also like to thank the faculty of the Philosophy and Religious Studies Department at Christopher Newport University, whose support and encouragement were instrumental for my progress. Finally, I would be remiss if I did not acknowledge the help of the library staff of the American Religions Collection, Department of Special Collections, at the Donald C. Davidson Library, University of California, Santa Barbara. In addition to donating the materials I perused there, J. Gordon Melton also was able to guide some aspects of my research.

ABSTRACT

Although religious innovation in America historically has been the norm rather than the exception, mainstream Americans have often viewed new religious movements with suspicion and occasionally with outright alarm. The question motivating many studies of new religious movements has been "why would someone join these religions?" In this book, I offer at least one answer to this often repeated query. I argue that followers of new religious movements in the 1960s-1980s, specifically the Unification Church, Feminist Wicca and the Nation of Yahweh, considered these religions to be legitimate because they offered members a personal religious experience, a connection to an ancient tradition, and agency in improving their world. Utilizing an historical approach, I consider the conversion narratives of adherents and primary literature of the formative years of these movements, which demonstrate that the religious experiences of the adherents and a resonance with the goals of these religions propelled individuals into social action.

INTRODUCTION

Although religious innovation in America historically has been the norm rather than the exception, mainstream Americans have often viewed new religious movements with suspicion and occasionally with outright alarm. Leaders in established religions, the media, and sometimes religion scholars have warned that these "alternative" religions are deviant and perhaps even dangerous for Americans to join. In this book, I argue that followers of the Unification Church, Feminist Wicca and the Nation of Yahweh considered these religions to be legitimate because they offered members a personal religious experience, a connection to an ancient tradition, and agency in improving their world. These new religions developed in the 1960s through the early 1980s and offered their potential members a vision of a more inclusive, more morally responsible American society during a time of cultural upheaval and uncertainty. Previous studies of these new religious movements have overlooked their complexity, their humanness, and their conceptual organization of the world.

The new religious movements described in the following text were surrounded by social controversy in various ways. For instance, many Americans in the 1960s and 1970s believed that the Unification Church brainwashed its young members, forcing them to leave their families and disassociate from the ones they loved. The Reverend Sun Myung Moon, the founder of the Unification Church, spent time in prison for tax evasion, and the media has condemned the movement for its financial success for many years. American society also criticized Feminist Wicca, with its links to the feminist movement, for its woman-centered ideology. Many Americans considered Feminist Wiccans to be "man-haters" intent on using magic to emasculate American power structures. In addition, Feminist Wicca's links to Wicca and witchcraft left it open to charges of devil worship by Christians misunderstanding Wicca's ideology. Very few people have focused on the ideology of the Nation of Yahweh, since the media was understandably more interested in its criminal activities. Yahweh ben Yahweh, the founder of the Nation of Yahweh, and seventeen of his followers, were convicted on charges of racketeering in Miami, Florida in the 1980s. The charges included firebombing a Miami neighborhood, conspiracy to commit murder, and a host of other violent crimes. While I do not wish to condone or ignore the controversial aspects of these new religious movements, I argue here that members of these religions were acting in accord with religious ideologies understood in the context of their religious experiences. Adherents believed that their actions were part of a larger plan to bring about a better America.

The Unification Church, Feminist Wicca and the Nation of Yahweh appealed to people who considered themselves outsiders in American society. They were not outsiders by choice; they yearned to be a part of American society without sacrificing their uniqueness. They would have rejected the premise of Israel Zangwill's World War I play *The Melting Pot,* which invoked the sentimental notion that different races, ethnicities and religious beliefs combined in America to make something new.[1] The young Americans drawn to these new religious movements thought that Zangwill's vision of a "land of opportunity where race, religion, and national origin should not be a barrier to social mobility"[2] was a naïve notion. Clearly, for many of them, race, religion, gender, and national origin continued to be barriers to social mobility. In addition, they did not wish for the variety of ethnic, religious, and national identities evident in America to be "melted" into a monolithic mold.[3] These idealistic people, most of them young, argued that America's praise could not be sung in a single voice. It required harmony sung in dozens of parts, the combination producing the necessarily nuanced chorus of their country's diverse culture. Each voice longed to be individually recognized, no longer overshadowed by the melody.

Many Americans discontented with what they believed was a culture obsessed with consensus sought both secular and religious solutions. Along with the "new left," the "civil rights movement," and the nascent "neo-conservative" movements in the 1960s and 1970s, emerged a smaller, but equally zealous faction hoping to change the world through their religious visions of what America could become. These optimistic believers chose to reject traditional religions in order to join new religious movements that promised to make them active agents for social change in America.

This study focuses specifically on those who embraced the ideologies of the Unification Church, Feminist Wicca, and the Nation of Yahweh in 1960s and 1970s America. Many devotees of these new religions felt disillusioned by their childhood religious traditions, considering them to be complicit in quieting their voices. While those attracted to these groups wanted personally to reconstruct American society, they felt they lacked the individual status needed to achieve change. Some felt too young. Some believed skin color or ethnicity disenfranchised them from secular power.

Many were overwhelmed at the enormity of their task, whether they worked individually or together in like-minded communities.

In these new religious movements, members found a combination of factors they believed was missing in traditional religions and certainly in secular social movements: a personal religious experience, a connection to an ancient religious tradition, and the imminent possibility of improving their world. The Unification Church, Feminist Wicca and the Nation of Yahweh promised to make the voices of their membership heard in the larger American chorus. The conversion story of Teresa, a young woman from New York who joined the Unification Church in the 1970s, bears witness to this search for a relevant religious experience:

> I am 25 years old, and have been a member [of the Unification Church] for 2½ years. I was born in Long Beach, New York, the second of five children. I attended Long Beach Catholic School for 8 years, went to Mass regularly, was a good student and have only good memories attached to my childhood years.
>
> When I was 15, our family bought a new home further out on Long Island in East Setauket. I attended a public high school and had no trouble making friends and adjusting in the new neighborhood. I did begin to realize, however, that it was becoming increasingly difficult to avoid situations where drinking, smoking, and sex weren't the main activity or topic of discussion.
>
> Later on, drugs came into the picture and it seemed as though the ideals of faith, hope, love, and strength were disappearing from the hearts of a good part of my generation. My trust in God remained, though I couldn't find the answers to many of my questions in the church, in the Bible, or reflected anywhere in the world around me. Still, I knew that the words of Jesus were true and absolute whether or not society in general or I individually chose to maintain the standard he taught and lived by.
>
> I decided to investigate what different groups and organizations were studying and doing toward improving the present situation of the world and of themselves. I, along with my mother, became part of a Catholic Charismatic group where we could feel a new awakening of spirit for the first time. It emphasized the guidance and healing that could come from total reliance on the work of the Holy Spirit in our lives. It was through this experience that my heart and mind were open at the time I met the Unification Church.
>
> Though I had many physical blessings, the moment of truth came when I realized that it was up to me to decide just how much I was willing to sacrifice to follow what I believed to be true. Frankly, I never expected that someday I might be called to devote my life to serve God HIS way, and not mine. This was the real awakening.
>
> I'm deeply grateful that I am able to participate in this movement right now, which has strengthened and cemented what basic moral values I had,

only from Reverend Moon I've learned not to compromise. I deeply
respect and admire him for his humility before God and the love he has for
mankind. Example, once again, is the best teacher.
    I also want to mention that my mother and two of my sisters are also
active members of the Unification Church as well. Truth knows no age.
Since they joined two years ago, our love has grown deeper and broader in
knowing that only through our unity can God's will on earth be understood
and accomplished.[4]

The Unification Church's call for personal sacrifice as a way to bring
about a more moral society influenced Teresa because she had been
looking for a way to improve herself while changing her world. The
Unification Church appeared to be a legitimate faith to Teresa because she
had a religious experience as part of her conversion. While earlier
involvement in a Catholic Charismatic group also gave her a "religious
awakening," the Unification Church challenged her personally to become
an agent for change. This charge inspired her to embrace a larger religious
vision.
    Following the sometimes hedonistic upheaval of the Sixties, young
people such as Teresa searched for a similarly radical, but very different
kind of revolt – a revolution that turned religious faith into a catalyst for
both personal and social change as surely as the Pill.   Part of their
transformation included the rejection of traditional religions.   Potential
participants in these new religious movements believed that "mainstream"
churches had fallen short in their efforts to recreate American society.
Moreover, future members of these alternative religions concluded that
Christianity, specifically, was not merely missing the solution, but in fact
was part of the problem. They believed that Christianity reinforced the
larger American culture's moral worldview. These young people argued
that Christianity accepted, and occasionally propagated, sexism and
racism. In that way, conventional Christianity lost legitimacy for some of
its believers, driving them to look elsewhere for spiritual grounding. Some
found the answers they sought in the emerging new religious movements.
    The Unification Church, Feminist Wicca, and the Nation of Yahweh
promised to equip members with the tools they needed to be personally
involved in remaking their world. The Unification Church offered a way to
purify the morally corrupt American society and the rest of the world
through perfected families. It pledged that individual sacrifice would
prepare the world for God's forgiveness and salvation. Feminist Wicca, on
the other hand, proposed a vision of a peaceful American society in which
women and men shared power equally. Wiccans offered ancient Goddess
religions as a model for an egalitarian society, which they believed would

end gender disparity in America. The Nation of Yahweh claimed that American blacks descended from the ancient Hebrews, the chosen people of God. Since the Nation's members professed to be the true Jews, they laid claim to their God-given right to govern themselves under His guidance. They declared that once blacks (and whites) knew the "true" identity of American blacks, American society would correct its racial inequities.

The Unification Church, Feminist Wicca, and The Nation of Yahweh not only supplied solutions to their members' problems on these fronts, they also explained the failures of traditional religions. In spiritual terms, new religious movements provided direction, meaning and power for potential members: the elements of an obtainable goal. The Unification Church explained that Christian churches had misunderstood the "true" mission of Jesus. They claimed that God sent Jesus to create the perfect human family, which would restore the relationship between God and humans. Unificationists believed that if they led perfected lives and created families who sacrificed their needs for the Church, members could help restore God's will for humanity. Wiccans insisted that the Judeo-Christian traditions failed women because these established religions offered theological validation for the oppression of women. They maintained that the Christian male deity reinforced the patriarchal order. Feminist Wiccans asserted that seekers could find solutions to these problems in the ancient goddess religions, which proclaimed women as equals and which could, in modern America, legitimize women's role in shaping not only religion, but public policy. Finally, amidst widespread racial discrimination, The Nation of Yahweh offered members a vision of a refined American social order for blacks in which power shifted in their favor. The group's leaders believed that white slave owners and others claiming Jewish descent had intentionally withheld knowledge of blacks' Hebrew identity. The Nation of Yahweh taught its members that if they reclaimed their Hebrew heritage, they would achieve a kind of parity in a white-dominated society, bringing about their desired social goals. While their approaches differed, each of these new religious movements shared a critical optimism: each offered an explanation of why traditional religions had failed, and each offered hope for an American society that would incorporate their various visions in ways that would make the nation a better place.

In addition to the grand visions of a reformed American society, new religious movements offered potential members the prospect of improvement on the individual level. In other words, everybody won. Society would improve, but so would members of these new religious movements. The Unification Church, Feminist Wicca, and the Nation of Yahweh promoted a personal relationship with their deity and a meaningful religious experience. The Unification Church offered a connection with the Christian God who had suffered, been misunderstood, and only wanted the best for his children. Feminist Wicca provided women with the goddess, a deity with whom women, who had been oppressed by the male God of patriarchal religion, could relate on a more personal level. The Nation of Yahweh claimed a fatherly black deity, the God of the ancient Hebrews, who gave black members a sense of status and entitlement.

The "religious experiences" offered by each of these religions differed and were closely tied to the personal relationship with the deity. None of these religions dictated what constituted an authentic religious experience by an individual. It could be a feeling that they were on the right path, a mystical vision, a deep emotional connection with the deity, or a feeling of belonging to the community. While I will describe some of the religious experiences in the following chapters as related by adherents, I am more interested in the response to the experience than the encounter itself. I argue here that the religious experience served to authenticate the new religious movement for persons and was a catalyst for their social action.

Although these religions professed to offer a new religious path, each of them also claimed connections with an ancient religious tradition. This lent them some authority to spread their religious views. History provided the affirmation. While they claimed to be starting something novel in the 1960s and 1970s, American new religious movements, including those discussed in this book, tended to appropriate many of their so-called "new" ideas from existing religious traditions. This connection resonated with people raised in organized religions; these links with the past (to a certain extent) endowed the new religions with legitimacy for potential adherents. Aidan Kelly, an adherent and scholar of Neo-Paganism and Wicca, accordingly observed: "All religions begin as new religions at some time and place; almost all of them proceed to claim a great antiquity for themselves as part of their foundational myth."[5]

Whether new religious movements claim roots from ancient Asian traditions such as Hinduism and Buddhism, or from Judaism, formative Christianity, Islam or Celtic traditions, most new religions adapt ancient tradition to suit contemporary worldviews. New religions of 1960s and 1970s America hoped to ground themselves in historical religions through such a process of adaptation. The Unification Church asserted that it taught the original intent of God for Christianity in their perfected families. Feminist Wicca professed that ancient goddess religions offered the answer to America's gender conflicts. The Nation of Yahweh, meanwhile, maintained that American blacks were descended from the ancient Hebrews, and therefore inherited the promises in the Hebrew Bible made to the chosen people of God.

New religious movements had many reasons to incorporate ancient religious traditions in the formation of their religious identity. The most important was to establish credibility with their potential adherents. Successfully making the case for historical connections gained the new religions a certain amount of authority for attracting potential members. Aligning themselves with ancient religious traditions accordingly became a statement of identity for these new religious groups; connecting to the past kept newcomers and outsiders from dismissing the movements as come-lately crackpots. Claiming old traditions, then refining them, meant sacredness, not sorcery. History gave the beliefs and values – whatever they were – authority. These connections placed the new religions into a familiar framework of thought—the recovery of a usable historical past—that allowed them to claim more easily a place in contemporary culture.

An Historical Approach to the study of New Religious Movements

Many religions have the goal to make their vision of the ideal world a reality. While new religious movements share this same objective, they have become widely misunderstood. Sometimes biased histories by members or outsiders cause confusion about these religions. Adherents often wrote histories about their religious movements because they wanted their religion viewed through a particular ideological lens. In addition, some scholars in the past were interested in showing how these movements deviated from "traditional" religions or how aspects of their beliefs compared to similar movements. These previous histories of new religious movements failed to take into account the religious experiences of adherents or how the teleological vision of these movements affected the practical application of their beliefs. In addition, early scholarship on new religious movements used the terms "occult," "cults," or the kinder term, "alternative" to refer to these religions, which already held negative connotations in the larger American culture. In many cases, scholars were interested in one facet of the religion without taking the cultural context into consideration. In this text, by contrast, I demonstrate that these religious movements are far more complex, visionary, and concerned with individual members than previously shown.

Often, new religions are misunderstood because their religious practices or beliefs are unfamiliar to "mainstream" America. Typically, scholars have either assumed that new religious movements indicate a social problem needing to be solved or they approach new religions as oddities needing to be defined and ennumerated.[6] Thus, in order to facilitate a conversation between members and non-members of new religious movements, much scholarship on new religious movements tends to be phenomenological. Hence, it is mostly concerned with describing the beliefs and practices of these movements. Many scholars, such as J. Gordon Melton and James Lewis, have formulated reference texts for studying new religious movements, such as Lewis' *Cults in America: a Reference Handbook*.[7] These texts give a brief historical background of the development of new religious movements, information about their religious leaders, and a description of their beliefs and practices. While immensely helpful as reference tools for scholars and students, these types of texts are descriptive, rather than analytical or explanatory.

While phenomenological approaches are important for approximating an objective perspective in the study of religions, scholars also need to examine how members of new religions comprehend their place in the world. Lorne L. Dawson, a sociologist at the University of Waterloo, contends that "new religious movements grow out of a desire to satisfy certain spiritual needs of humanity that have a reality and importance independent of our other social and psychological needs."[8] In order to understand new religious movements, Dawson explains that one must make sense of them within the context of the circumstances and perspectives of the actions of their members. With Dawson's recommendations in mind, this book is geared toward understanding the worldviews of its subjects in all of their complexity.

The unfamiliar practices and worldviews of new religious movements of the 1960s and 1970s sometimes embroiled these religions in cultural controversy. Thus, several scholars became interested in studying the reactions of the surrounding society to the beliefs and practices of these new religious movements. These scholars examined the responses of other religions, the media, and secular culture to the alternative religions they studied.[9] Jim Beckford, a British sociologist at the University of Warwick, charted the development of the "cult controversy" as a social phenomenon. In *Cult Controversies: the Societal Response to New Religious Movements*, he explains that while insights from psychology, history and religious studies are helpful in studying new religious movements, scholars must "explore the social processes whereby the interactions between humans can generate controversy."[10] Beckford believes that studying the relationships linking members to their movements, and the movements in turn to the society, allows the scholar to more easily make comparisons across space and time.[11] I take one of my leads from Beckford in writing about new religious movements in this book (additionally I place the religious movements within the historical context of their emergence).

Understanding the dialogue between new religious movements and their surrounding culture is certainly important. This conversation reveals much about the agendas of all parties involved. The discourse surrounding new religious movements affects members of the movement, their families, the media, and those engaged in traditional religions. Because new religious movements make claims that are unfamiliar to those entrenched in "mainstream" religions, controversy often surrounds these movements. Sometimes parents or the media accuse the new religions of "brainwashing" their converts. Also, because many new religions have unusual eschatological claims and some have been involved in mass suicides or political scandals, the larger American culture distrusts them.

Since the new religious movements in this study were among those surrounded by controversy, most contemporary scholars have attempted to "step back" from the contentious aspects of the study of new religions in the interests of maintaining some objectivity. Others approach new religions in a more comprehensive fashion. John A. Saliba, religious studies professor at the University of Detroit, in *Understanding New Religious Movements*, argues that scholars must attempt to comprehend these movements from the perspectives of the movements themselves.[12] Benjamin Zablocki and Thomas Robbins, both sociologists, in their text *Misunderstanding Cults: Searching for Objectivity in a Controversial Field*, call for a middle ground between "cult bashers" and "cult apologists."[13] In several incisive essays, they have commented on what makes experts disagree about cults. While I agree that objectivity is essential in comprehending religious views that vary significantly from traditional beliefs, I argue in this study that scholars must make an attempt to understand the religious motivations of the members of these movements. Thus, taking a cue from Zoblicki and Robbins, I do not intend to either "bash" new religious movements, nor "apologize" for them.

Religious beliefs can be powerful motivating factors. James Lewis worries that scholars often discount the religious experience of adherents when they research new religious movements. Lewis has authored two studies in which he offers an approach for studying new religions. In the first, entitled "The Scholarship of 'Cults' and the 'Cult' of Scholarship," Lewis notes the cultural bias of scholars against new religious

movements.[14]   He maintains that scholars try to explain how "cults"
deviate from mainstream culture, discounting any possible meaningful
religious experiences that adherents might derive from these movements.
In *Legitimating New Religions*, Lewis states that phenomenologists who
have studied new religious movements in the past have failed to consider
the meaning that the religious experience holds for members of new
religious movements. Furthermore, Lewis claims that many scholars
presume that the founders of the movements intentionally fabricate
religious phenomena.[15]   Instead of operating under these assumptions,
Lewis claims, scholars studying these religions should understand that
religious experiences can be powerful motivating factors.

I agree with Lewis that the religious experience of the members of new
religious movements needs to be at the center of investigating these
religions. This religious experience is often what endows the new religion
with authenticity for adherents. While this religious experience differs for
each person, it seems to be the factor motivating them to embrace the
religious ideologies in these new religious movements.   In order to
understand why people joined new religions in the 1960s and 1970s, it is
necessary to comprehend the particular meanings that the conversion
experience held for believers. I argue in the following pages that devotees
of new religious movements believed that their new religion could only be
successful through their individual involvement, as they conceived it
through their religious experience.

The following study is limited to the study of the Unification Church,
Feminist Wicca, and the Nation of Yahweh. Scholars have given these
movements short shrift by underestimating the significance of the
adherents' religious experiences. In the following chapters, I detail the
previous scholarship on these traditions. Each of these religions was
surrounded by controversy, somewhat blinding outsiders to the
motivations behind these movements. What has been lacking is a history
that takes into consideration the religious experience of the adherents
alongside the goals of these movements. These new religions did not
appear from a vacuum. Instead, they formed during the cultural turmoil of
1960s and 1970s America. They sought to restore order through their
religious visions of a more morally upright, inclusive nation.

The new religious movements described in this book constructed their
own group cultures, differing in certain ways from the prevailing
American culture. They wished to change beliefs and values of the larger
community. While apparently political in nature, each of the movements
chose several distinct cultural avenues, based on their religious beliefs, to
make their visions for America a reality. The Unification Church instilled

its ideas about how to purify the moral decadence in American life through small networks of families working in communities. They also became involved in academic conferences and special interest groups in order to make their vision a reality on a larger scale. Feminist Wiccans, while interested in seeing change in legislation concerning women, believed that in order for that to happen, they would need to first change how American culture perceived women. They therefore worked at the grassroots level and instilled in their members a sense of purpose and personal authority. The Nation of Yahweh drew strength from a small committed community of like-minded followers. They believed that their plans for racial equality could occur in America only if both blacks and whites understood their "true" historical identity. Thus, each group had political goals, but worked toward them through unconventional routes. A historical treatment of these religions needs to take this complexity into consideration.

The term "culture" as used in this text refers to a group's shared values, beliefs, and patterns of meaning.[16] According to Clifford Geertz, culture is a context, webs of significance humans themselves have spun, within which social events, behaviors and institutions can be intelligibly described.[17] A community's values are evident in every area of their collective lives: in governmental institutions, political movements, religious communities, educational institutions, language, art, literature, film, and music, just to name a few. America as a nation has a collective culture that reflects shared values, beliefs, and patterns of meaning. America also encompasses a variety of cultures. There are ethnic, racial, gender, and religious cultures along with professional and academic cultures, for instance. Individuals learn what to believe, who they are, and how they should behave from the different elements in the various cultures to which they belong. Culture reflects a society's collective knowledge, which in turn, molds what an individual learns and believes.[18]

The Unification Church, Feminist Wicca, and the Nation of Yahweh made historical claims informed by American culture and their own "local" religious cultures. The Unification Church, immersed in its own conservative culture and Christian restoration plans, drew membership from the emerging religious right movement in America. Feminist Wicca formed its own innovative goddess culture borrowed from ancient goddess religions and the feminist movement. The Nation of Yahweh, while instilling in its membership a Hebrew identity and culture, appropriated rhetoric and strategies from the Black Power Movement. The current study is a cultural history of these new religions.

The converts of The Unification Church, Feminist Wicca, and the Nation of Yahweh in the 1960s and 1970s sought to define American public culture through the lens of their own newly-constructed "local" cultures. They believed that their religious symbols and meanings could benefit the ordering of American life. According to sociologist James Davison Hunter, public culture consists of "procedural norms and legal codes, symbols of national identity, shared notions of civic virtue and the common ideals of the public good, and collective myths" of past and future.[19] Members of these new religious movements aspired to influence each of these areas of American culture. The Unification Church, reflecting the interests of the growing religious conservatives, believed that its religion could cleanse the moral decadence it thought was leading America into decline. Feminist Wicca offered a new vision for elevating the status of women in American life through ancient goddess myths. The Nation of Yahweh believed that its religion could raise the social position of African-Americans through proper adherence to Hebrew Scriptures and the teachings of its leader, Yahweh ben Yahweh.

Because these groups based their proposed cultural changes on religious ideas, a careful examination of those religious beliefs and motivations is necessary. As Rhys H. Williams argues in "Religion as Political Resource: Culture or Ideology?" the historian needs to be aware that the terms "culture" and "ideology" do not signify mutually exclusive realities.[20] While researching a group's culture might allow for an examination of their beliefs, an ideological study might more readily be conducive to understanding individual motivations. However, when studying religious movements, Williams concludes the historian must examine the religion in light of individual motivations informed by group ideologies. He states:

> Religion is a useful resource for social movements because it is a great source of what I have called both 'culture' and 'ideology.' Religion shapes identity, the sense of solidarity, and the moral outrage that are integral to social-movement cultures. Motivated believers are the core of any collective action. At the same time, religious doctrine and theology can offer coherent and elaborated cognitive rationales that diagnose social problems, prescribe possible solutions, and justify the movement's actions—often in the cause of universal verities. Thus, religion as a political resource is both culture and ideology, with both theoretical and empirical significance for the study of politics and collective action.[21]

As Williams argues, the relationship between individual believer and religious movement is complex. While religion shapes believers' identities and engenders moral "outrage" over societal problems, it also offers solutions justified through theological discourse.

While the new religious movements in this study each had political aspirations, they also sought to shape the values of American society. They wished to utilize the beliefs of like-minded idealistic individuals to enact social change in America. The religions in this study are limited to those formed in the late 1960s and the 1970s. The Unification Church, Feminist Wicca, and the Nation of Yahweh responded to the late 1960s and early 1970s cultural environment in constructing and promoting new religious ideologies through which they intended to influence American life. To that end, the literature I review here and the conversion stories I analyze are limited to those written or given orally during the formative period of each religion.

Thus, research for this book included consulting archives, as well as primary and secondary literature, for the new religious movements included in this study. Each of these movements has an array of primary literature. These include texts written by founders of each religion during the historical period under study, newsletters for each, and brochures advertising meetings and agendas for the Unification Church and Feminist Wicca. The University of California-Santa Barbara's special collections library houses the latter, along with various unpublished works. In addition, newspaper articles revealed how each of these traditions viewed themselves and how aspects of American culture viewed them during their formative years. In the following chapters, I specify the literature and secondary research consulted for each religion.

Conversion narratives for each new religious movement represent the most important aspect of this research. These narratives, recorded during the 1960s and 1970s give the views of adherents at the times when they joined these movements. One challenge encountered during the research for this study was problematic data. Part of this was due to missing or fragmentary witness accounts that had a mediating source. Also, because this study considered three very different religions, the sources of information varied a great deal. However, the available interviews help to explain devotees' motivations. This is important for this manuscript for two reasons. First, conversion stories explain what factors led to an individual's interest in a particular new religious movement. Converts to each of these religions commonly desired to change the world in a meaningful way. They believed that something the religion offered could help them accomplish that goal. For instance, if the convert felt that American society was "out of control" and spiraling toward moral collapse, they might have been more apt to look for a movement like the Unification Church, which offered a way to give America a moral compass. Second, conversion stories disclosed what significance, if any, historical claims had in drawing in potential adherents. For example, Feminist Wicca claimed that ancient goddess religions offered a blueprint for how the revival of goddess worship could create a more egalitarian American society. Women and men searching for an historical precedent for a society that valued the contributions of women were attracted to this movement.

Because historical associations claimed by these new religious movements appealed to potential members, studies of new religions must analyze these assertions. These claimed historical connections lent the religions a certain amount of legitimacy for prospective adherents. Scholars generally take for granted that new religious movements claim ancient historical identities in order to be seen as legitimate by mainstream America. However, this assumes that new religious movements constructed their religions to appease the surrounding culture. Instead, new religious movements were often critical of their surrounding culture and, at least in their formative years, were less likely to seek its approval. It appears that prospective members were more influenced by the new religions' claims of antiquity than the larger American culture. Hence, the process of legitimation for new religious movements is a far more complex process that deserves analysis.

Max Weber suggested that religions use three methods to establish their authority with adherents: charismatic appeals, rational appeals and traditional appeals.[22] While the new religious movements in this study employed all three of the strategies described by Weber, I focus mostly on the third: tradition. Although Weber used the term "strategy" to explain the process of gaining members, I would caution against assuming that this was a conscious effort by leaders of these groups. Instead, I argue here that new religious movements during the 1960s and 1970s sought converts more than the consent of society at large. Leaders of these groups sought to spread their message among like-minded individuals. Attracting members consisted of several steps: 1) a believable message considered legitimate by believers; 2) an authoritative source (claims of antiquity help here); and 3) a credible messenger. The first three steps, moreover, were accompanied by what members believed to be a religious experience.[23] This study offers the first analysis of these steps with regard to the Unification Church, Feminist Wicca and the Nation of Yahweh.

Max Weber further explains the use of historical associations as they pertain to religions in *Economy and Society*. In this text, Weber notes that new religions appeal to traditional religions for their authority. He explains that "authority" can assume legitimacy in the eyes of the believer in several ways: it can appeal to tradition, emotion, or rational beliefs, or appeal to something whose legitimacy is beyond questioning.[24] While the new religious movements in this study utilize a combination of these claims of authority, the appeal to tradition (ancient religions) is of particular interest here. Weber explains that when a movement is consciously creating new authority, it tends to claim new revelation or prophecy, unless it asserts that it offers an ancient truth that had already been established as valid. In cases of the latter strategy, the movements alleged that their truths were obscured for a time, but were "now being restored to their rightful place."[25] These are precisely the types of claims made by each of the new religious movements in this study. Thus, the word "tradition" used in this book will refer to a historical, established religious group.

Summary

In addition to the considerations outlined above, there are two historical studies that shape the approach I have taken in this book. R. Laurence Moore's *Religious Outsiders and the Making of Americans* argues that new religious movements are the epitome of what makes American religions particularly American.[26] For Moore, most people in America gained a sense of what it meant to be an American "by turning aspects of a carefully nurtured sense of separate identity against a vaguely defined concept of mainstream or dominant culture."[27] According to Moore, the separatist tendency in American religions points to a paradox. "The American religious system may be said to be 'working' only when it is creating cracks within denominations, when it is producing novelty, even when it is fueling antagonisms. These [religions] are not going on at the edges or fringes of American life. They are what give energy to church life and sustenance to the claim that Americans are the most religious people on earth."[28] Moore argues that the language of dissent has a long history in the United States, and it often manifests itself in the search for a unique religious identity apart from mainstream culture.

In another study of new religious movements during the 1970s, Stephen A. Kent analyzes the identity-forming process of radically political youth who chose to follow non-traditional religious paths. The young Americans in Kent's study, *From Slogans to Mantras: Social Protest and Religious Conversion in the Late Vietnam War Era*, abruptly shifted from political means of transforming society to spiritual means, "reinventing" themselves in the process.[29] Kent argues that this shift happened because these political radicals had negative experiences with their respective protest movements. They had been disappointed with the sluggish and often nonexistent results of their secular efforts to transform American society. Kent claims that the "increasing costs and diminishing returns of political action" caused many of these young people to convert to new religious movements that offered the same goals through spiritual means.[30]

Like Moore and Kent, I believe that an historical approach offers the most comprehensive route to understanding why converts chose to join new religious movements in the 1960s and 1970s. While Moore argues that new religious movements develop because they are continuing the tradition of dissent in America, Kent believes that particular social ideologies cause people to turn to new religious movements rather than established religions. Like Moore, I argue that new religious movements are continuing a pattern of innovation in the process of dissent. Like Kent, I argue that, to a certain degree, the feeling of powerlessness in their respective societal situations led some young people to turn to these new religious movements in the 1960s and 1970s. However, I would add to these assertions, that perhaps a more persuasive factor may have been the promise that members would be personally involved in bringing about their religious visions of a better America.

Thus, I argue that people converted to new religious movements—specifically the Unification Church, Feminist Wicca, and the Nation of Yahweh—because they believed these movements offered the most viable path toward their respective societal visions. These religions claimed that established religious traditions were no longer credible because they were complicit in creating the problems in American society. New religions drew converts with promises of personal involvement in creating an ideal America, using ancient religions as their inspiration.

In addition, in this text I describe the individual new religious movements that form the core of the following chapters. While much information is available on the Unification Church, an analysis of its conversation with the emerging religious right has been lacking. Both Feminist Wicca and the Nation of Yahweh have attracted little scholarly attention, and a history of the emergence of these movements is needed. The overall goal of the research for this study is to show the importance of historical associations for these new religious movements. Within their cultural contexts, these links to the past were critical to attracting membership and for shaping their religious visions for an improved America.

Finally, in the following chapters, I offer some suggestions as to why and how new religions form. This study proposes that new religions take shape in response to a particular need of potential members and a perceived failure on the part of established religious traditions to effect necessary change in American society. The religions in this study offered a combination of both new and old ideas. While the Unification Church, Feminist Wicca and the Nation of Yahweh in the 1960s and 1970s incorporated ideas from ancient religious traditions, these religions adapted those ideas to suit contemporary visions of America. Each of these religions sought to shape American society while offering adherents a closer, more personal relationship with their deity.

Although this study is limited to three new religious movements that emerged in 1960s and 1970s America, it sheds some light on larger questions in the study of religion and American culture. This project suggests what factors in society lead people to form new religious movements and what elements give authority to new religious ideas and new religious leaders. It answers, in part, why young people in the 1960s and 1970s chose new religious movements and rejected already-established religions. In addition, I offer fresh criteria for grouping new religious movements. In classifying new religious movements by their claim of ancient origins, scholars will be able to learn more about how these religions view themselves.

The first chapter of this book analyzes the conversion experience of members in the 1960s and 1970s Unification Church. Utilizing ideas and rhetoric of the emerging conservative movement, the Unification Church explained that Christian Churches overlooked Jesus' true mission on earth. This new religious movement offered potential converts an understanding of a relationship with the Christian God who had suffered as a result of his children's failures. Unificationists declared that purification of the morally corrupt American society was necessary. This cleansing of America would make salvation possible for humans in the world. In this chapter, I argue that converts were drawn into the Unification Church with the promise of a "true" Christian religious experience and the pledge that their self-sacrifice would become an integral part of bringing about a morally pure America. Because the Unification Church claimed to be restoring the original mission for Christian Churches, they appealed to formative Christianity and the creation story in Genesis for this inspiration.

In chapter two, I demonstrate that Feminist Wicca appealed to women who experienced discrimination from the patriarchal American establishment and who were in search of a religious path to their political goals. Feminist Wicca explained to their potential adherents that Christianity was responsible for stamping out the ancient goddess traditions and had instituted an age of patriarchal religions that validated secular patriarchal power structures. Feminist Wiccans offered their adherents a vision of a peaceful, egalitarian American society that was concerned with confirming the worth of women, issues of the family, and a healthy environment. They promised women a female deity that understood their point of view and gave them legitimacy in relationships of power. They claimed that ancient goddess religions offered a model for their version of the ideal American society.

The last chapter concerns a black Hebrew Israelite tradition, The Nation of Yahweh. This new religion denounced Christianity as the religion of the white power structure. Leader Yahweh ben Yahweh also condemned black Christian ministers for compromising their black heritage and working in complicity with whites to keep blacks a subordinate race in America. The Nation of Yahweh instead offered a vision of a more desirable society for blacks in which the power structure shifted into their favor. The Nation's leaders assured their members that they would have a meaningful relationship with the black, powerful, vengeful God of the ancient Hebrews. They claimed that American blacks were descendants of the ancient Hebrews and thus were entitled to the promises made by God to His chosen people. I argue in this chapter that the Nation of Yahweh appealed to blacks frustrated with their lack of social progress and those who were intrigued with membership in the "chosen" people of God.

The conclusion of this study will discuss the benefits of categorizing new religious movements by the historical roots they claim. Grouping new religious movements in this way gives scholars a new view of how these movements perceive themselves. The Unification Church in this study professed an ancient Christian heritage. Feminist Wicca asserted that their religious beliefs and practices had roots in prehistoric goddess worship. The Nation of Yahweh claimed to be descendants of the original ancient Hebrews. While the new religious movements asserted connections with these venerable traditions, they also claimed new insights or revelation that changed the original religion. Thus, they could profess to be identified with an ancient religion, while still claiming to be a new religious movement. This association lent the new religions some legitimacy for their potential adherents, but it also offers scholars some insight into their worldviews.

The following chapters are presented chronologically, beginning with the Unification Church, formed in the 1960s, then moving to Feminist Wicca, which took shape in the late 1960s and early 1970s, and then finishing with the Nation of Yahweh, which formed at the end of the 1970s. The chapters will set each new religious movement in the historical context of its formation and give a history of the movement. Each chapter will then demonstrate how potential adherents were drawn into these new religious movements by their rejection of Christianity, their visions of an improved American society modeled after an ancient religion, and promises of personal religious experiences and agency in bringing about an improved American society.

CHAPTER ONE

THE UNIFICATION CHURCH
AS A RESTORATION MOVEMENT

God Blessed America to save the world.
—Reverend Sun Myung Moon

In the 1970s, the Unification Church was drawn into the public eye when the media dubbed it a dangerous cult, prompted by anxious parents and leaders of some traditional Christian churches. In the midst of the controversy, few people tried to genuinely understand why young people were drawn to this new religious movement. Most parents and other outsiders were content to accept that members had been misled or brainwashed into becoming "Moonies," instead of believing that the Unification Church could offer its members a meaningful religious experience. This chapter argues that the Unification Church appealed particularly to young people who were frustrated with what they believed to be the moral decay in America. The Church promised its members that they could be personally involved in cleansing the impurities in American culture, and together they would bring about a unified world under their vision of a restored Christianity.

Beatriz Gonzales gave the following conversion story as a testimony for potential adherents:

> As a child, I attended segregated schools and worked in the fields together with my brothers and sisters in order to support our family. Because of the oppressive environment that surrounded us, by the age of 12 I had cultivated a deep awareness of the suffering of man and had developed a strong sense of responsibility for ending the injustices of discrimination, war and poverty. At 18, I joined the civil rights movement and began to march for equality in education, labor and government for blacks, Latinas, and Indians.
>
> In the beginning we shared much hope for advancement as the government poured millions of dollars into our communities. Soon, however, our own leadership became greedy with the funds, leaving little with the people; the coalition meetings turned into battlefields of

accusation among the different races; and our elected minority representatives turned out to be no less corrupted than all the rest.

After seven years of bitter fighting, it was clear to me that the potential for discrimination, corruption and wrong doing transcended all races and nationalities. In fact, the solution I sought actually lay in changing the hearts of men. I had once looked into communism, thinking it might be the answer, but it was purely materialistic. I knew that only an ideology centered on God could change men's hearts.

I searched for a leader. I had learned that the greatest leader was not he who could rally masses of people behind a cause, but he who by his example of sacrifice and service for others could raise up his followers to become as great or greater than himself.

It was in the Unification Church movement that I found God, a God-centered theology, and a leader of men who lives totally for God and the world. Reverend Sun Myung Moon teaches us that as God's creation, we are all a part of a greater whole in which God longs to see Himself reflected. How can we but love what in God's eyes is so precious? Truly, there is no room for discrimination.

Here, people of all races, ages and nationalities work side by side as true brothers and sisters for the highest purpose of all—to unite as one family, one nation and one world—under God.[31]

Beatriz longed to be part of a solution "centered on God" for the problem of injustice in America. Like Beatriz, the Unification Church attracted many young people in the 1960s and 1970s because it promised to involve them in purifying an immoral American society and to unify the peoples of the world through the Christian faith. Utilizing rhetoric from the conservative movement and promising to restore Christianity to God's original purpose, the Unification Church offered its members an explanation for why Christianity had failed in its attempts to combat immorality in America. In addition, it promised its members a personal religious experience, a special relationship with God, and the possibility of transforming their world. "Mainstream" Christian denominations lost authority for many potential members of the Unification Church, who believed that Christian churches had failed in their moral guidance of America. In turn, the Unification Church gained legitimacy because it offered potential members explanations and possibilities through claims to restore Christianity to what they perceived to be God's original purpose.

Based on its intention to correct Christian teachings, I argue that the Unification Church is a Christian restoration movement. Such movements believe that their doctrines and practices embody the spirit of the authentic message from God as represented by Jesus in his earthly teachings. Restoration movements are a category included in this study because they appeal to an ancient past to explain their current practices. The ancient tradition the Unification Church appealed to was "original," or formative, Christianity. Restoration movements are critical of the contemporary Christian churches for straying from their founding message. Some restoration movements include the Pentecostal Movement, the Unification Church, the Four Square Gospel movement, and Christian Science. The Unification Church is the restoration movement included in this study. The emerging conservative movement in 1970s American culture greatly informed this new religious movement in addition to what it perceived to be the decadence of the 1960s and 1970s undermining of the "Christian" nation.

This chapter begins with a literature review and a brief history of the Unification Church. It then shows that the Unification Church's conservative and Christian restoration rhetoric attracted new members. This chapter then proceeds to argue that the Unification Church appealed to its potential adherents because it offered them an explanation for Christianity's failure in America, a personal religious experience, and the possibility of restoring Christianity in order to end what they believed to be the moral chaos engulfing American society.

Existing Scholarship on the Unification Church

Most extant scholarship on the Unification Church focuses on its status as an alternative or new religious movement. Consequently, scholars often discuss the beliefs of the Church and its relationship with the larger American society. Many examine the charges of brainwashing leveled against the Unification Church during the late 1960s and early 1970s, or the charges of financial misdealings leveled against Sun Myung Moon.

Unlike previous scholarship that presents the Unification Church as opposed to American society, I argue that the success of the Church was a product of that same culture. While it developed in Korea, the Unification Church focused its efforts on the United States from its inception, believing that the struggles in America to maintain a democratic society had universal implications. The Church evolved in the United States, responding to the moral chaos it perceived was destroying the country. Using rhetoric borrowed from the newly-resurging conservative movement, the Unification Church appealed to young people intent on saving their nation from destroying itself from the inside out. Potential members believed the Unification Church was a legitimate religion for three reasons: it used familiar rhetoric from the conservative movement, it claimed to be restoring the original Christian Church, and it offered a personal religious experience along with the possibility of personal involvement in improving the world.

While scholars have written numerous texts and articles about the Unification Church, none have argued that the success of the movement was dependent on its interaction with American culture. John T. Biermans has written a text about the Unification Church's struggle to be considered a legitimate religion in *The Odyssey of New Religious Movements: Persecution, Struggle, Legitimation: A Case Study of the Unification Church*.[32] This text is concerned with the dialogue between the Unification Church and the larger American society. Biermans disabuses the reader of the notion that the church brainwashed its converts and explains many of the previously misunderstood beliefs of the movement. Biermans' rejection of the brainwashing charge lends support to the idea that adherents voluntarily remained in the movement. I submit that church members chose to join the Unification Church because its religious and social goals closely coincided with their own.

An insider history has been written by Michael L. Mickler entitled *A History of the Unification Church in America, 1959-1974*.[33] Mickler argues that when the Church established a presence in America, the various factions settled their differences and united their movement under the direction of the Reverend Sun Myung Moon. Mickler's history details the development of the different factions and the effect of Reverend Moon's presence in America. While Mickler is not as interested in describing beliefs and practices, other scholars are, including Massimo Introvigne's *The Unification Church: Studies in Contemporary Religion*[34] and George D. Chryssides's *The Advent of Sun Myung Moon: The Origins, Beliefs, and Practices of the Unification Church*.[35] In this chapter, I show that an examination of the historical development of the Unification Church and the teleological visions of its founder and members give insight into the beliefs and practices of this movement.

Other scholars have been concerned with why people joined the Unification Church, which is a question central to this study. Roger Allen Dean addresses the psychological aspects of this question in *Moonies: A Psychological Analysis of the Unification Church*.[36] Along these same lines, Joseph Fichter presents the narratives of members who joined the Church in the 1960s and 1970s in *Autobiographies of Conversion*, with the intention of understanding the motivations of new adherents. I have found the autobiographies in Fichter's text immensely helpful for this study, because he allowed the subjects to speak for themselves. Likewise, Eileen Barker studied conversion experiences in her text entitled *The Making of a Moonie: Choice or Brainwashing?* Leaders of the Unification Church allowed Barker unprecedented access to their records and interviews with current and former members. She concluded that members chose to join the movement of their own volition and were not brainwashed. There are also numerous articles concerned with the possibility of brainwashing or mind control tactics during the conversion experience of Unification Church members. Instead of examining conversion stories for evidence of societal problems, however, I suggest that these narratives give insight into the beliefs and practices that Unification Church members found particularly meaningful.

Other scholars interested in various aspects of the intersection between the Unification Church and particular facets of American culture include: James H. Grace's text *Sex and Marriage in the Unification Movement: A Sociological Study*,[37] Irving Louis Horowitz's *Science, Sin, and Scholarship: The Politics of Reverend Moon and the Unification Church*,[38] and Kathleen S. Lowney's *Passport to Heaven: Gender Roles in the Unification Church*.[39] These scholars examine how the Unification Church views marriage, politics, and gender. Each of these authors compares and contrasts the Unification Church's ideas with those of the larger American culture on these topics. This type of cultural comparison is applicable in this text. Below, I analyze the similarities and differences between the rhetoric of the Unification Church and the American conservative culture in particular. The Unification Church promised its members to save American society from its moral decline, a concern they shared with the conservative movement.

While many scholars have written about the Unification Church, none have discussed why its restoration claims were necessary for survival in the larger American culture. In fact, the conservative rhetoric and restoration claims of the Unification Church lent the movement authority to thrive within the American culture it sought to repair. Converts were convinced that their individual work in this religious movement would save Christianity and in turn, God would save America.

The research for this study not only included the literature reviewed above, but the following primary documents from the Unification Church during the 1960s and 1970s. The *Divine Principle* and sermons of Reverend Sun Myung Moon written during the movement's formative years present its beliefs and doctrines. Reverend Moon also published many of his speeches in newspapers around the country, which outline his views on how the movement could "save" America. Joseph Fichter recorded conversion stories of members from the early years of the movement, which include the motivations of new adherents. The special collections archives at University of California, Santa Barbara contained more conversion stories in various 1970s brochures. In addition, scholarship on the conservative movement during 1960s and 1970s America shed some light on the motivations of this movement.

I begin this chapter with a brief history of the Unification Church in the United States. I then proceed to show how the Unification Church utilized rhetoric from the conservative movement and from restoration Christianity to draw in converts. While the Unification Church's rhetoric was convincing, several members reported that their religious conversion was the factor that convinced them to remain committed to the new religion. Therefore, I next argue that the Church gained authority with its new adherents because it offered an explanation of why Christianity was in need of restoration, in addition to promising them a personal religious experience. Finally, I show that the ultimate purpose of membership was to save America from its moral decline. Lofland and Stark called members of the Unification Church "World Savers," because they believed that their actions as members of this community had universal implications.[40] While members believed they were saving America from its moral decline by restoring Christianity to its original purpose, they trusted that these actions would not only save America, but save the world. They therefore felt that their individual contributions to the Unification Church had ultimate significance.

History of the Unification Church

Both Michael Mickler and Eileen Barker offer historical information about the beginnings of the Unification Church, upon which I rely for much of the following. The founder of the Unification Church, the Reverend Sun Myung Moon, was born Young Myung Moon in 1920. Moon's family converted to Christianity when Moon was ten years old, joining the Presbyterian Church.[41] Moon claimed that he received the revelation that spurred him to begin the Unification Church on a Korean hillside, Easter morning in 1936. He was 16 years old. In this vision, Moon reported that Jesus appeared to him in spirit and asked him to be an instrument of God for bringing about a new age for humanity and to complete the work of redemption that Jesus had left unfinished when he was crucified.[42] Moon claimed that his visions continued over the next nine years "through prayer, meditation, the study of religious scriptures, and spiritual communications with such key religious figures as Jesus, Moses, and Buddha, and directly, with God Himself."[43] His followers recorded his revelations in an early text published in 1957. A later version of the text was translated and published in English as the *Divine Principle,* which became the Unification Church's companion to the Christian Bible.[44] After some reflection, Moon came to believe that God meant to complete the restoration of Christianity in the United States.

Moon founded the Holy Spirit Association for the Unification of World Christianity, later known as the Unification Church, in Seoul, Korea on May 1, 1954.[45] His interpretation of the Hebrew and Christian Bibles became the *Divine Principle*, published in 1976. According to Moon, part of the divine plan of Jesus was to marry, which would have restored the world to its creation-state, but Jesus was murdered before he was able to complete this divine directive. Moon taught that the mission of Jesus was not a complete failure: he was able to accomplish the spiritual marriage required for the restoration through a union with the Holy Spirit. Therefore, Moon claimed that a perfect human marriage was needed in order to complete God's plan. Moon explained that his own marriage, in addition to the mass marriages that his movement performed, was an effort to restore the world to its innocence before the fall in the Garden of Eden. The Unification Church wished to save humanity from the influence of Satan by delivering humans back into the dominion of God. This could only succeed by the restoration of humanity, which could be accomplished, according to Moon, through marriage and family and the continued sacrificial work of church members in this world.[46]

After Moon's vision at age 16, he began a period of inner searching while he finished high school and went on to study electrical engineering at Waseda University in Japan.[47] After World War II, in 1948, Moon returned to North Korea to preach about his revelations from God. The introduction of the *Divine Principle* explains that Moon was sent as God's messenger and he endured much persecution for his beliefs.[48] He reportedly suffered for his faith in communist North Korea throughout his twenties and thirties, including beatings, tortures, and imprisonment.[49] Moon was sent to a prison camp from 1948-1959. He was freed when United Nations forces liberated the camp and he returned to North Korea to continue preaching his understanding of God's will for the world.

Moon's message of unity appealed to the Korean community where he began his movement after the war. His church reportedly started in a small hut built by church members from the debris of the war, but grew after he organized the Holy Spirit Association for the Unification of World Christianity. They sent their first missionary to Japan in 1958.[50] The church sent its first proselytizer to the United States, Young Oon Kim, as a student to the University of Oregon at Eugene in 1959. She was responsible for the first center for teaching the *Divine Principle* in the United States, as well as the first translation of the text into English.[51]

Miss Kim had converted to the Unification Church in 1954, after her short career as a professor of New Testament and Comparative Religions at Ewha University in Seoul and her postgraduate work in Canada from 1948 to 1951.[52] Kim said that she converted because of three factors: she was convinced of the teachings on creation, she felt the members' testimonies were authentic, and she experienced healing during her first encounter with the teachings.[53] She became active in the movement and agreed to become the first missionary to the United States in 1958.

By 1971, there were several groups representing the Unification Church in America including Mr. Choi's International Re-Education Foundation in San Francisco, Miss Kim's Unified Family in Washington D.C., and David Kim's United Faith, Inc. in Portland, Oregon. Each group had its own newsletter, membership, and interpretation of the Principle. The Reverend Moon toured the Unification centers in the United States in 1965, 1969, and 1971.[54] During his visits, Moon became concerned that the various factions teaching his revelations would eventually divide his new religion.

Hence, in 1972, Moon moved to the United States in an effort to unite the many small divisions that had appeared in the American centers teaching the *Divine Principle*.[55] He called for unification of the movement in his "One World Crusade," and considered it essential for the mission of the Unification Church to succeed. As part of his One World Crusade, he held a series of rallies called "Day of Hope" in many major cities.[56] Local newspapers often printed his speeches from these rallies. From 1972 to 1982, he also began small fundraising groups modeled after those that had been successful in Japan called MFTs (Mobile Fundraising Teams).[57] The MFTs sold candles and other small items in an effort to keep the movement financially afloat. To further disseminate the beliefs of the church, Moon decided to open a Unification Theological Seminary in Barrytown, New York in 1975. The seminary was designed to train future leaders for the movement.

Many of Moon's methods for spreading his beliefs in the United States have been controversial. He supported Nixon during the Watergate scandal, and he was investigated by a Congressional committee for trying to buy political influence for South Korea. In 1982 he was convicted of tax evasion by the Internal Revenue Service.[58] In addition, he founded daily newspapers in both New York and Washington D.C., in an effort to disseminate his views in a nationally-recognized forum. In the 1970s and 1980s, he also organized scientific and scholarly conferences, inviting academic professionals to give papers on a range of topics. He sponsored a peace academy and a Washington think tank, and he invested large sums of money in primarily conservative political lobbying groups.[59]

After a student rally at Berkeley in 1974, the Unification Church came under attack by some Christian groups and the anti-cult movement. At this rally, organized by the Christian Student Coalition, the Christian students disavowed "any spiritual kinship with the Unification Church and its founder, Sun Myung Moon."[60] The Unification church became the target of "an increasing number of Christian organizations and individuals, particularly those of a right-wing, fundamentalist or evangelical persuasion …who declare(d) that Moon and his beliefs were not Christian but, according to a few, Satanic."[61] Opposition to the Unification Church included political antagonism stemming from Moon's alliance with President Nixon and the disapproval of some Christian clergy, who called him a false prophet.[62] After this, the Unification Church became the focus of the anti-cult movement, drawing the negative attention of the media. The anti-cult movement brought together "specialists" designed to explain why "deviant" religious movements attracted young people.

In the beginning, the "anti-cult" movement consisted mostly of worried family members of Unification Church adherents. These groups later rallied against not only the Unification Church, but also against other new religious movements at the time, particularly the Hare Krishnas. The anti-cult groups distributed information about new religions through newsletters and the media, lobbied government and other officials, and employed a number of ways to restrict the practices of new religious movements. This included attempts to persuade individual members to sever their association with their new-found religions, which anti-cult groups called "cults." The methods of inducement ranged from informal counseling, during which devotees were free to come and go as they please, to illegal kidnappings and "deprogrammings."[63]

Despite evidence to the contrary, the anti-cult movements accused the Unification Church of "brainwashing" its members so they could not leave of their own free will. These groups borrowed the term "brainwashing" from techniques used by Chinese and European communists many years earlier that produced conversion of political beliefs or false confessions by the war prisoners held against their will.[64] Anti-cultists accused the Unification Church of using tactics to force potential recruits to accept their messages, such as sensory deprivation, emotional blackmail, repetitive chanting, concealment of their real intentions, and deliberate attempts to alienate members from all outside influences.[65]

The problem with using the term "brainwashing" to describe the conversion experiences of members of the Unification Church was that members were free to leave at any time, as evidenced by the small percentage of potential members who actually joined the movement. As many as nine out of ten people who went to open houses did not join at all or only joined for a short time and left.[66] In addition, observers and former members concur that church members did not deprive potential converts of food or water nor did they force converts to endure torture tactics. Lee Coleman, a psychiatrist, suggests that "brainwashing is simply an explanation for behavior with which people disagree."[67] When parents could not accept that their children would willingly adopt the beliefs of the Unification Church, they rationalized that the new religious movement must have brainwashed their children.

The anti-cult movement influenced public and private organizations with the intention of making the existence of the Unification Church difficult within American culture.   Anti-cultists described what they termed "brainwashing" techniques: they characterized members of the church as walking zombies, and they related "testimony" of disaffected members of the movement. Even more damaging were the actions taken by other social institutions to exclude the Unification Church from conventional social networks. Some communities tried to ban Unification Church fundraising on their streets. The New York board of Regents denied academic accreditation to the seminary at Barrytown, the Unification Church was denied membership in the New York Council of Churches, and many college campuses refused to allow the Unification Church to establish campus organizations. In addition, several states held hearings aimed to distinguish "cults" from "legitimate" churches.[68] Also, the U.S. Immigration and Naturalization Service began to deny extensions on tourist visas for many of the international Unification Church missionaries.[69] While these measures were legally questionable, their affect was to establish in the court of popular opinion that the Unification Church was a deviant religious movement.[70]

Reverend Moon fought against this negative characterization of his movement by finding ways for the Unification Church to be recognized as a legitimate religious institution in America. He began by organizing days for parents to visit their adult children in Unification Church centers, by allowing scholars to assess his new religious movement on its merits, and by becoming even more involved in political groups working toward restoring morality to American culture. Starting in the 1970s, the Unification Church began to focus on world peace through inter-religious dialogue.   The movement organized many groups with these aims including the Professors World Peace Academy, the Women's Federation for World Peace, the Inter-religious and International Federation for World

Peace, and the International Religious Foundation.[71] These groups claimed that their goal was to help people of different religious faiths find some common ground in their search for peace. These movements attempted to realize Reverend Moon's vision of all religions unified in a universal religion in a world-wide culture.[72]

The Unification Church is alive and well in the twenty-first century. While membership numbers are down, Reverend Moon continues to perform mass wedding ceremonies and work toward a unified Christianity. Church members understand inter-religious dialogue to be part of the process of restoration between humanity and God. Members therefore continue to be involved in the church's seminary and peace movements around the world. The mission of the Unification Church requires the universal acceptance of the truth of their theory as a condition for the restoration of humankind.[73]

The Conservative Movement and the Unification Church in the 1960s and 1970s

Because the Unification Church emerged in America during the late 1960s and early 1970s in response to the perceived decline in moral values, the Church was drawn to the ideology of the neo-conservative movement. Unificationists agreed with many aspects of conservative ideals, thus it was natural for Reverend Moon and his missionaries to utilize the rhetoric of the American conservative movement in their efforts to unify Christian churches, beginning with new members.

Conservatism emerged after World War II, but did not become a viable political force until the late 1960s and the 1970s. Historian Gregory L. Schneider has argued that conservatism in the 1960s developed a critique of the reigning liberalism with particular focus on "the economy, foreign policy, and culture."[74] Conservative ideas tended to favor limited government, veneration of the constitution, moral traditionalism, Christian religious heritage, anti-communism, and free-market economics.[75] Many conservatives, calling themselves "traditionalists," believed that established traditions, such as religion, law, or politics, maintained a stable social order.[76] The conservatives' rallying cry in the 1960s was to end the moral chaos that they perceived to be taking over American culture and to return to "traditional" family values. Conservatives considered the anti-war movement to be composed mostly of left-wing student radicals, pacifists, and communists, combined with a "growing specter of revolution in the wider society prompted by urban rioting, widespread drug use, and growing permissiveness."[77] This perceived loss of governmental control over American society prompted a backlash against the liberal Johnson administration in 1966. During that midterm election year, conservative Republicans made some crucial gains in local and state elections.[78]

Ann Burlein, in her critique of James Dobson's Focus on the Family, suggests that the conservative movement's call for a return to the 1950s family values was a "counter-memory." By this, she means that the emerging conservative movement in the 1960s and 1970s exploited people's desire for a particular view of the family against the cultural realities of family life. Specifically, they invoked nostalgia for the traditional Bible-based family with a working father, a stay-at-home mother and their children, "pitting the way we are against the way we wish we were."[79] The religious right offered this imagined ideal past as a goal for the foreseeable future. While Burlein's article concentrates specifically on the tactics used by the religious right in the 1970s, this same strategy of revising history was also utilized by the conservative movement in general.

Historians David Farber and Jeff Roche complain that most historians miss the rise of the conservative movement because the left held such sway over American culture in the 1960s. They note that while the "radical left" held protests against the Vietnam War or demonstrated in favor of civil liberties, conservative grassroots movements were also active. Conservative women began movements against national education reforms including "sex education, experimental pedagogy, and 'progressive' textbooks."[80] On college campuses across the country, the Young Americans for Freedom organized protests against what they perceived to be liberal policies of school administrations.[81] Conservatives gained footholds in many local elections. Even militant volunteer civilian border patrols were actively fighting what they perceived to be the encroaching threats from across America's borders in the late 1960s.[82] Following many of the urban race riots in the 1960s, conservatives complained to their politicians about "crime in the streets" and demanded that "law and order" be restored in America.[83] While the liberal left gained much media attention, the neo-conservative movement operated largely under the media's radar.

Part of what alarmed conservatives about the liberal left's control over the government was the perceived decline in moral values in American society. Conservatives pointed to increased drug use among young people, promiscuity, teen pregnancies, a rise in the divorce rate and similar moral "decadence" as proof of a dangerous slide from traditional American values. Robert Welch, author of *The Blue Book*, an anti-communist manifesto, claimed in 1968 that, "except for the diminishing number of fundamentalists of all religions, and the increasingly but still comparatively small percentage of the human race which has fervently accepted Communism as a religion, all faith has been replaced, or is rapidly being replaced, by a pragmatic opportunism with hedonistic claims....you can see the magnitude of our loss, as to a base for our morals, our purposes, and our aspirations."[84] The solution, for conservatives, was to revive in the American government a moral compass based on Christian values.

In the 1960s and into the 1970s, liberal politics added to their social and economic liberalism a cultural liberalism that pushed many political moderates to turn to the conservative agenda. The new moderates felt that the United States government was spending an increasing amount of public moneys on behalf of minority cultures. According to historian William C. Berman, it seemed to many of these swing-voters that "liberalism had become a vehicle for big governmental spending programs for blacks...and in the words of journalist Harold Myerson, 'the one against the many—*not the many against the powerful.*'"[85] These same moderates, encouraged by conservative rhetoric, were concerned that the programs of "big government" infringed on their personal liberties. So conservatives across the country in the 1960s and into the 1970s gained support for their politics of family values, patriotism, and fighting crime and moral corruption.[86]

During this emergence of the neo-conservative movement, the Unification Church, under various names all teaching Moon's *Divine Principle*, entered the United States. As mentioned above, while Reverend Sun Myung Moon did not come to America until 1972, his missionaries began small communities in the United States starting with Dr. Young Oon Kim at the University of Oregon, where she was enrolled as a student in 1959.[87] By 1971, there was Mr Choi's International Re-Education Foundation, Miss Kim's Unified Family (Washington, and the Bay Area), and David Kim's United Faith Inc. Each group had its own newsletter, membership, and interpretation of the *Divine Principle*. Miss Kim was concerned with "the spiritual life," Mr Choi stressed the utopian community, and Mr. Kim called for the unification of all religions under the *Divine Principle*.[88]

Like the conservative movement, the Unification Church emphasized the need for Americans to return to a morally pure life. In the early years of the movement, they primarily recruited young single members. They insisted that unmarried members of their church remain abstinent from sexual intercourse until Reverend Moon chose a mate for them to marry. The Church prohibited drinking alcohol or using drugs and promoted honest hard work and living "God-centered" lives. To achieve unity and high moral standards, members worked together as a family. The members of the church believed that if they worked industriously and "centered their actions on God," they could save the world from its moral decay. In addition to agreeing with the conservative movement that Americans needed to turn toward a "traditional" moral life, the Unification Church also agreed that embracing the nation's Christian religious heritage, rejecting communism, and encouraging free-market economics were necessary for saving America from her decline into virtue-less decadence. Like conservatives, the Unification Church believed that America's return to the tradition of Christianity would restore social order in the United States.

By advocating a rehabilitation of Christian values in American culture, the conservative movement gained more ground in the 1970s. They were able to attract new voting constituencies, such as Catholics and evangelical Protestants. These religious groups were disturbed by what they perceived to be the growing moral decay in American culture and the "liberal" Supreme Court, with controversial decisions such as Roe v. Wade.[89] Couching their rhetoric in specifically religious terms enabled the conservative movement to appeal to the moral conscience in their potential supporters.

According to Moon, the moral decline in America in the 1970s was evidence that Americans were pushing God away, rather than trying to restore their relationship with Him. Moon claimed that signs of American decline were evident in all aspects of the culture: drug problems that plagued America's youth, juvenile crime, the breakdown in families, the threat of communism, the economic crisis, and the lack of prayer in schools. Moon called attention to the relaxation of sexual mores in American culture as evidenced in pornography, widespread venereal disease, teenage pregnancies, and premarital and extramarital sex.[90] He called on Americans to bring God back "in your homes, your churches, your schools and your national life, our work for God's purpose must begin."[91]

Reverend Sun Myung Moon came to the United States in 1972 to bolster his movement's already significant growth. At that point, Moon took charge of uniting the various Unification families in America into one movement. The church's connection to conservatism grew more entrenched with the charismatic presence of their founder. Moon's support of President Nixon during the Watergate scandal brought increasing negative publicity and public opinion against the Unification Church from late 1973. Moon's response to Watergate was: "America must live with the will of God, and God's command at this crossroads in American History is

Forgive, Love and Unite."[92]   President Nixon invited Moon to a prayer breakfast on January 31, 1974 during which Moon had a twenty-minute audience with the President.

In addition, Moon's church began donating to several political groups with conservative ideals and those who were anti-communist, particularly. In addition, he urged his church members to be active agents for change in their neighborhoods. In the late 1970s, as part of his support of a return to family values, Moon began the "home church movement" within his church communities.   The Unification Church gave its members a geographical area around their residence where they would visit and chat with 360 families in their neighborhoods.   The Church charged its members to help elderly people with their shopping, offer to baby-sit for young couples, and provide whatever other services people needed. During the 1970s Moon's movement became part of the American conservative culture at the same time that many considered the movement to be a radical "cult."

The late 1960s and the 1970s saw a boom in religious "fringe" groups, what many in America at the time termed "cults." This was not a new phenomenon, but since it was the most recent "cult boom" since the 1940s, Americans became alarmed at the unfamiliar religions sprouting up. Philip Jenkins claims that cult-like movements have a long history in America.[93] Cults, according to Jenkins, are small groups that are organized around a charismatic leader with unconventional religious ideas.[94] Because the Unification Church claimed many Christian ideas and resonated with the conservative movement's agenda, they were accepted for a short time. When outsiders learned that their Christian ideas differed dramatically from the mainstream, that they recruited heavily among young single adults, and that they had a charismatic leader called "father," the mainstream churches withdrew support from the movement and began to describe the movement as a "cult." This did not deter Moon from his advances into the conservative movement, although he began forming focus groups that did not use "Unification Church" in their title. Moon's connection to conservatism was never severed; it just became less obtrusive.

Meanwhile, the Unification Church focused primarily on single college students and professionals. Many young people involved in the secular reform movements in the 1970s began to believe that their social activism was not producing results and others became disgusted with the drug culture. Steven Kent, in his *From Slogans to Mantras*, claims that the radical youth in the 1960s wanted to change the world, but once they became disenchanted with the secular movements, they had to find new means. They wanted to heal the moral ills of society. Many of them found their answers in the emerging alternative movements like the Unification Church and the Hare Krishna movement.[95] These religions promised that morally and socially responsible people could be personally involved in changing the world.

If Barbara W. Hargrove is correct that much of the Unification Church theology is based on ideas that Moon encountered in the conservative Christianity of his youth in Korea, then it would appear that themes such as a tendency toward biblical literalism, strict personal moral conduct (no liquor, no tobacco, no drugs, no extramarital sex), and a strong work ethic are consistent with the stance of conservative Christians on such matters.[96] These themes attracted to the Unification Church many young people who wanted to change the world and create a just and moral society. The search for a more virtuous America led the Unification Church to be more actively involved in American culture, from science and academics, to media and business, to supporting various charitable projects.[97]

Like the conservative movement's view that strong family values could help heal society, Moon's movement wished to create strong families centered on God, as a way to begin the restoration process. Neil Albert Salonen, then President of the Unification Church of America, stated in 1976 that "a strong family is the key to a moral society, yet in America the breakdown of the family is accelerating at an alarming rate. The Unification Church believes that the family can stand only with God at the center."[98] This focus on strong families was drawn from Moon's background in Korea and his exposure to Confucianism there. Moon stated in a lecture in 1975 that American families lacked the filial piety evident in Asian families. Filial piety requires one to serve one's parents and for the parents, in turn to serve their children. Each must sacrifice their own needs to meet the needs of the family. He claimed that through love, whether parental love, conjugal love, or children's love, one can reach God.[99] Moon believed that this absence of filial piety in American families was one reason for their decline.

Another subject on which the Unification Church agreed with the conservative movement was communism. This was not a subject that Moon borrowed from the conservative movement, however. His personal experiences, including his imprisonment for preaching his message in Korea, certainly informed his stance against communism. One of his teachings explained the "three major headaches of God: the conflict and disunity among the world's religions, the increasing immorality in society, and the expansion of atheistic communism."[100] Moon taught that communism was the source of the destruction of extended families among the Chinese.[101] Moon's anti-communism made him a supporter of both the Vietnam War and Richard Nixon. In December 1973, more than a thousand of Moon's followers demonstrated their support for President Nixon and the war during the annual lighting of the White House Christmas Tree.[102] Moon saw the fight between democracy and communism to be an ideological battle with spiritual implications. For him, if communism won, Satan would establish his rule over the material world.[103] Part of the Unification Church's mission, then, was to ensure that democracy prevailed, thus paving the way for the consolidation of the world's religions under a single Christianity.

Although its perceived status as a "cult" movement may have pushed the Unification Church out of the center of conservative politics, the Church nevertheless resonated with the ideals of American conservatism. Its use of conservative rhetoric attracted new members: both movements decried America's moral decline, both stressed the need for a return to a traditional Christian moral center, both showed alarm over the threat of communism, and both claimed that a stronger Christian nation could be built on the foundation of the family unit. The sentiment of the emerging conservative movement was integral to the success of the Unification Church during the 1960s and 1970s.

What the Unification Church Offered its Members

In addition to its use of conservative rhetoric, another way that the Unification Church appealed to potential members was that it offered them a chance to personally make a difference in the world. The Unification Church presented its members with an explanation of why Christianity had failed to create a moral America, but more importantly, it claimed to offer a religious solution to this problem. The Unification Church asserted that it could restore Christianity to God's original purpose while saving America from its moral decline. Church leaders promised potential members that their personal relationship with God would prepare them to be active participants in changing American society. The Church claimed that if members restored Christianity and lived "God-centered" lives, that God would enable them to save America, and ultimately, the world.

Explanation of Why Christianity Needed Restoration

When Reverend Moon claimed to have received his first vision on that early Easter morning in Korea in 1954, he was a member of the Presbyterian Church. Moon's intention, from the beginning, was to restore Christianity to the "original" purpose of God revealed to Moon through his visions. However, his understanding of how this restoration would occur developed over time, as evidenced by his sermons and the conversion stories of congregation members. At first, they seemed to view their movement as a new beginning for the existing Christian church. Later, this view evolved into a belief that the movement had come to replace the extant Christianity as the "true" Christian vision of God. In either case, the Unification Church offered its members an explanation of why Christianity needed to be restored.

Moon made his feelings about Christianity's ineffectiveness quite clear in the *Divine Principle*, published in America in the 1960s and 1970s. In the introduction, he explained that "today's religions have failed to lead the present generation out of the dark valley of death into the radiance of life, so there must now come a new truth that can shed a new light."[104] Moon's new truth was his teachings, found in the *Divine Principle*. He further claimed that the "new truth" would explain all the "difficulties" evident in Christianity and clarify the relationships between God, Jesus and Humans.[105] He asserted that Christianity had lost its way and become corrupt, no longer leading its members to the "light of faith."[106] Moon taught his members, through the *Divine Principle*, that the "true" mission of Christianity was to "restore the one great world family which God had intended at creation." This was to be accomplished by finding the "True Parents" of humankind from whom all could become "children of goodness through rebirth." Moon claimed that Christianity was the "central religion" that would accomplish the "purpose of God's providence of restoration."[107] Since Moon reasoned that Christianity had failed in its mission, he aspired to "return" the Christian Church to what he understood as God's original purpose for it.

The Reverend Moon thus stressed that Christianity had failed in combating the moral decline in America. Also in the *Divine Principle*, Moon stated that "Christianity is in a state of confusion. Split by the chaotic tide of the present generation, it is unable to do anything for the lives of the people who have been drawn into today's whirlpool of immorality."[108] Later in the text, Moon claimed that Christianity was different from other religions, because its purpose was to "restore one great world family which God intended at the creation."[109] This established the eschatology of the Unification Church: the belief that all religions would be united into a unified Christianity.[110]

Toward this goal, Moon gave a speech in 1973 claiming that Christianity had begun to decline in America because Christians felt the need to "subjugate other religions and have all people under one religion, rather than uniting them."[111]   Similarly, when Moon spoke in 1972, he "stressed the Christian side of Unification beliefs, and he urged America to turn again to God. The advent of the Messiah [was] announced, but audiences [were] not given much information on this subject other than the warning that if they fail to recognize him, Christianity will have no hope."[112] His vision was thus to unite all religions in the common purpose of bringing about peace in the world and restoring humanity to its relationship with God through a renewed Christianity.

Because Moon utilized rhetoric emphasizing the restoration of Christianity, many of his early followers did not believe that they were abandoning their Christian backgrounds. New converts reported that they had found the true meaning of Christianity in the *Divine Principle*. For example, "Charles," who was a Catholic seminary student when he joined the Unification Church in the late 1960s, believed that his Catholic background taught him obedience. He believed that following the *Divine Principle* was following God's calling and he had no other choice.[113] He explained that he did not give up his Catholic faith when he became a Unificationist. Rather, he stated "I live my Catholic beliefs more intensely now and with a greater awareness of their meaning."[114]

Likewise, "Eugenie" from Texas, who joined the Unification Church in 1974, said that people misunderstood the movement when they called it "new" or deviant from Christianity. Instead, she felt that part of her job as an adherent was to help "revitalize" Christianity. Her statement to that end follows:

> One of the important aspects of our movement that outsiders do not understand is that we do not want to be labeled as a new and different Christian denomination. Maybe it's too late in America to change the image that people have of us as a new and separate church. We know that is not Reverend Moon's message, nor his purpose. Our task is to revitalize World Christianity, to widen its embrace so that we include all religions, as well as all nations and races. The Kingdom of God, toward which all of humanity is moving, will certainly not be exclusively for Christians, or Westerners, or Unificationists. In a sense, we are doing in a modern movement what Jesus intended for all his followers: that they reach out to all the world. We like to think we are redoing his mission and not starting something that is brand new out of Korea.[115]

While adherents in the 1970s felt that they could be loyal both to Christianity and the Unification Church, they felt that Moon's movement was the next step. "Andrew," a disillusioned Catholic, saw Moon as the "successor to the earthly tasks of Jesus."[116] Likewise, another young convert named "Patricia" stated: "this is why I don't think it is correct to say that we shift from our religious affiliation when we join the Unification Church. We continue to represent the church we used to attend but with a different emphasis and more accurate destination."[117] The conversion narratives show the Unification Church's early emphasis on the reformation of Christianity, rather than the emergence of a new denomination. Members of this movement believed that the revelations of Reverend Moon were God's way of restoring Christianity to its original purpose.

Unlike many Christian denominations, Reverend Moon taught that Jesus was not the human incarnation of God. Instead, he explained that Jesus was a reflection of God; he was the messiah in the image of God. According to Moon, the savior of humanity was not supposed to die. Instead, God intended for Jesus to create the perfect family on earth for the restoration of the relationship between humans and God. Because Jesus was killed before completing his mission, God made it possible for him to complete part of this restoration—he sent the Holy Spirit as the bride of Jesus so that Christians could be spiritual children of God. Jesus completed the spiritual portion of the restoration, but was unable to accomplish the requirement of mortals. Thus Moon taught that the incomplete task of Jesus caused the need for another savior. This "lord of the second advent" would consummate universal restoration, which must be done through the perfect human family.[118]

The Unification Church raises the question of what it means to be a Christian, and more importantly, who has the right to claim that title.[119] Moon asserted that the new revelation in the *Divine Principle* gave Unification Church members the privilege of carrying the Christian label. Church members believed that this revelation was the key to interpreting biblical questions that Christian leaders had previously "misinterpreted," such as the nature of original sin and the role of Jesus for salvation.[120] While Unificationists claimed to be restoring Christianity to the original intent of God, their model of a messiah was closer to the Jewish expectation of a human leader sent by God to lead his chosen people in the restoration of the kingdom of God, than to the traditional Christian view of a sacrificial messiah.[121]

In light of their vision of a restored Christianity, the Unification Church sought acceptance into the Christian community. On September 4, 1975, the Unification Church filed a notice of petition in the Supreme Court of the State of New York identifying itself as "a Christian Church committed to the ministry of spreading by word and deed, the gospel of the Divine Lord and Savior, Jesus Christ." It filed under the name "The

Holy Spirit Association for the Unification of World Christianity" requesting membership in the New York Council of Churches. Following this petition, The Commission of Faith and Order of the National Council of the Churches of Christ, U.S.A. declared that the Unification Church was not a Christian Church and must be denied membership in the New York Council of Churches because:

> Its doctrine of the nature of the trinity is erroneous; its Christology is incompatible with Christian teaching and belief; and its teaching on salvation and the means of grace is inadequate and faulty. We further conclude that the claims of the Unification Church to Christian identity cannot be recognized because the role and authority of scripture are compromised in the teachings of the Unification Church; revelations invoked as divine and normative in the *Divine Principle* contradict basic elements of Christian faith; and a 'new, ultimate, final truth' is presented to complete and supplant all previously recognized religious teachings, including those of Christianity.[122]

The Churches of Christ denomination conducted the study of the Unification Church. This commission was concerned with distancing the Unification Church from Christianity because it felt that Unification Church doctrine was not compatible with traditional Christian teachings.

Whether or not they were accepted by "mainstream" Christian churches, the goal of the Unification Church was to restore the original vision of Jesus for his church. A late 1970s Unification Church pamphlet claimed: "Modern Christians must look beyond symbol, dogma, and ritual to the original intent of his [Jesus'] message."[123] While acceptance by the existing Christian denominations would have gone far in reaching the goals of the Unification Church, it was more important for them that their members and potential converts believed that they were doing the work of God. Because the Unification Church relied on its members to do the labor required for restoration, their acceptance of Moon's teachings was critical for the movement to continue.

Following the rejection of Unification teachings by many Christian churches, Moon claimed that Christianity had lost its chance to be involved in saving the world. He said in 1976: "God wanted all Christians to be willing to give themselves for the salvation of the world. However, today Christians of the world are not even close to realizing the heart of God."[124] He claimed that Christian churches were falling away from their relationship with God. Likewise, Reverend Ken Sudo, director of training at Barrytown Unification Seminary, in 1975 declared that Jesus came to earth "to realize the world of love. Every one of us is here to fulfill what Jesus should have done…Christians couldn't realize this. They thought he came to die to give life through the resurrection…Jesus should have gotten married sinlessly and had sinless children to realize the sinless family."[125] Christian churches, thus, according to the Unification Church, had misunderstood the role that Jesus was meant to play in the salvation of humankind.

Moon believed he was sent by God to bring Christianity back into its role as the instrument of salvation for humanity. In a lecture at Goucher College in 1972, he stated: "If all people understood the existence of God everyone would want to follow in His direction. However, I don't think there are many people who really understand the existence of God. Even among Christians, among Christian ministers and Christian leaders, I say there are many who don't understand the existence of God."[126] Moon felt that the teachings in the *Divine Principle* were the answer for bringing humanity closer in their relationship to God. A 1977 Unification Church brochure claimed "Today, what Christianity needs is not another human interpretation of the Bible, but God's interpretation."[127] Moon thus claimed that his teachings were God's plan for returning Christianity to God's original purpose for the world.

Offering an explanation of why Christianity had failed to provide a moral American society showed potential adherents that Christianity had lost legitimacy. It also explained that the Unification Church could engender a moral society through the restoration of the Christian Church. This connection with the primitive Christian church, an ancient established religious tradition, gave members the sense that they were embarking on a sanctioned quest. However, in order to retain members, the Unification Church also offered them another type of authority that gave them the assurance that they were involved in a legitimate religion: a personal religious experience and a special relationship with God. These led members to believe that their individual role in saving America had cosmic implications.

Personal Religious Experience and a Special Relationship with God

While the rhetoric of the conservative movement and Christian restoration drew members to the Unification Church, many stayed in the movement because they believed their work for the church led them to experience God in a personal way. This intimate religious experience helped to persuade many new members that the Unification Church was a legitimate religion. Members of the church stressed to potential converts that they must read the literature and search their hearts to know that the

Unification Church spoke the "truth."[128] This assertion indicated that the church recognized that the potential adherents sought a personal religious experience over revelations, teachings, or leaders' authority.

Unification Church members described their conversion experiences in terms similar to those of traditional Christian adherents. They characterized their transformation as part of a longer journey toward God. What marked their conversion was "a rather dramatic event whereby they [were] confronted and challenged by the need to travel this road with greater seriousness and urgency. They [were] made aware of just how far they really [were] from the goal of achieving Godliness, but [were] given fresh perspective and a clearer roadmap with which to hasten the journey."[129] Adherents of the Unification Church felt that their participation in the movement advanced their own religious journey, as well as involving them in the restoration of the relationship between humankind and God. This gave members the sense that their own work for the movement had cosmic implications.

Moon described the relationship between God and humans as reciprocal. According to Moon's *Divine Principle*, God created humans in order to "feel joy upon seeing His goal realized. Therefore, the purpose of [a human's] life is to return joy to God."[130] In other words, God created humans in order to participate in a relationship with Him. Moon described the relationship as "the four position foundation," which can be depicted in a picture of a cross. God would be at the top as the origin, husband and wife as the creation at either end of the cross-section, and their offspring as the result of their unity at the bottom of the cross.[131] When Adam and Eve brought about the fall of humankind, they broke this perfect relationship. According to Moon, if husband and wife were to live a life "centered on God," their children would bring joy to God and bring about the fulfillment of God's purpose of creation and a part of the restoration of the relationship between God and humans.

The Unification Church taught that God was perfect and the source of love. Moon explained that people could love one another through the example of God. Since God was the source of love for others,[132] one could experience God through parental love, conjugal love, or children's love. Moon also taught that when humans established ideal families, centered on God, then God "comes not as the ideal God, but as the living God in our lives."[133] In other words, the idea of God becomes real in members' experience. In the *Divine Principle*, Moon explained that "the purpose of truth is to pursue and to achieve goodness, and the origin of goodness is God Himself. Therefore, the world attained through this truth would be one in which all men would live together in wonderful brotherly love under God as our Parent."[134] Humans could then experience God personally and become true children of God.

Moon explained that one could come into a personal relationship with God by "centering one's life on God," which he described as perceiving the world through God's eyes and experiencing what God felt. He taught that if one sensed how God loved humans, one would want to love others in a similar fashion. This love would lead to an aversion toward harming others, making sin obsolete.[135] Working on their relationship with God gave new converts an opportunity to be involved in bringing about a purified society. Moon taught that the new sinless world created by this relationship with God would bring about the Kingdom of God on Earth.

The adherent of the Unification Church learned that seeing the world as God viewed it gave individuals the chance to become perfected and attain a level of divinity. For Moon, the perfection of the individual was only possible through a realization of the relationship between God and humans. He explained this transformation in the following passage from the *Divine Principle*:

> The man whose mind and body have formed a four position foundation of the original God-centered nature becomes God's temple (I Cor. 3:16) and forms one body with Him (John 1:20). This means that man attains deity. Feeling exactly what God feels and knowing God's will, he would live as God would want. A man with his individuality thus perfected would have perfect give and take between his mind and body. In uniting together, his mind and body would form a substantial object to God. In that case, God becomes happy because He can feel His own character and form objectively through the stimulation coming from such a substantial object. Man's mind as subject feels the same way in relationship to his body. Therefore, when man has realized God's first blessing, he becomes a good object for the joy of God. A man with perfected individuality feels all that God feels, as if God's feelings were his own. Consequently, he cannot do anything which would cause God grief. This means that such a man could never fall.[136]

As part of discovering the world anew through the eyes of God, Moon taught converts about the "broken-heartedness" of God. Moon explained that the fall of God's children left Him lonely and yearning for the relationship with humans denied by their disobedience.[137] Members were encouraged to understand that God was miserable and lonely and longed for a true family because the sin of Adam and Eve had effectively separated humans from God. Moon taught that identifying with the suffering of God and seeing the world from God's point-of-view would draw members into a closer special relationship with Him.

The experience of identifying personally with God appealed to many new members. Charles, who was a Catholic seminary student when he converted to the Unification Church in 1968 in St. Louis, felt that the teachings in the *Divine Principle* offered him an immediate experience of Jesus. He felt that he could most relate to the "human struggles of Jesus."[138] He also identified with the idea that God needed the love of humans and suffered from the separation caused by original sin. He claimed that focusing on God's feelings made him feel closer to God. He believed that following the teachings in the *Divine Principle* meant that he was obeying God's will for his life.

This feeling of closeness with God that "Charles" mentioned in his conversion narrative is similar to a story related in a study done by scholars in the early 1980s. One person in the study found the Unification Church appealing because of its belief in selflessness: "I don't like the idea of only looking inside yourself to see God. I feel we should look to see God in each other rather than in ourselves. This seems so much less self-centered and so much more loving. I, therefore, think the Unification Church has more validity than the cult of Guru Mahaj-ji, because they believe in finding God in others."[139] Like Charles, this convert was looking for a close experience of God and felt that she had found it in the teachings of the Unification Church. She was able to make the connection with God by "seeing God in others." She determined that the Unification Church was a legitimate religion because she experienced God through love of others.

Like the person above, Moon's teachings led many in the 1960s to experience God through their relationships with others. The conversion story of Beatriz, given at the beginning of this chapter, is a good example. She felt that the solution for the corruption she found in American society lay in "changing the hearts of men," so she looked for a movement with an ideology centered on God. She felt that she found God in the Unification Church movement.

> I found God, a God-centered ideology, and a leader of men who lives totally for God and the world. Reverend Sun Myung Moon teaches us that as God's creation, we are all a part of a greater whole in which God longs to see Himself reflected. How can we but love what in God's eyes is so precious? Truly, there is no room for discrimination. Here, people of all races, ages, and nationalities work side by side as true brothers and sisters for the highest purpose of all—to unite as one family, one nation and one world—under God.[140]

Beatriz found God in the eyes of others. She believed she had to work to unite everyone in God's love. She decided this unification could be accomplished through her work in the Unification Church. This need to change the world through a morally upright movement seems to be true of many Unification converts.

Like Beatriz, Andrew wanted to serve God through ministering to others. The Catholic faith lost legitimacy for Andrew because he did not see people's behaviors transformed as a result of their religious rituals. For instance, he explained that the Catholic Church taught that one experienced God through the Eucharist. However, after one service, he saw a woman making derogatory comments about other parishioners. He believed that if she had felt the presence of God in the Eucharist, it would have been impossible for her to behave negatively toward others. He came to the conclusion that she must not have experienced God through the Eucharist, and, he explained, "I wanted to experience God."[141] He believed he found an intimacy with God through the Unification Church. Andrew was also convinced that Reverend Moon exemplified what humans should strive to become. "I really believe that he is closely cooperating with Jesus. I don't conceive of him as divine, but he is a supreme example of a man who has total self-mastery."[142]

The personal religious experience that many members encountered through the Unification Church gave the new religion legitimacy for them. Whether they were drawn in by the conservative rhetoric or the Church's teachings of restoration, many stayed in the movement because of their personal relationship with God and a religious experience. However, for these converts, the teachings had a purpose—to save an immoral American society. In order to do that, Moon taught that they had to first repair the broken relationship between God and humans.

A Role in the Restoration of Christianity

Ultimately, the promise that they could actively participate in changing the world was the deciding factor for many converts of the Unification Church. While they resonated with the rhetoric of the conservative movement and were convinced that the Christian Church was in need of restoration, they were idealists. American members wanted to personally play a part in cleansing an immoral nation. Restoration has two functions for the Unification Church: they believe they are restoring humans to a right relationship with God, and they believe they are restoring the Christian Church to God's original purpose. Members were persuaded by Unification Church teachings that through their efforts to save the world, they must first save America. This lent their vision cosmic significance. The Unification Church also convinced potential members of the urgency of their mission; they instilled the idea that hesitancy was a sign of spiritual weakness in the minds of adherents.[143]

According to Unification Church theology, the method for individuals to be practically involved in cleansing their world was to "save" the institution of marriage and establish holy families centered on and devoted to God. Marriage and family are the central concepts in Unification Church theology.[144] Because of this focus, the majority of the church's beliefs tend to be concerned with the preservation of family through proper sexual conduct.[145] Moon's upbringing in a primarily Confucian society likely influenced his ideas about the family.[146] His notions of familial piety were drawn from his own background in Korea. Moon taught that the head of the household had an obligation to be a role model for the other members of the family, who in turn, were to obey and trust his guidance.

One of Moon's chief revelations from God concerned how original sin was introduced into the world. Moon noted that the common Christian interpretation of the Genesis story, which concerns Eve and Adam eating forbidden fruit, was often taken literally. Instead, Moon claimed that the "fruit" was symbolic of a forbidden sexual union. Adam and Eve were meant to "attain perfection and unity in heart with God" becoming God's objects of love. They were meant to become "eternal husband and wife, forming a heavenly family...God gave them the ability to bear children so that they could experience with their own children the vertical love that God has for us."[147] In order for their marriage to be considered sacred, it required two blessings from God. When created, Adam and Eve were given the "first blessing" by God and were to remain abstinent until God gave them the second blessing, which would consecrate their marriage.[148] Moon thus claimed that the forbidden "fruit" was actually forbidden sexual union. Had they stayed sinless and been blessed a second time by God, Adam and Eve would have produced the sinless children intended by God.

Instead, according to Moon, Satan caused the fall of humanity by entering into an unholy trinity. Satan tempted Eve into a sexual union with him. Eve told Adam about her illicit sexual union with Satan out of guilt. Rather than bringing Eve to confess the sin to God, Adam engaged in premarital sexual union with Eve, creating a trinity of Satan, Eve and Adam, rather than the holy trinity that God intended of God, Adam and Eve.[149] Moon explains that the marriage of Adam and Eve produced the children of evil because they were born of "false love, false life and false lineage. Thus, when the last days come we can expect the increase of moral decadence among young people to arise as a global phenomenon."[150] Moon saw the moral decay and sexual misconduct of America's youth as a result of the forbidden sexual relationship in Genesis, which made all humans the children of evil.

Moon believed that in order to restore humanity into a right relationship with God, the holy family must be restored. Salvation must happen in the realm of humans because "humanity is the mediator and the center of harmony between the [physical and spiritual] worlds."[151] Moon taught that humans were a combination of flesh and spirit; the spirit of a person could be perfected only through the physical body.[152] Moon believed that God sent Jesus, a perfect human, for the purpose of saving humankind. Jesus was to be the second "Adam," the second sinless son of God. His mission as a sinless human was to get married and produce perfect children. This would have realized the sinless family.[153] While Jesus was not able to fulfill his mission to create a sinless mortal family, God sent the Holy Spirit in the place of Jesus' spouse, to create a spiritual family. Moon taught that this marriage begat Christians as the spiritual children of Jesus and the Holy Spirit. Importantly, this fulfilled *part* of the requirements for restoring the relationship with God.

Moon thus asserted that the original mission of the Christian Church was to engage in sinless marriages to take part in the final restoration of the relationship between humans and God. A third Adam was needed to complete this restoration. This Adam, a sinless human, would enter into a marriage centered on God, creating the first sinless human family.[154] The restoration, or the elimination of original sin, is referred to as "indemnity" by Moon and his followers.[155] Moon and his wife are considered to be the True Parents, creating with their children, the True Family, also calling themselves the "Unified Family."[156] While the True Family refers to Moon's family and those families born of unions presided over by Moon, the Unified Family came to mean the Unification Church family. The True Family is believed by Church members to be the way for the restoration of humanity. Moon explained it this way in 1972:

> When we establish this ideal family God can come down among us. God then comes not as the ideal God but as the living God in our lives. When we usher in the True Parents and establish the True family the ideal world will grow from this—the ideal world of happiness, the ideal world of unity, the ideal world of peace will spring for mankind. Then we can all become children of God.[157]

Moon taught that the relationship with God, disrupted by original sin, could be restored through the creation of a perfect family centered on God.

Indemnity was an important concept in Unification theology, because it allowed a practical path for humans, or members of the Church, to realize their goal. Moon's understanding of God did not include a doctrine of grace, such as that found in traditional Christianity. Instead, God demanded payment in kind for the sins of humanity. His perfect justice did not allow Him to overlook sin without proper restitution. However, God did set up conditions that offered the possibility of restoration for those willing to meet them unconditionally.[158] Moon taught that humans could take practical steps toward making amends for the sins of humanity, restoring the relationship between humans and God.

Individual adherents could personally participate in the restoration process by "initiating proper moral standards and practices, forming true families, uniting all peoples and races, resolving the tension between science and religion, righting economic, racial, political, and educational injustices, and overcoming God-denying ideologies such as communism."[159] These practical actions allowed members to be individually and communally engaged in changing the world. Members believed that their individual involvement in the Unification Church had significance in the larger struggle to procure salvation for humankind. In this way, members believed they were restoring religion as the essential function of the family, which in turn, would return humans into a right relationship with God.[160]

To participate in this restoration, Moon encouraged his followers to first focus on cultivating their personal relationships with God. In addition, the Unification Church required members to follow a strict personal moral code forbidding the consumption of alcohol, drugs or tobacco, and extramarital sex. According to Moon, in order to center one's life on God, one was expected to practice prayer and live a strictly moral and selfless life. The selfless way of life required one to "think beyond himself and his family and live for the greater purpose of the nation and the world."[161] Adherents of this faith worked for the movement, whose goal was to share how reconciliation with God was possible. They were not to focus on marriage for themselves; instead, they were to concentrate on perfecting themselves in the eyes of God. Their work consisted of witnessing, raising money for the movement, converting new members (called their "spiritual children"),[162] organizing retreats, learning more about God's plans, serving their communities, and organizing various events scheduled by Moon. Members called this work "living the selfless life."

Part of living the selfless life involved joining the Unification Church's family. Reverend Ken Sudo, director of Training at the Barrytown Seminary, explained to his students that they must see each member as Jesus. "We should love each other as brother and sisters. But that is not enough. We are here as a small messiah to make up for Jesus' resentment of love."[163] He felt that the success of the *Divine Principle* depended on love: "Give the most precious thing you have to others, to brothers and sisters...It is by giving that you are given to...It is by sacrificing ourselves that someone can sacrifice for us." Therefore, the selfless life involved loving others and the sacrifice of self for the higher good of humankind.

Members of the Church believed that the selfless life meant becoming servants to the larger community. Judi Culbertson, an adherent in 1968, explained the selfless life in her conversion story: "My heart now burns for all of mankind, not just one individual."[164] Another adherent, named Gertrude also had this to say about the selfless life: Reverend Moon "practices what he preaches: you sacrifice yourself for the world, and you place the world before your family. In order to love your family you have to love God first. There is deep sincerity in his actions and his beliefs and the members of his family love him dearly."[165] Members believed their personal sacrifices served God's higher purpose.[166]

According to Moon, the family must be centered on God and must exemplify love. He stated in a conference in 1976, that humans must learn love from God:

> Since the ultimate source of love does not come from man but from an absolute, unchanging and causal subject, the family of love centered around the causal being is the basic unit for realizing the ideal in human society. To realize an ideal of absolute value, we must begin with this family of love and expand to the scope of the nation and the world to reach an ideal world of unity where eternal happiness of absolute value is promised.[167]

The salvation of the world, according to Moon, starts with the family centered on God in a relationship of love. "The family will always be the basic unit of happiness and cornerstone of the kingdom of god on earth and thereafter in heaven."[168] Moon thus stressed the family as the foundation of the restoration structure.

In accordance with its beliefs about original sin, the Unification Church required its members to abstain from sexual relations until they were married. This might be referred to as a "premarital apprenticeship," during which converts strived to perfect their character.[169] The Unification Church required its members to be celibate for at least three years and be a minimum of 24 years old before they could be considered for marriage.[170] In the early period of membership, the convert participated in a "fictive kinship system: Moon and his wife are designated as True Spiritual Parents and other members are 'brothers' and 'sisters.'" During this period, the convert learned to love his or her other church members spiritually and to center his or her life on God.[171] They understood that these relationships would be the basis of the salvation of an immoral American society.

Because devotees of the religion understood that Reverend Moon would choose their spouse, the Unification Church discouraged unmarried members from thinking about who their potential mate might be. This unwise focus distracted one from his or her primary purpose of learning to love one another spiritually. Moon taught that one must learn to love God before one could learn to love another. In addition, this period functioned to allow the convert to understand the "broken-heartedness" of God. Since the member experienced loneliness during this apprenticeship, they could understand how God felt since the fall of his children.[172] Moon taught that only in this state of celibacy and focus on God could one truly understand the suffering of God. Identifying with God in this way drew members into a closer personal relationship with Him.

When Reverend Moon felt an individual was ready for marriage, he would match that person with another member. The couple often had not previously met, so they were given some time after the match was made to discuss the possibility of marriage. If they agreed to the match, the Reverend Moon would announce the engagement. They often waited another two years, sometimes working in separate areas, before they were married. Reverend Moon periodically performed mass weddings to join many of these engaged couples. The Unification Church taught that these large public weddings demonstrated that marriage was not just a private contract between the couple, but rather a part of a much larger religious family under the fatherhood of God.[173]

In an official program of a mass wedding held in New York City in July of 1982, the expectations of married couples starting "blessed families" was clearly stated:

> Until today, the eyes of the world have been upon our Church; after today the eyes of the world will be upon you and your families. Remember three things above all in your life together:
> 1.   **The eternal union of husband and wife**. Your marriage is not merely "until death do us part," but for all time eternal. Each spouse is a great key to ever expanding and deepening our understanding of the

infinite God. In your marriage, God's love is consummated and together
you are able to receive His total love.
2.   **The tradition of family love.** After seeking ideal marriages it is
your responsibility to educate your children with a commitment to moral
excellence. Before you can freely invest your love and energy in other
dimensions, you must by all means fulfill your responsibilities as a loving
parent.
3.   **The Ideal World.** Heaven is a world of heart, where all may trust
and unite with one another in love. But there will be no true heaven for
anyone while people are still in want, in need or in pain—physically or
spiritually. You must all accept your responsibility to work as world
citizens so that the legacy you leave to your children and grandchildren
will be the harmonized world of God's love.

God bless you in all that you undertake and may He give you the vision
and strength you need to realize His Kingdom on earth. That is the task
facing us all.
Reverend and Mrs. Sun Myung Moon[174]

These couples shared the responsibility with other Unification Church
families of creating an ideal family. The Unification Church expected the
formation of these families to be an integral part of realizing the Kingdom
of God on earth.

Once married, the couple not only had one another for family, but the
entire kinship network of the Unification Church. James Grace notes that
"these men and women bring to the marriages many shared concerns.
Even before joining the group, they probably held in common a sense of
alienation from American society, an idealistic view of marriage, and a
commitment to change the world."[175] The couple learned even before they
were married that the community came first, and that their marriage was
part of a larger vision of restoration.

Members of the Unification Church believed that families begun in
marriages performed by Reverend Moon were the beginning of the
restoration of Christianity. These marriages would ultimately bring about a
moral American society and save the world. However, Moon taught that
this would not remove sin from the world all at once. In 1974, when
members wondered about how soon original sin could be removed, the
"Blessings Monthly Newsletter"[176] gave answers to these concerns.
According to Mrs. Shin Wook Kim, the dedication of a baby born of a
Unification couple would not remove original sin. "The original sin will be
removed in three generations' time." Kim explained that the marriage
blessing removed 30% of original sin, the children of a blessed marriage

were 50% cleansed, grandchildren of the blessed couple would be 70% cleansed, and the great grandchildren would be free from original sin.[177]

When the anti-cult movements in the 1970s charged that the Unification Church was breaking up families because of its recruitment of young people, they were attacking one of the most fundamental beliefs of this new religious movement. In a case study of the movement, John T. Biermans explains that because the main emphasis of the Unification Church was on family ties, family relationships of members were important to the church. He notes:

> Many members have developed much closer relationships with their families because of their experience in the Unification movement. This is based on Church teachings which emphasize the eternal bonds that exist in all family relationships as well as the importance of the respect and care for elders. It might also be added that in recent years church leaders have explicitly urged members to resolve difficulties that may have existed in the past [with their family members].[178]

Reverend Ken Sudo, in a speech given at Barrytown Unification Seminary in 1975, likewise explained to his students that because they did not want parents to worry, the church invited them to open houses and had the children serve their parents to see how loving they had become because of their involvement in the movement. However, if their parents still disapproved, he reminded his students not to be shortsighted because "true love is from God."[179] The church went to great lengths to convince parents that their motivations were pure, but were not averse to advising their young recruits to choose the church as their new family if necessary.

While the Unification Church tried to reach out to members' disgruntled families after the difficulties with anti-cult movements, early seminary training literature claims that the best way to draw in members was to slowly convert entire families. Moon advised converting children first, then mothers and then fathers. "If you convert daughters and son, mother is very easy to convert also. Then you can convert a whole family to *Principle*. You are using that strategy to save that family, not for your own good."[180] However well-meaning Moon's intentions, these conversion policies often led to divisions in families; children in the movement sometimes left their families when their conversion was rejected. When their parents refused to join the Unification Church, members were convinced that their parents had been duped by the powers of Satan. Adherents then determined to save their families along with the rest of humanity through their actions as members in the movement.

As part of the restoration process, adherents of the Unification Church believed that repairing the relationship between God and humans would bring about the kingdom of God on earth. In order for restoration to happen, Unification theology asserted that there needed to be an experience of heaven on earth. As a 1970s Unification Church brochure explains:

> Heaven is the realm in the spiritual world where perfected people dwell in oneness with God, as one family of the heavenly father. But heaven must be experienced on earth before we can dwell in it eternally. Therefore Jesus came to bring the Kingdom of Heaven to earth and he left the keys to it with Christians on earth.[181]

Thus, according to Moon's teachings, the Kingdom of God would begin on earth with the True Parents chosen by God to create a heavenly family.

Moon's theology regarding the True Parents was possibly drawn from his contact with Confucianism as a child in Korea. There had been a religious sect connected with Confucianism during the Ming Dynasty in China called *Wu-shen Lao-mu*. This sect declared that there would be a new heaven and earth for the perfect family of humankind under a pair of "Eternal Parents." These parents would give refuge to the disinherited and dispossessed.[182] Likewise, Moon claimed that the True Parents of the Unification Church would help bring about the kingdom of God for all of humankind. As mentioned previously, Moon also borrowed ideas about filial piety from Confucianism.

Conservative individuals with traditional family expectations tended to be drawn to the Unification Church in the 1970s by the Church's adoption of conservative Christian rhetoric. In a study done by Bromley, Shupe and Oliver, Fifty-five percent of their respondents believed that the husband should have the final word in important family decisions and eighty-one percent felt that the husband should be the primary income-producer. Both male and female members were respondents in this survey.[183] Potential members tended to treasure traditional family values.

"Mary," who joined before 1975, said that several things convinced her to join the Unification Church. She was attracted by the "loving family spirit of the members," the teachings about family and parenthood, and her desire to "transform the world, establishing ideal families and an ideal world."[184] She envisioned the ideal world as one where the Kingdom of God transcended all religions, cultures and all races. She wanted to change the world and she saw in the Unification Church theology regarding family a way she could participate in that mission.

Members of the Unification Church believed that their sacrificial work could save the world, but that this happened in steps. Through their perfected families, members intended to rescue America from its moral decline and restore it back to a democratic Christian nation. Once this was achieved, the church could begin its efforts through peace movements to integrate religions around to world into a unified Christian Church family. Restoring America's moral compass was the key to the salvation of humankind, according to Unification Church teachings.

America's Role in the Restoration of Christianity

In 1976, Reverend Moon stated that God always chose a central religion and a nation to receive the messiah. [185] The first religion had been Judaism, the second was Christianity, and the third was the Unification Church. These religions, he felt, "must unite in America and reach out to unite religions of the world." Moon claimed that America was chosen to receive the new messiah because it was "already a model of the unified world." [186]   Moon believed that the whole world was represented in America because all the different races and nationalities of the world lived in harmony in the United States. Moon felt that America was a "microcosm of the world. Transcending nationality and race, America had created a model of the ideal world." [187] Therefore, he taught that the United States needed to "realize that the abundant blessings which God has been pouring on this land are not just for America, but are for the children of God throughout the world. [She has] a responsibility as a world leader and the chosen nation of God." [188]   While this responsibility would save all of humankind, it would save America herself, as well. Moon felt that the depravity of American society was proof that God had started to move away from the nation. Therefore, turning toward God would save America and in turn the rest of the world.

While he understood God to be the source of the independence of America, Moon also saw in this independence the potential for self-centeredness. Hence, Moon pleaded with America to center herself on God so that she would enjoy prosperity. [189] In his speeches in the 1970s, Moon showed some hope for American society: "I know that in spite of America's rebellion against Him, God will not abandon this country. His will is to make America an example of a Godly nation that the nations of the world might follow. I know God's will is to save the world, and to do this, America must lead the way." [190] This idea, that America must become a model for Christian perfection, echoes the Puritan idea of becoming a "City on a Hill" that would have caused the Church of England to mend

her ways.[191]   Moon reasoned that if America became a God-centered
moral nation, the other nations of the world would follow her lead. Moon
saw America as the "central nation in God's providence."[192]

During the Watergate scandal, Moon was concerned that the crisis
would lead America further from her role in humankind's restoration. He
called people to forgive the administration and move ahead. He felt that
"the American nation seems mortally wounded in spirit and soul by the
tragedy of Watergate."[193]   The title of his speech printed in the *New York
Times* in 1973 was "Forgive, Love, Unite."   His close ties with the
administration notwithstanding, Moon felt that the Watergate crisis could
be the undoing of the nation. He beseeched Americans to forgive Nixon's
shortcomings. He declared: "God says 'Forgive.' If we want God to
forgive us, we have to forgive others first."[194]   Moon felt strongly that
Nixon needed to retain his position as president, because he believed that
God had chosen Nixon to lead the country.   According to "Lionel," a
convert in the mid-1970s, Moon saw the celebration of the bicentennial of
America as an opportunity to stress the providential destiny of America.[195]

Distraught by what he understood as the moral decay in America,
Moon tried to call its citizens to task in 1976: "In the 1960s, America
seemed to be the hope of the world...today, however, the world has lost
faith in America. Her cities have become jungles of immorality and
leprosy."[196]   He felt that if Americans could only recognize their moral
backsliding, they could begin to turn toward God and start the
reconciliation process. He wanted to help America lay the foundations for
creating the kingdom of God on earth. Neil Albert Salonen, President of
the Unification Church of America in 1976, said that the mission of the
Unification Church was "based on a new revelation from God given
through Reverend Moon to prepare the world for the return of Christ. The
sole mission of the Church is to bear witness to this revelation and to lay a
foundation for the kingdom of God on earth."[197]   Moon felt that America
had a crucial part to play in the restoration process and in the kingdom of
God.

Many converts joined the Unification Church due to its eagerness to
save America from her depravity. Thus, they felt strongly about how to
accomplish the purification of their country.   "Walter" joined the
Unification Church when it was called the "Unified Family" in California.
He joined the movement because it "had a vision and a discipline for
changing this world and the energy and the program to do it, but was
spiritual and not atheistic."[198]   The means of salvation and cosmic
significance of the Church's mission were an important impetus for
Walter's conversion. Like other Unification Church members, Walter

believed that members' practical steps of self-perfection and ideal families could save America from her depravity and from there, save the world.

Others felt that the day-to-day steps of witnessing to potential adherents would ultimately yield the most results toward saving America. Jeff Tallakson, a former member of Campus Crusade for Christ and new adherent of the Unification Church noted, "The most important of our goals for 1969 is witnessing, because this is the basis upon which our purpose here in Berkeley rests. We must advance upon Satan's front line so we can be creative behind the lines. We are developing new ways of witnessing and finding new battlegrounds."[199]

Likewise, Philip Burley, a new member to the Church, was more concerned with daily efforts toward restoration, "In our life there are high points of joy and success and creativity, but the major pattern is the day-to-day small, steady progress. Often this does not seem to show great results, and it is easy to get discouraged. But it is only through this steadfastness that we can remain faithful."[200] These Unification Church converts, while cognizant of the goal of restoration, believed that emphasis needed to be placed on the practical, day-to-day application of the message.

Other members felt that this focus on witnessing was short-sighted and would not produce results in the larger vision for the Unification Church in America. Farley Jones, a Princeton University graduate and member of the Washington DC group explained, "There was a time in our movement when we truly believed that to build the Kingdom of God in America, we had only to witness every day and teach as many people as possible…Our belief…was not misguided, only very childlike."[201] Instead, Jones felt that individual efforts needed to concentrate on creativity. He believed the movement needed to focus on patterns that were working in Korea and Japan to fashion something that would facilitate America reaching her goals.

Recruitment was seen as instrumental in the early years because of the urgency of the task at hand. While much early recruitment was done through the Mobile Fundraising Teams (MFTs), selling candy, plants, candles door-to-door and flowers on street corners, those efforts were curtailed in the late 1970s and early 1980s. By then, most members were working in the many industries owned by the Unification Church including dry-cleaning, stationary stores, and fish markets, as well as distributing ginseng and the operation of the two daily newspapers *Newsworld* and the *Washington Times*, among many others.[202] The Unification Church may have chosen to be involved in these industries in order to change their public image, in addition to providing opportunities to disseminate their message in previously unavailable avenues. The Unification Church also organized public entertainment such as orchestras, choirs, dancers, martial arts, and theater productions.[203]   While these groups entertained at Unification Church events, they also toured widely as a promotional tool for the church. Finally, from its inception in the United States, the Unification Church relied on campus recruitment for the infusion of new members into its movement.

Those members of the Unification Church who joined the movement in America tended to focus on the means to combat the moral decline they saw in their society. They wanted to be a part of "restoring" America to its Christian moral compass.   While they were drawn into the movement through conservative rhetoric and restoration claims, their personal religious experiences lent them a sense that they were involved in a legitimate religious movement. The church taught that recruiting new members, focusing on self-perfection and their relationship with God, and forming ideal families in accordance with the teachings of Reverend Moon, were steps leading toward "saving" America from moral chaos. The daily religious practices of converts became for them a way to be personally involved in saving America from its moral decline.

Summary

Why did some young people in 1960s and 1970s America join the Unification Church? Members were not coerced into membership. Rather, they willingly became involved with the Unification Church because they were intrigued by the movement's vision for America and for the world. In addition, adherents reported that they encountered meaningful religious experiences as a result of their involvement with this religion. Since many new adherents believed that Christianity misunderstood Jesus' role in the salvation for humankind, and furthermore had failed to prevent the decline in American morality, they chose this alternative path. The Unification Church persuaded these adherents that their Church had the proper understanding of God's message and a vision to save humankind. Furthermore, the Unification Church promised to involve members in its plan to restore the relationship between humans and God, which they claimed would first save America from its moral depravity and then save the world. The Unification Church offered its members a personal religious experience and a special relationship with God. This lent religious authority to the Church in the minds of its adherents. Converts to the Unification Church believed that their actions within that movement had cosmic significance—they intended to rescue the world.

Because the Unification Church emerged in America in the 1960s and 1970s, it addressed the upheaval and restructuring of America during that time period. Since the Unification Church taught that the "rampant" drug use, teenage pregnancies, premarital and extramarital sex had their roots in a religious problem, the movement offered a religious solution. The Unification Church leaned toward the emerging conservative movement, which had a similar rhetoric and solution. Both movements felt that the answer to America's moral decline was the return to their definitions of traditional Christianity and "family values."

Ultimately, the Unification Church's version of Christianity led many Americans to conclude that the Unification Church was a "deviant" religious movement, or a "cult." While conservatives and the Unification Church had a similar agenda, they viewed Christianity differently. Conservatives stuck to the "mainline" churches' definition of Christianity, while Reverend Sun Myung Moon offered a divinely-revealed new understanding of what God originally intended for the Christian community. This is why the Unification Church can be considered a restoration movement: they believed they were "restoring" God's original plan for Christianity. They asserted that personal sacrifice and adherence to God's purpose for marriage would reinstate the relationship between humankind and God.

In order to disseminate his message to a larger cross-section of Americans, Reverend Moon took advantage of the means available to him in the culture. In the early years of the movement, devotees were visible signs of the movement in their street corner carts hawking their wares and in university organizations across the country. Later, the Unification Church bought small businesses that contributed proceeds to the parent organization. The Church staffed these small businesses with church members, integrating them into productive society. Moon also purchased two daily newspapers in major American cities to voice his religious message. Additionally, he held scholarly conferences and created several non-profit organizations working toward religious tolerance. Finally, his entrenchment in the conservative movement in America gained his ideas admission into the political circles of the emerging Religious Right. While these were various routes to ensure that Moon's religious message was heard, they also secured his religion's representation in the discourse of American culture.

The success of Reverend Sun Myung Moon's Unification Church hinged on the universal acceptance of its message. In order for this movement to unite the Christian churches of the world, all Christians needed to agree that Moon's revelation was God's plan to restore humanity into a right relationship with Him. Since the National Council of Churches declared the Unification Church was not a Christian church, the American "mainstream" Christian churches considered the Unification Church to be a deviant religion. Others in America were convinced of the questionable nature of the Unification Church because of negative media coverage prompted by anti-cult groups. This aberrant status likely thwarted Reverend Moon's mission to finish the work that he believed Jesus had started.

While Moon could have started a movement claiming a new revelation from an unknown source, Moon's revelation came from the Christian God with a message for Christians. This is important for a few reasons. First, Christianity is a known religion with global visibility. Christianity has the institutions and sheer numbers in place to start the process of changing the world. Because potential members primarily came from Christian backgrounds, they understood the worldview from which the Unification Church drew its theology. Second, Christianity already has a tradition of newer denominations claiming to practice what God originally intended for the Christian church. Therefore, potential converts would not have immediately dismissed the new religious movement, since restoration claims are common in Christianity. Third, Moon appealed to "tradition," which was the language of the emerging conservative movement at that time. Tradition meant that the Christian ideas, practices and values had been handed down from generation to generation, making it more acceptable in the eyes of American culture.[204] This lent Moon a certain amount of legitimacy within the segment of the American population from which he was most likely to attract followers.

While Moon persuaded converts that he had a genuine restoration message, members' personal religious experience and their sense of success in their goals to save the world ultimately led to their conversions. Members participated in strict moral discipline and meditation on the suffering of God. They actively engaged in the conversion of new members and formed committees for world unity and peace. This personal experience of God and active participation gave members the sense that they could achieve their goals of changing the world. Because the Unification Church arrived in America during a time of cultural upheaval and uncertainty, its claims of an ancient Christian message gave potential members a sense that they were joining a long tradition. While Moon claimed a new revelation, this message was grounded in a conservative Christian model, one with which new members could identify.

CHAPTER TWO

FEMINIST WICCA,
A NEOPAGAN RELIGIOUS MOVEMENT

i found god in myself
& i loved her/i loved her fiercely
—Ntozake Shange[205]

While the Unification Church appealed to conservative American youth intent on purifying a morally corrupt nation, Feminist Wicca drew women frustrated with their subordinate status in America. Although they engaged a different demographic and worked toward very different goals, the strategies of the two movements had some similarities. Both offered a plan for otherwise disempowered people to be personally involved in improving their society. Unlike secular social movements of the 1960s and 1970s, however, the Unification Church and Feminist Wicca promised their constituents spiritual rewards for their work in America: a personal relationship with their deity and a religious experience that would enable them to transform their world.

Feminist Wicca, one of many Neopagan new religious movements, specifically appealed to women from the feminist movement using familiar feminist rhetoric and claims that it was resurrecting the worship of the ancient goddess. This modern witchcraft religion offered its potential members a religious path toward ending patriarchy. Many converts to Feminist Wicca in late 1960s and early 1970s America believed that Judaism and Christianity were complicit in their oppression and for that reason, had failed to create a better society for women. Feminist Wicca promised to help women re-envision the deity through the lens of ancient goddess worship, which would give them a personal religious experience and a special relationship with "the goddess." Most importantly, Feminist Wiccans believed that their new religious movement gave a model and the means for ridding America of her patriarchal power structure.

Jean and Ruth Mountaingrove, the editors of the quarterly magazine called *WomanSpirit* in Oregon in the 1970s, intended to print the voices of women involved in emerging religious movements. Specifically, they

were interested in those who were in the process of discovering a
connection between ancient goddess religions and the contemporary
feminist movement. They described their work as follows:

> We feel we are in a time of ferment. Something is happening with
> women's spirituality. We don't know what it is, but it's happening to us
> and it's happening to other people. *WomanSpirit* is trying to help facilitate
> this ferment. Ruth and I feel that women's culture is what we want. We
> want so much to live what we can glimpse. Now that we understand what
> our oppression has been, and have fantasized what it would be like not to
> be oppressed, we want to *live* like that. That is what we are looking for; we
> want the world to be a wonderful place for us to live in; and we don't want
> it in three thousand years; we want it this afternoon; tomorrow at the
> latest.[206]

Like Jean and Ruth, many women in the 1970s were drawn to Feminist
Wicca, which revered ancient goddesses, because the new religious
movement offered them a glimpse of how the world could become better
for women.

The term "Neopagan" is a broad term that describes many new
religious movements claiming to be resurrecting ancient earth-based
religions.   These groups believe their ancestors passed down these
religious rituals by word of mouth for hundreds or thousands of years.
The ancient healers whom members identify as their religious ancestors
were often marginalized and persecuted by Christian churches.
Neopagans reject the separation of spirit and body and give nature and the
earth divine qualities.[207] Most see the earth as "Mother," to be revered and
protected.

Neopagan movements in America claiming ancient origins include
Wicca, Druidism, Pagan Reconstructionists, The Church of All Worlds,
the Fellowship of Isis, and various Neopagan witchcraft groups. This
study focuses on the Feminist Wicca practices of Neopagananism that
emerged in America in the 1960s and 1970s from the feminist movement
of that era. Feminist Wiccans claimed to be recovering an ancient
European goddess religious tradition. Feminist Wiccans declared that they
were perpetuating the ancient practice of witchcraft, passed on from
mother to daughter for centuries. In addition, they believed that the power
of goddess worship impacted the political actions of women, enabling
them to shape their future by following a model of an idyllic past. These
women believed that the personal religious experiences offered by their
movement would give members the incentive to act in the American
political sphere. Feminist Wiccans integrated an ancient religious tradition
into a new religious movement in order to improve their world. They

believed that their appropriation of ancient goddess worship could help them to end the patriarchal power structure in America.

This chapter offers a brief literature review of the scholarship on the religion of Wicca. It then summarizes the history of Feminist Wicca, as it developed out of a combination of the feminist movement and the Wicca religion in the late 1960s and early 1970s. I then explore the two types of rhetoric that attracted potential members to Feminist Wicca: feminism and the "re-emergence" of the Goddess. Section two of this chapter explains what Feminist Wicca offered its prospective members. First, I show that Feminist Wiccans clarified for potential adherents how women's childhood religions failed them. I then proceed to describe the personal religious experiences and the special relationship with the Goddess promised to potential members. Finally, and most importantly, this chapter explains how Feminist Wiccans believed their newly appropriated ancient religion would dismantle patriarchy in America.

Existing Scholarship on Feminist Wicca

Most of the scholarship on Wicca, or contemporary witchcraft, in the United States focuses on the versions that came to America via English immigrants. Few specifically address Feminist Wicca, which changed "traditional" Wicca to suit its own needs. However, the scholarship on Wicca does identify the claims of antiquity, which is of particular interest here. This study shows that Feminist Wicca, along with Gardnerian Wicca, appropriated an ancient heritage because this mythological golden age offered a model for an ideal future. The following literature review demonstrates that scholars have been most interested in either disproving the antiquity of Wicca or describing it as a religious phenomenon. Many scholars also claim that the appeal for women lay in the feminine divinity, who, they assert, enabled women to take control over their lives. These particular scholars explain that this identification with the goddess gave women the authority to be leaders in their religious and secular lives.

Historians have long debunked the theories of Wicca as a continuation of an ancient witchcraft religion. According to Margot Adler, author of *Drawing Down the Moon*, British historian Norman Cohn insisted in *Europe's Inner Demons* that the lineage of witchcraft was a delusion.[208] He claimed that many societies had stories about small groups engaged in secret religious practices in the midst of a larger society. However, he believed this was a common fantasy. Since no one had ever come across a society of witches secretly practicing their religion, he reasoned, they could not exist. Rather than a group fantasy, H. R. Tevor-Roper, another

British historian, suggests in an essay entitled "The European Witch Craze and Social Change," that witchcraft was a political creation.[209] This theory proposed that the Inquisition devised the idea of witchcraft in order to bring rural areas into conformity with the Christian church's beliefs. In other words, witchcraft was a notion created by the Christian Church that did not exist before the Inquisition.

Aidan Kelly, a Neopagan practitioner and scholar, also questions Wicca's claims of antiquity, as evident in his introduction for Gordon Melton's *Cults and New Religions*. Kelly traces the roots of Wicca to Gerald Gardner, who claimed to have recovered the ancient tradition of witchcraft and renamed it "Wicca." Kelly reasons that it is more likely that Gardner created the rituals himself from other widely available religious sources. Like Kelly, Jacqueline Cooper questions Wicca's history in an article entitled, "Comprehending the circle: Wicca as a contemporary religion." Although somewhat critical of the formation of Gardnarian Wicca, Cooper's thesis is that Wicca should be considered a new religious movement, or in her terminology, a contemporary religion. In arguing that Gardner may have created the religion, she also questions the ancient historical roots that Gardner claimed for Wicca.

Agreeing with Kelly and Cooper, two historians have recently questioned Gardner's historical claims. In 1998, Philip G. Davis, a professor of religion at the University of St. Edward Island, published *The Goddess Unmasked: The Rise of Neopagan Feminist Spirituality*.[210] In this text, he also claims that Wicca was created by Gerald Gardner and, like Ronald Hutton, a British historian of pagan religions, could not find any evidence of the coven into which Gardner claimed he had been initiated. Hutton, in his 1999 text *The Triumph of the Moon*, gives the history of the development of Wicca and comes to the conclusion that, while there may have been some folk witchcraft in Britain, Gardner invented the new religious movement of Wicca.[211]

Cynthia Eller also discussed the historical claims of contemporary witchcraft in her early scholarship observing: "Neopagans believe they are reviving (and sometimes creating anew) ancient nature religions. They usually trace their genealogy to Europe, and sometimes even more narrowly to Britain."[212] She also noted the importance of the historical claims for practitioners of new religious movements, arguing that: "Especially in its early years, hereditary witchcraft was very important to Neopagans as proof that the religion they practiced had a real tradition behind it."[213] However, Eller claimed "Wiccan lineages and ancient practices are of less and less importance nowadays, as Neopagans feel more secure in the religions they have created (or maybe only more certain that their hereditary claims will be disproved)."[214] Eller has most recently written a text debunking this ancient goddess history entitled *The Myth of Matriarchal Prehistory: Why an Invented Past Won't Give Women a Future*. This text explains why the plans of Feminist Wiccans to offer an ancient model for a future end of patriarchy will not be successful.[215]

While most scholars question the antiquity of Wicca specifically, Mircea Eliade, an American scholar of comparative religion, argued that witchcraft generally has ancient roots. He noted that stories about witches were found in many ancient religions and indigenous traditions. He believed that the contemporary practice of witchcraft probably survived in part from ancient folk culture, which is closer to what Neopagan witches believe themselves.[216]

While I agree that the antiquity of Wicca is questionable, I argue in this chapter that the function of these claims is more important than their historical veracity. Appealing to an ideal past allowed members of Feminist Wicca to posit a vision for an ideal future. The function of the ancient goddess myth will be the subject of much of this chapter.

While many scholars have debunked the historical roots of Wicca, others are interested in the function of the divine feminine in this religion. These scholars have suggested that the feminine divine in Wicca was a draw for women in the 1970s. Carol P. Christ and Judith Plaskow explain that women felt oppressed by the male deity of western religious traditions. They point out that "God in 'his' heaven is both a model *of* divine existence and a model *for* women's subordination to men."[217] Christ also claimed that women needed to, "Name the great powers or powers of being…from their own perspective and to recognize their participation in them. Women need to recognize that their participation in the life and death forces in all natural processes means that they have as much right to exist and to affirm their value as every other being."[218] Cynthia Eller agrees, and explains that the goddess myth offered women an improved self image.[219] Lynda Warwick, a religious studies scholar, suggests that claiming a connection with a feminine deity was a source of empowerment for women.[220]

"Empowerment" is a term often used by feminists to denote the assumption of power, the ability to take control over their own lives.[221] This idea grew out of the slogan "the personal is political" first coined by Carol Hanisch, a leader in the radical feminist movement.[222] Women in the Feminist Wicca movement felt that a personal religious experience with a goddess would propel members to work together in a common cause for women in America. The yearning for power to define the self and one's relationship with the world is of much interest in this study and will be discussed at length in subsequent sections of this and the next chapter.

In addition to historians and religion scholars interested in claims of antiquity and the image of the goddess, some scholars have been more concerned with making primary source material and reference material about Wicca available to researchers. James Lewis, a scholar of American new religious movements, offers a reference text of Wicca entitled *Witchcraft Today: An Encyclopedia of Wiccan and Neo-Pagan Traditions*.[223] This text describes the belief systems of various Neo-pagan groups and has biographies of their leaders. Likewise, J. Gordon Melton's reference text, *Neo-Pagan Witchcraft I*, is an introduction to a collection of primary source material from Wicca and other forms of witchcraft in England and America.[224]

While the above scholarship ranges from those debunking the historical claims of witchcraft to those offering reference information on the movements, not many scholars have analyzed the motives of the movement. The only explanation of the intentions of the various goddess movements offered was by Christ, Plaskow, Eller and Warwick—that it gave women a sense of "empowerment." However, for Feminist Wicca, Goddess worship was even more calculated. Unlike previous scholarship, I show in this study that these claims of antiquity had a compelling purpose. Asserting that Wicca was a direct descendant of ancient goddess worship gave women in Feminist Wicca a sense of legitimacy. They felt that ancient goddess worshipping societies, which they understood to be peaceful and respectful of nature, offered a precedent for a comparable contemporary American society. They believed that the success of ancient goddess religions assured the potential triumph of a similar contemporary religion that would imbue its values into American culture. In addition, since Feminist Wiccans concluded that American patriarchy was legitimated by a male deity, it stood to reason that offering a female deity would make an egalitarian society equally legitimate.

The research for this chapter not only incorporates the secondary literature reviewed above, but primary documents from the main voices of Feminist Wicca in the 1970s. In this chapter, I reference Zsuzsanna Budapest's *The Feminist Book of Lights and Shadows* and Starhawk's *Spiraldance* for rituals and theological beliefs of the leaders in the movement. These books also give voice to some of the members. Margot Adler's *Drawing Down the Moon* has both primary and secondary material. In addition to a chapter on Feminist Wicca, Adler presents some of the viewpoints of women in the movement. In order to encompass additional viewpoints of the adherents of Feminist Wicca, I also include excerpts from the 1970s newsletter entitled *WomanSpirit*.

Since I wish to present the perspective of Feminist Wiccans, I also summarize the myth of ancient goddess cultures as described in Merlin Stone's *When God Was a Woman* and Riane Eisler's *The Chalice and the Blade*. Since the cultural historical context is vital in order to understand how women became alienated from their childhood religions and attracted to a new religious movement, I also integrate information from a variety of scholarship on the feminist movement and women's spirituality in 1960s and 1970s America.

The thesis of this chapter illustrates that Feminist Wicca utilized rhetoric from the feminist movement and the myth of the ancient goddess in order to attract members to its religious movement. Potential members were women who felt disenfranchised from the patriarchal power structure of American religious and secular society. Thus, Feminist Wicca offered prospective adherents reasons that the Judeo-Christian religions had failed women, a personal religious experience with a special relationship with the deity, and the possibility of dismantling the patriarchal power structure in America. Many potential members had previously been involved in the secular feminist movement in the 1970s. Feminist Wicca promised a religious approach to women's secular goals of advancing the status of women in America.

Thus, the first section of this chapter addresses how the two types of rhetoric that drew potential members into Feminist Wicca: feminism and the "re-emergence" of the goddess, informed the history of the movement. Section two explains what this religious movement offered its prospective members. First, it shows how Feminist Wiccans clarified the failure of traditional religions for women. Next, this chapter proceeds to describe the personal religious experiences and special relationship with the Goddess that Wicca promised its followers. Finally, this chapter shows that Feminist Wicca assured women that their involvement in the religion would help them realize their goal of dismantling patriarchy.

History of Feminist Wicca

Wicca has two histories—the myth of antiquity and the history of its "revival." The ancient goddess myth is integral to understanding the movement's modern history, because many of the claims of modern witches refer to the story of ancient goddesses and the tradition of witchcraft practices. Feminist Wiccans claim that before patriarchal cultures existed, there were ancient societies that worshipped a goddess. In these peaceful cultures, men and women were valued equally for their contributions to their communities. Contemporary witches found hope for women in this ancient myth. The rhetoric of the ancient goddess myth will be discussed at length later in this chapter.

While most Wiccans would have agreed in general about their origin myth, their opinions differed about who "revived" the ancient tradition. Important figures in the development of early Wicca included Margaret Murray, the writer of *Witch-Cult in Western Europe*; Charles G. Leland, who wrote books about pagan cults that survived in Italy; Robert Graves, the author of *The White Goddess*; and Gerald B. Gardner, who wrote *Witchcraft Today* and *The Book of Shadows*.[225] Many Wiccans read these books at the time of their publication, but contemporary Wiccans searching for their "roots" have also read these texts.

Of these early influences, many contemporary Wiccans credit Margaret Murray with being the first to propose that ancient pagan folk customs in Britain survived in a limited form into the modern age. While many scholars and adherents consider her work to be filled with errors, she was nevertheless influential in shaping early witchcraft thinkers. Several later writers cite her as a source for their assertions that witchcraft practices survived from ancient times. In addition, Charles Leland's *Aradia, or the Gospel of the Witches* (1899)[226] was a significant contributor of ideas for early revivalist witches. This work concerns a Romanian myth describing a Queen of the Witches (Diana, or Tana) who sends her daughter, Aradia, to earth as a messiah figure to teach the arts of witchcraft to the poor and oppressed of humanity.[227] Another frequently-cited source of inspiration for the witchcraft revival was Robert Graves' *The White Goddess*.[228] Often discredited as an anthropologist, Graves in fact saw himself as more of a poet. He offered, in *The White Goddess*, another mythology for modern witches. He argued in this text that several covens of witches survived from ancient Britain until modern times. He claimed inspiration from Margaret Murray's work, which he believed made a revival of witchcraft possible.[229]

While the above texts were certainly important for the "revival" of witchcraft, most scholars generally credit Gerald B. Gardner with founding contemporary witchcraft. This is most likely because he was one of the earliest people to publish a book of spells and ritual practices. Gardner (1884-1964) was active in this movement in the 1940s. He claimed that a circle of witches initiated him into their coven in an English forest in 1939. Gardner wrote a descriptive volume about witchcraft entitled *Witchcraft Today* in 1954. Gardner asserted in this text that he was recording the practices of a dying religion. Gardner formed a coven with whom he practiced the rituals as set forth in *Witchcraft Today*, and in this coven Gardner established a magical system and a set of rules for Wicca.[230] He published these practices in a text entitled *The Book of Shadows*. Gardner reportedly passed on these rituals to initiates such as Alex Sanders, who proceeded to form their own covens.

While Gardner claims that he borrowed the rituals described in his books from ancient witchcraft practices, it is more likely that he invented and appropriated much of the information. Ronald Hutton, British historian of modern Pagan witchcraft, notes that not only did academic historians not take Gardner's claims seriously, but his rituals and belief system were dismissed by the journal of the British Folk-Lore Society, which found Gardner's rituals far removed from those of "traditional" witchcraft researched by them.[231] Gardner's religious ceremonies contained dances and ceremonial feasting. The practitioners performed the dances naked, since they wished to promote fertility. In these rites, believers venerated a god and goddess while the members of the group worked in a sacred circle. Wiccans used particular tools, such as a knife, chord, and censor in the rituals. In addition, part of ritual practices included trance and ecstasy, giving the members a personal experience with the divine.[232] Each group was called a coven, led by a high priest and priestess.

While many witches in America called themselves Wiccans and used Gardnerian-inspired rituals, others devised their own sets of practices. Gleb Botkin, the son of the court physician to the last Russian Tsar founded the first of these and the oldest Neopagan church in America, called the Church of Aphrodite. He established this religious community in Long Island in 1938. The mission of the religion was to "seek and develop Love, Beauty and Harmony and to suppress ugliness and dischord."[233] Members practiced these rituals in order to bring themselves into a "right" relationship with the Goddess. The rituals were inspired by ancient Greek myths and Russian folklore.

In addition to the Church of Aphrodite, other small pockets of pagan groups also sprang up in mostly rural areas around the United States from immigrant families in the 1930s and 1940s.[234] Vance Randolph's survey of the Ozark highlands in 1947 found evidence of European pagan religious practices in these areas.[235] These "family" witches claimed to practice rituals passed down through descendants of older relatives from Europe. The rituals mostly consisted of the healing arts and divination. However, the witchcraft that had been percolating in England in the 1930s and 1940s finally arrived in force in the United States during the 1960s and 1970s. Some Americans were reading Murray, Graves and Gardner during that time, and the immigration of English Wicca practitioners further spread Neopagan ideas and practices in America.[236] According to Ronald Hutton, the unique contribution to Neopagan witchcraft was its assimilation into the women's spirituality movement—the marriage of feminism and goddess worship, called Feminist Wicca.[237]

The first indication of this blend of ideas was the formation of the group called WITCH (Women's International Terrorist Conspiracy from Hell) in 1968 in New York.[238] They claimed that the link between women, witchcraft and political action was ancient:

> WITCH is an all-woman Everything. It's theater, revolution, magic, terror, joy, garlic flowers, spells. It's an awareness that witches and gypsies were the original guerrillas and resistance fighters against oppression— particularly the oppression of women—down through the ages. Witches have always been women who dared to be groovy, courageous, aggressive, intelligent, nonconformist, explorative, curious, independent, sexually liberated, revolutionary. (This possibly explains why nine million of them have been burned.) Witches were the first Friendly Heads and Dealers, the first birth-control practitioners and abortionists, the first alchemists (turn dross into gold and you devalue the whole idea of money!) They bowed to no man, being the living remnants of the oldest culture of all—one in which men and women were equal sharers in a truly cooperative society, before the death-dealing sexual, economic, and spiritual repression of the Imperialist Phallic Society took over and began to destroy nature and human society.[239]

This manifesto claimed that, to gain freedom, women needed to become witches again simply by being female, untamed, nonconformist, and intelligent. To be a witch, one only had to claim the title. WITCH was involved in several protests, but disbanded in 1969. Although American feminist witches did not pick up all of the ideas of WITCH, they did borrow some: the ideas that patriarchal institutions have historically oppressed women, that the witchcraft trials killed thousands of women, and that women needed to claim the witch as a positive political symbol, all were eventually blended into feminist witchcraft ideas.

Several important American feminist writers also informed the newly-evolving Feminist Wicca movement in the United States. Mary Daly, a Catholic theologian, believed that witches throughout history had been independent women. Andrea Dworkin, an American radical feminist, asserted that the witchcraft trials had been "gynocide," or intentional extermination of females. Both Barbara Ehrenreich, social critic and essayist, and Deirdre English, former editor of *Mother Jones* magazine, claimed that ancient witches had been the healers and midwives in their small rural communities and that the witch trials had not only eliminated female power but also traditional medicines.[240] Most of the American feminist writers also blamed the 15th century Christian *Malleus Maleficarum,*[241] drawing quotations from it liberally. Andrea Dworkin said that the *Malleus Maleficarum* proclaimed women to be naturally carnal and that women's innate nature made them more amenable to sin and partnership with Satan. According to feminists, the beliefs espoused by this document were to blame for the thousands of women killed in witch trials in the Middle Ages.

Feminist Wiccans, along with many women in America, were also influenced by women's literature in the 1960s and 1970s. Women writers described the impact of the era's political upheavals on American women in their poetry and novels. Poet Sylvia Plath described her personal struggles with her father in her poem, "Daddy," (1963) as having political and theological implications.[242] Jean Temperman also reflects the idea of rebellion in her poem "Witch," (1973) in the lines "We are screaming/we are flying/laughing, and won't stop."[243] While rebellion was a common theme, so was the search for an answer to the subjugation of women. Adrienne Rich describes the search for a common language for women to communicate with one another, define and reinvent themselves in her "Transcendental Etude" in *The Dream of a Common Language.*[244] While American women's literature in the 1960s and 1970s is far too extensive to enumerate here, it is clear that women's discontent had far-reaching implications in American culture. Women meant for their voices to be heard and, as Mary Daly explained, women intended to "spook" the patriarchy with all the weapons at their disposal in American culture: "theater, satire, explosions, magic, herbs, music, costumes, cameras, masks, chants…[their] own boundless, beautiful imagination."[245]

While most feminists, including women involved in WITCH, drew on the witch as a purely political reference in the 1970s, other groups, beginning in California, began to appropriate the witch as a religious symbol for the advancement of feminism. Since many women believed that the religions of their childhoods had failed them, some feminists sought alternative religions, particularly those with a female deity. Their specific explanations of Christianity's failure will be discussed later in this chapter. Some of the religious groups with a feminine divine were already established, such as Wicca, however, others sprung up from discussion groups organized by grassroots feminists.

The "women's spirituality movement" drew many women in the late 1960s and the 1970s. While this movement defies definition, according to Cynthia Eller, the practitioners of women's spirituality, while extremely diverse, held many things in common. Virtually all participants believed that the movement was empowering for women; that ritual was an important tool of authority and communication with the sacred; that nature was sacred; that women's reproductive functions were holy; that female symbols gave significance to women's experience; and that the worship of the Goddess had historically lent women more power in their societies.[246] Eller believes that the movement of women toward spirituality was inevitable, because the experience of some women with feminism was all-encompassing and because their beliefs had grown too far outside of any extant orthodox faith.[247] In the 1970s, the women's spirituality movement was in its infancy; it took hold more widely in America in the 1980s.

The women's spirituality movement was loosely organized and its followers held different beliefs about its meaning and practices. Ronald Hutton notes that for some it was a "general female right to a separate spirituality, while for others it implied the spiritual power within women."[248] For others it was the general belief in the mythology of the ancient Goddess cultures and the promise it held for contemporary women. Some believed that the implications of the goddess were personal, while others felt that there were religious and political ramifications of their beliefs.   What the women's spirituality movement lacked was a common doctrine and prescribed religious rituals. The ideas promulgated by the women's spirituality movement were widespread, however unorganized. Many women exposed to these ideas became involved in feminism and some became involved further, into Feminist Wicca.

Wicca drew some feminists because it offered an established religion with a divine feminine, which was deficient in the women's spirituality movement. However, when feminists entered Wicca, they changed the practices of the religion to suit their particular spiritual and political needs. Wicca had an existing religious structure and working theology, which the women's spirituality movement lacked. While most Wiccan covens had a dual male/female godhead, the female was the more powerful of the two. Most covens in the 1970s originally had both male and female members. When feminists joined the movement, however, many chose to begin their own covens that worshipped only the goddess and were exclusively for women.   The beliefs and practices of the strictly female covens came to be called Dianic Wicca.   Others continued to have both males and females, but their agenda was feminist-driven.

This re-envisioning of the godhead as primarily female gave feminists a way to identify personally with the deity. In *A Feminist Philosophy of Religion*, Pamela Sue Anderson observes that this need for identification with a female deity arose because women felt excluded from sexual difference by "the unfair privilege of dominant figures of male selfsameness and the exclusive use of reason."[249] She asserts that the dominant religious philosophy had equated males with God and reason as the exclusive dominion of men. Thus, Feminist Wiccans meant for the female deity to equate emotion and sensuality with power for women. They believed that a transfer of the deity's gender would make these qualities valued by the culture and provide women a higher status.

However, Feminist Wiccans felt uninhibited by either restrictions of male deities or reason. They sought to embrace a religion that valued them and gave them a sense of control over their lives. According to Margo Adler, who administered a survey of Neopagans in the late 1970s, Neopagan witchcraft in general embraced the values of

> spontaneity, nonauthoritarianism, anarchism, pluralism, polytheism, animism, sensuality, passion, a belief in the goodness of pleasure, in religious ecstasy, and in the goodness of this world, as well as the possibility of many others. They have abandoned the 'single vision' for a view that upholds the richness of myth and symbol, and that brings nourishment to repressed spiritual needs as well as repressed sensual needs. 'Neopagans,' one priestess told me, 'may differ in regard to tradition, concept of deity, and ritual forms. But all view the earth as the Great Mother who has been raped, pillaged, and plundered, who must once again be exalted and celebrated if we are to survive.'[250]

Many Neopagan Wiccans in the 1970s did not embrace political action. They kept their religious and secular lives separate. Their religious practices "provided a spiritual and religious framework for celebration, for psychic and magical exploration, and for ecological concern and love of nature."[251] Wicca, as a religion, was based on personal experience. While many were members of covens, just as many were sole practitioners. Its ethical standards "an it harm none, do what ye will' and the laws of three-fold effect (whatever one does will come back to one three-fold) articulated the belief that one must be responsible in one's religious practice.[252] While women represented the goddess in ritual, these leadership roles often did not extend into the secular lives of Wiccan women.

Feminist Wiccans, however, insisted that the personal *must* be political. They asserted that one's deeply held religious beliefs should affect one's political views and one's actions within the society. Through "consciousness raising groups," women involved in the feminist movement learned that they shared powerlessness with other women. They came to realize that women's' relationships with men, whether personal or otherwise, were dominated by unequal distributions of power— educational, economic, religious, social, political and physical.[253] Feminist

Wiccans took this a step further and declared that one's personal relationship with the goddess would necessarily provoke one to be politically involved in changing the status of women in society.

Interviewing Susan Rennie and Kirsten Grimstad, editors of the *New Woman's Survival Handbook*, Margot Adler learned that feminist witches around the country in the 1970s understood themselves as a source of power that, although it had been repressed, had enormous potential for active change:

> They put forth the idea that women have an even deeper source of alienation than that which comes from the imposition of sex roles; that, in fact, patriarchy has created the erroneous idea of a split between mind and body and that women's exploration of spirituality is 'in effect striving for a total integration of wholeness,' an act that takes the feminist struggle into an entirely new dimension. 'It amounts,' they said, 'to a redefinition of reality,' a reality that challenges mechanistic views of science and religion as well as masculine politics.[254]

Feminist witches equated women with the goddess. The goddess as feminine divine had power over the earth. She therefore gave legitimacy to the idea that women could have power over their worlds. They saw the "witch" as an "extraordinary symbol—independent, anti-establishment, strong, and proud. She is political, yet spiritual and magical. The Witch is woman as martyr; she is persecuted by the ignorant; she is the woman who lives outside of society and outside of society's definition of woman."[255] The feminist witch, therefore, while a strong independent agent outside of mainstream society, channeled her powers from the goddess to enact change for the betterment of women *within* American society.

Thus, Feminist Wicca in the 1970s was concerned with engaging women to enact change in society. One practitioner in the late 1970s, Leigh Star, explained:

> The union of female self-identification and mysticism is witchcraft. Politically, it has been/is ultimately threatening in its implications for the radical restructuring of man's world. It was once subjected to brutal control under patriarchy, now it is being subjected to extremely subtle control…It is being done in a manner which ensures that the connections between feminism and wholeness will not be made.[256]

Star believed that this worldview could empower women to radically change the male-dominated world. In addition to validation, adherents saw Wicca as offering women more opportunities in their religious and secular lives, and greater personal insight than monotheistic traditions such as Christianity.

Theories of a long-ago universal age of goddess worship or a universal age of matriarchy appealed to Feminist Wiccans. They believed that during this age, women had been respected and had held positions of power. These peaceful societies flourished and were bastions of art, literature and music. While scholars such as Elliot Rose and Norman Cohn have debated whether or not such an age actually existed, this did not diminish the power that such an idea had for many women during the formative years of this movement.[257] This mythical golden age sparked the imaginations of many feminist witches who felt that it offered a potential model for how society could be restructured in the present generation. Feminist Wiccans chose to envision a future based on a past paradise. Zsuzsanna Budapest, a Dianic priestess, told Margo Adler, "After all, if Goddess religion is sixty thousand years old or seven thousand, it doesn't matter. Certainly not for the future! Recognizing the divine goddess within is where real religion is at."[258] Visions of the past goddess cultures, whether real or imagined, and finding the goddess within, ignited in Feminist Wiccans the spark needed to fuel the fire of societal change.

However, the marriage of feminism and Wicca was not an easy one. Many Wiccans were unhappy with the restructuring and revisioning that the feminists proposed when they came into the existing movement. Kelley Schara, in trying to reconcile the two movements, agreed that "every aspect of women's lives have been oppressed by both Eastern and Western religions."[259] However, she feared that feminists focusing on political ideals would swing the movement too far away from its spiritual base. The new feminist members of the movement did not hesitate to change rituals, organization, and beliefs to suit their needs. An anonymous Sacramento Wiccan said "for feminists, the Goddess is a new discovery, and getting a lot of attention accordingly. Like a pendulum, a person must swing to both extremes before reaching the middle…For general exposure, then, perhaps accuracy isn't as important as contrast to the prevailing Judeo-Christian thought."[260] This woman felt that feminists might be able to add something to their new religion in the long run. Other Wiccans, however, resented the move away from their established religious practices.

One self-proclaimed "Old Guard Pagan" complained that Starhawk's book *Spiraldance* in 1979 was to blame for a "massive influx of people into feminist traditions of Wicca" and a subsequent shift in ideology.[261] He complained that Feminist Wiccans did not hesitate to begin new circles and start new rituals, whereas an "old guard" pagan would rather join an existing coven. Existing covens, he believed, could pass down centuries-old secrets through oral traditions for the novice to learn. He complained that the "old ways" would be lost if the feminist witches continued to begin new covens and create new rituals.

When feminists joined the Neopagan movement, they changed the emphasis and language of many rituals. They pointed out that this female-oriented religion usually had male spokespeople, such as Gerald Gardner, Alex Sanders, Ray Buckland, and Leo Martello. Feminists noted that while Wicca gave women some stature within the religion, women members of the movement were not taking that experience and acting upon it in the wider society.[262] Feminist Wiccans sought to change this, and thus formed feminist covens. In their covens, the Goddess was emphasized, women were in leadership positions, and members took the empowerment gained in the religious rituals to challenge patriarchal American institutions. Z. Budapest and Starhawk were the most vocal feminist Wiccans.

Z. Budapest was an early creator of Feminist Wicca. She was a catalyst for changing the Wicca religion to suit the needs of feminists. She firmly believed that personal beliefs were ultimately political. In her 1976 version of *The Feminist Book of Lights and Shadows*, she asserts: "What people believe (faith—religion) is political because it influences their actions and because it is the vehicle by which a religion perpetuates a social system. Politics and religion are inter-dependent."[263] Budapest and a few friends started a Feminist coven in 1971, calling it the Susan B. Anthony Coven Number 1. They named their group after the famous suffragette because they respected her ability to act on her beliefs. When asked what she would do in the afterlife, Susan B. Anthony replied: "I'll tell you: When I die I shall go neither to heaven nor to hell, but stay right here and finish the women's revolution."[264] They, therefore, felt that they were carrying on her heroic work for the women's movement in their coven. They intentionally started this group as a feminist coven, set apart from the larger Wiccan community. Originally, the coven was for women only, although they later allowed men to participate. The members explained that they began it in order to "resurrect, remember, and invent women's religious experience."[265] The manifesto of the Susan B. Anthony Coven #1 states:

> We believe that Feminist witches are wimmin who search within themselves for the female principle of the universe and who relate as daughters to the Creatrix.

We believe that just as it is time to fight for the right to control our bodies, it is also time to fight for our sweet womon souls.

We believe that in order to fight and win a revolution that will stretch for generations into the future, we must find reliable ways to replenish our energies. We believe that without a secure grounding in womon's spiritual strength there will be no victory for us.

We believe that we are part of a changing universal consciousness that has long been feared and prophesized by the patriarchs.

We believe that Goddess-consciousness gave humanity a workable, long-lasting, peaceful period during which the Earth was treated as Mother and wimmin were treated as Her priestesses. This was the mythical Golden Age of Matriarchy.

We believe that wimmin lost supremacy through the aggression of males who were exiled from the matriarchies and formed the patriarchal hordes responsible for the invention of rape and the subjugation of wimmin.

We believe that female control of the death (male) principle yields human evolution.

We are committed to living life lovingly towards ourselves and our sisters. We are committed to joy, self-love, and life-affirmation.

We are committed to winning, to surviving, to struggling against patriarchal oppression.

We are committed to defending our interests and those of our sisters through the knowledge of witchcraft: to blessing, to cursing, to healing, and to binding with power rooted in womon-identified wisdom.

We are opposed to attacking the innocent.

We are equally committed to political, communal, and personal solutions.

We are committed to teaching wimmin how to organize themselves as witches and to sharing our traditions with wimmin.

We are opposed to teaching our magic and our craft to men.

Our immediate goal is to congregate with each other according to our ancient womon-made laws and remember our past, renew our powers and affirm our Goddess of the Ten-thousand names.[266]

This manifesto shows that members of this Feminist Wicca coven intended for their religious beliefs to affect how they responded to the world. They believed that they were fighting to save women from an oppressive, dangerous patriarchal society. They wished for their beliefs about ancient Goddess worship to inspire their imaginations to improve American society for women. Budapest's *Feminist Book of Light and Shadows* and its later adaptation *The Holy Book of Women's Mysteries* were instrumental in many feminist witches' early development. Budapest later founded the Women's Spirituality Forum in 1986 with the purpose of bringing Goddess consciousness to the center of the feminist movement.[267]

According to a press release, Zsuzanna Budapest was born in Budapest on January 30, 1940. She came to the United States in 1958 at the age of 18, after escaping the Russian occupation of Hungary. Her fiancé from Hungary found her in the United States, and they married that same year. She had two sons by the time she was 21. She became involved in the feminist movement in the late 1960s, developing a female-centered theology declaring the Goddess to be Mother Earth. In 1970, she and her husband Tom divorced and she moved to California. She subsequently formed her coven and Women's Spirituality Forum in 1971. In the late 1980s she also hosted a cable television show entitled "13th Heaven" that promoted worship of the Goddess.[268] In addition, Budapest was an active member of NOW, a board member of Women and the Biosphere, and co-producer of the Defend the Children Rally.[269]

Z. Budapest claimed that her Hungarian family had roots in witchcraft dating back to 1270 CE. Her family history, written in a family Bible, included a long line of women herbalists and healers and male military leaders and church bishops (serving a double life of pagan priests after Christianization). Budapest's grandmother was an herbalist and was politically active in Hungary before World War I. Her mother was a ceramics artist whose work depicted the goddess. Budapest also claimed that her mother was a gifted medium, communicating with the dead and delivering messages for the living. University of Budapest scholars identified the language of one of these channeled spirits as ancient Egyptian.[270] Budapest asserted that many of the rituals she adapted for feminist Wicca were remembered from her mother. Zsuzsanna Budapest, who taught from the beginning of this movement that the ancient goddess religion gives contemporary women a vision of a future America, has been at the forefront of Feminist Wicca since its inception.

Starhawk, the author of *Spiraldance*, was another important voice for feminist witchcraft in the 1970s. Like Budapest, she called women to realize a new future for women in America through re-enacting ancient Goddess religious rituals. She called her style of witchcraft "reclaiming," because she asserted that it resurrected the ancient practices of goddess worship. She affirmed that the practices described in her book express a "deep, spiritual commitment to the earth, to healing, and to the linking of magic with political action."[271] This was another form of feminist witchcraft, which she insisted included "a radical analysis of power, seeing all systems of oppression as interrelated, rooted in structures of domination and control."[272] Starhawk described rituals using "elemental magic," or magic using the four elements (earth, air, fire, water), to enact change. She believed that these practices would "reclaim" ancient magical practices for contemporary women. The beliefs in *Spiraldance* were concerned with engaging spiritual women in political action. This book, first released in 1979, was an important contribution to the feminist witchcraft movement.

Starhawk, born Miriam Samos in 1951, created the "Reclaiming tradition," that sought to unify spiritual practices with political action. She was raised in the Jewish faith. She attended UCLA in the 1960s, getting involved in many political actions. Starting in the mid-1970s, she became a vocal feminist witch, teaching workshops and classes and performing public rituals. In addition, she was an activist, calling for non-violent reform of patriarchal institutions and environmental policies. She called herself an "eco-feminist, which, for her, meant that she was a feminist concerned about "mother earth."[273] She felt that her beliefs about the environment compelled her to political action on the earth's behalf.

While Starhawk's reclaiming movement was informed by what she believed were ancient goddess traditions, ultimately what was important for this movement was how this vision of the past could change the future. Starhawk stated "Looking back at the past inevitably leads to looking forward to the future."[274] However, claims of the antiquity are important:

> But Witchcraft is a religion, perhaps the oldest religion extant in the West. Its origins go back before Christianity, Judaism, Islam—before Buddhism and Hinduism, as well, and it is very different from all the so-called great religions…According to our legends, Witchcraft began more than thirty-five thousand years ago, when the temperature of Europe began to drop and the great sheets of ice crept slowly south in their last advance. Across the rich tundra, teeming with animal life, small groups of hunters followed the free-running reindeer and the thundering bison. They were armed with only the most primitive of weapons, but some among the clans were gifted, could 'call' the herds to a Cliffside or a pit, where a few beasts, in willing sacrifice, would let themselves be trapped. These gifted shamans could attune themselves to the spirits of the herds, and in so doing they became aware of the pulsating rhythm that infuses all life, the dance of the double spiral, of whirling into being, and whirling out again. They did not phrase this insight intellectually, but in images: the Mother Goddess, the birthgiver, who brings into existence all life; and the Horned God, hunter and hunted, who eternally passes through the gates of death that new life may go on.[275]

Feminist Wicca saw the goddess as Mother Earth, as the life-giver, and believed their religion to be a resurgence of an ancient earth-based tradition. Starhawk's book *Spiraldance* brought many feminists and environmentalists into the Neopagan community, and specifically Feminist Wicca.

In addition to groups begun by Budapest and Starhawk, an important vehicle for communication among American Neopagans in the 1970s was the monthly publication entitled *The Green Egg*, published and distributed by a Neopagan group called The Church of All Worlds. This group was formed in Missouri in 1967. They were inspired by science fiction and utopian writings.[276] The Church of All Worlds, in *The Green Egg*, defined Paganism as "a response to a planet in crisis, and its spiritual core lay in the concept of the earth as a single, divine, living organism. The mission of Pagans, was to save 'her' by a change in the values of Western society."[277] The importance of the Church of All Worlds and its publication the *Green Egg* was its ability to give a large number of individual groups a common language and purpose. They used terms like "pagan" and "neopagan" to describe the emerging earth-based religions, and the *Green Egg* gave these various groups a network for communication and terminology for identification.[278] Many Wiccans and Feminist Wiccans used the *Green Egg* as a tool to communicate their common ideas and goals with one another.

The newsletter entitled *Womanspirit*, was also an important communication device for many Feminist Wiccans. Jean and Ruth Mountaingrove, from southern Oregon, created the feminist magazine, *WomanSpirit* in 1978. The subject matter ranged from describing and affirming women's experience, to lesbian concerns, to the divine feminine. Women contributed articles, poems, and opinion letters. This magazine had a wide circulation and was an avenue for women to share their ideas and plans with one another in a semi-public forum.

In addition to communicating with one another through publications, Feminist Wiccans created covens in which they could share their experiences. The covens were communities through which they could personally encounter the Goddess and become active agents for change in the United States. Through their covens, women became involved in letter-writing campaigns, sit-ins, and protest rallies designed to advance the status of women in America. Many internalized their experiences of Goddess as earth and participated in demonstrations designed to heighten public awareness about the environmental dangers of big businesses and encroaching development. Most women involved in Feminist Wicca were radicals, in that they chose grass-roots avenues for change, rather than legislative or corporate routes.

While there were many types of Neopagan groups in the United States during the 1970s, Feminist Wicca made the most use of the ancient goddess religious tradition to effect political change for women. These groups used the imagery of the Goddess and the icon of the Witch as sources of empowerment. They imagined a glorious future that was patterned on an idyllic past. They were involved in the feminist and the environmental movements and used their religious ideas to shape their political actions. Feminist Wicca utilized rhetoric from the feminist movement and the image of an ancient Goddess religion to draw in potential converts.

Rhetoric of the Feminist Movement

Many members of Feminist Wicca had formerly been involved in the secular feminist movement in America. Therefore, the rhetoric of the feminist movement was a powerful means for communicating their ideas for change. The feminist movement in the 1960s and 1970s emerged in response to the recognition of discrimination against women in governmental policies, the educational institutions, the workplace, and in the home. Many of the women active in instigating change had been part of the radical sixties movements and thus learned strategies and rhetoric to help them in their own battles for equality.[279] Feminists intended to change the world by creating new language, changing perspectives, and posing solutions to the problems raised by a male-dominated society. This rhetoric made its way into Feminist Wicca, because the two movements shared the goal of ending patriarchy. The feminist movement was largely composed of white, middle class, educated women.[280] Women of color tended to be marginalized in the movement perhaps because of the perception of their association with other racial and ethnic minority groups.[281]

The feminist movement of the 1960s and 1970s sought ways to overthrow the oppression of women and to allow women to become equal independent agents.[282] Some scholars call this the second wave of feminism in America, the first wave having been during the women's suffrage movement.[283] Feminist rhetoric thus employed the claims that women suffered from inequality, oppression and subordination in the patriarchal society. By inequality, they meant that women were denied rights and privileges available to men. By oppression, feminists meant that women felt a weight pressing down on them: patriarchal ideologies, political forces, governmental policies, and economic disadvantages kept women below men in society.[284] Finally, feminists utilized the term "subordination" to identify men as the agents of oppression. Feminists claimed that men, as holders of the power in society, actively kept women

in a subordinate position.[285]   Feminists did not only point out the
oppression of women; they sought to change society so that women had
status and opportunity equal to that of men.

Feminists chose to adapt ideas from those created by male social
theorists designed to justify the social dominance of men. The idea was to
turn the men's arguments against them, and in the process justify a society
inclusive of women.[286]   While feminists borrowed ideas of equality,
democracy and freedom from Locke and Rousseau, these theories did not
take into account the social and economic degradation of women.[287]
Likewise, while Marxist theory provided a map toward equal social status,
Marxism's failure as a practical ideology caused feminists to continue
their search. Existential philosophers like Simone de Beauvoir, in
conversation with Sartre, offered some reflections on the relationship
between self and society; however, women craved practical application of
these theories.[288] Finally, feminists took into account the structuralist
theory of language, which located sexism at the point of language utilized
by the culture. Each of these theories partially informed feminists as they
strove to apply social theory to their movement toward social change, but
each theory had its drawbacks.

Andrea Nye, philosopher and feminist theorist, suggests that feminists
had difficulty deciding between the various theories because each had its
problems:

> Who is she to listen to?—the Marxist feminist who tells her she has
> abandoned poor women in her drive for equal democratic rights?; the
> radical feminist who tells her she has compromised her primary
> commitment to women in her involvement in leftist politics?; the lesbian
> feminist who tells her she is a collaborator because she lives with a man?;
> the French feminist who tells her that in being rational she denies her
> femininity?[289]

Nye points out a fundamental dilemma for feminists: how could one take
into consideration all the problems of women in devising a solution to
their societal difficulties? Clearly, women felt forced to choose different
routes to achieve the changes for which they felt most passionately.

Thus, women in the feminist movement took different courses of
action to achieve their goals of raising the status of women in American
society. Nancy Whittier, author of *Feminist Generations*, describes two of
these as "radical" and "liberal" feminists and she explains their different
strategies for achieving equality for women in America. Radical feminists
focused on grassroots issues like offering rape counseling, day care for
working mothers, self-defense training, and battered women shelters.

Liberal feminists, on the other hand, tackled legislative issues confronting women by organizing lobby groups for state and national governments, raising funds to elect candidates for political offices, and mounting court challenges against sexist practices.[290] In other words, while liberal feminists tried to work within existing social institutions for change, radical feminists created new social groups according to the needs of women. Women in Feminist Wicca tended to have come from the radical feminist movement; therefore they focused mostly on grassroots issues.

The radical feminist movement emerged in the late 1960s with the creation of "consciousness-raising" groups in urban centers. These groups were loosely organized and were designed to bring women of different backgrounds together to discuss the experience of "womanhood." The small groups of five to fifteen women selected a different discussion topic each time they met. They took turns speaking about the topic without interruptions or critique from the other women in the group.[291] They found that they had much in common and learned that they shared many of the same frustrations with regard to their role in the family, jobs and social institutions. By the mid-1970s, many of these smaller consciousness-raising groups had become more organized, often providing services most needed in that community. In addition, these groups also confronted sexist employment policies on a case-by-case basis and tackled the negative depictions of women in the media.[292] Feminist Wiccans used similar models to organize their small groups.

Feminists had learned how to organize, how to protest, how to get media attention, and how to create change from both inside and outside the system from the radical sixties movements. Feminist women who had emerged from the radical sixties movements "saw themselves as revolutionaries who were challenging and rethinking the meaning of revolution to include women's liberation."[293] They brought with them the notion that "the personal is political." This meant individual women worked for the benefit of womankind in America, creating new communities and new identities.[294] They found solidarity among the various women's groups in calling the whole collective the "sisterhood."

I refer to feminism as a movement because it was an overall worldview, not a collection of formal organizations. Feminist rhetoric claimed that women were denied economic, political and social equality because men held power in American institutions. Since men controlled societal institutions, women were often restricted from, or left out of, important decisions affecting themselves and their families. In addition, women felt that they were not treated as intellectual equals by men and were therefore denied opportunities in society. Women did not just want to be able to do what men had always done, they also wanted to be able to do what women had always done, and to have these actions valued.[295]

While the feminist worldview was fluid, so was the definition of the term "feminism." Women in the movement tended to describe their worldview and their definition of feminism in individual ways. What drew the movement together in the 1960s and 1970s were individual women who internalized a feminist worldview and then joined communities, social movements, and formal organizations that put their ideas into action.[296] Women diligently sought ways to make claims for the collective group of women, "the sisterhood," without reducing the broad spectrum of women's experience.[297] Feminism was engaged in changing the world. In order to do this, the movement created new language, new perspectives, and posed solutions to the problems raised by a male dominated society.[298]

While Feminist Wicca inherited this worldview, it expanded upon it by offering a religious solution to the problem of the oppression of women in America. Feminist Wiccans believed that worshipping the Goddess could bring about the ideal gender-equal society. They offered the blueprint of an ancient peaceful goddess culture for a contemporary egalitarian America. Like their counterparts in the feminist movement, Feminist Wiccans believed that the personal was political. They asserted that women's personal religious experiences would compel them to be actively engaged in toppling patriarchy in America. Part of their religious experience involved envisioning a new America based on an idyllic past goddess-centered society.

Rhetoric of the Re-emerging Goddess

Feminist Wicca was the result of the marriage of feminism and goddess worship. As noted in the survey of Feminist Wicca above, practitioners intended for their religion to spark women's imaginations to envision and bring about a better world for women. They believed that the spiritual lives of women should inform their political activism. Thus, Feminist Wicca offered the myth of ancient goddess-worshipping cultures, which they believed had been peaceful and concerned about the environment, literature and the arts. This myth was loosely based on archaeological and anthropological evidence.

Margot Adler, a scholar and adherent of Neopaganism, describes the myth of ancient goddess worship as follows:

> Witchcraft is a religion that dates back to Paleolithic times, to the worship of the god of the hunt and the goddess of fertility. One can see remnants of it in cave paintings and in the figurines of goddesses that are

many thousand years old. This early religion was universal. The names changed from place to place but the basic deities were the same.

When Christianity came to Europe, its inroads were slow. Kings and nobles were converted first, but many folk continued to worship in both religions. Dwellers in rural areas, the "Pagans" and "Heathens," kept to the old ways. Churches were built on the sacred sites of the Old Religion. The names of the festivals were changed but the dates were kept. The old rites continued in folk festivals, and for many centuries Christian policy was one of slow cooptation.

During the times of persecution the Church took the god of the Old Religion and—as is the habit with conquerors—turned him into the Christian devil. The Old Religion was forced underground, its only records set forth, in distorted form, by its enemies. Small families kept the religion alive, and, in 1951, after the Witchcraft Laws in England were repealed, it began to surface again.[299]

The following is a summary of how adherents interpret the myth according to Cynthia Eller:

In a time before written records, society was centered around women. Women were revered for their mysterious life-giving powers, honored as incarnations and priestesses of the great goddess. They reared their children to carry on their line, created both art and technology, and made important decisions for their communities.

Then a great transformation occurred—whether through a sudden cataclysm or a long, drawn-out sea change—and society was thereafter dominated by men. This is the culture and the mindset we know as "patriarchy," and in which we live today.

What the future holds is not determined, and indeed depends most heavily on the actions that we take now: particularly as we become aware of our true history. But the pervasive hope is that the future will bring a time of peace, ecological balance, and harmony between the sexes, with women either recovering their past ascendancy, or at last establishing a truly egalitarian society under the aegis of the goddess.[300]

This myth provided Feminist Wiccans with a model for a future America devoid of patriarchy. According to the myth, ancient matriarchal cultures were non-hierarchical, harmonious, and peaceful communities. To stress the peaceful nature of goddess cultures, academic writer Charlene Spretnak claimed that matriarchies such as Minoan Crete enjoyed one hundred years without war, and that defensive structures were unnecessary in ancient Europe before the northern invasions.[301] The ability to demonstrate the past success of goddess cultures was the cornerstone upon which the argument for a contemporary non-patriarchal society rested for Feminist Wiccans. In pointing to an ancient version of their goal for a future America, Feminist Wiccans were claiming that their new ideas were based on tradition. This lent their plan for a patriarchy-free America some legitimacy.

The myth of ancient goddess worship began with the writing of feminist authors about archaeological artifacts that suggested the worship of an ancient goddess. Marija Gimbutas was one of the first archaeologists to claim that ritual artifacts supported the ancient goddess theory. Gimbutus explained that many prehistoric European cultures worshipped a goddess and were women-centered, and that patriarchal institutions had destroyed these cultures.[302] Gimbutas was widely-read among feminist authors, who began to believe that the ancient goddess cultures constituted a precedent for women gaining power in society. Readers believed that the worship of a female deity improved the status of women in those ancient societies and thus, women began to look to history for their models. Many came to the conclusion, through studying the work of feminist archaeologists and historians, that women had not always been oppressed by men.[303] They began to assert instead, that women had once been revered and respected. Supporters of the ancient goddess theory believed that historical records suggested that societies that worshipped a Mother Goddess were peaceful, ecologically responsible, and cultured. They asserted that the worship of a goddess also granted women a higher status in those societies.[304]

According to Merlin Stone, the author of *When God Was A Woman*, the existence of ancient goddess worship is based on three lines of evidence. First, supporters of this theory point to "anthropological analogy" to confirm their argument that matriarchal societies existed. This chain of reasoning relies on the premise that the mystery of the process of conception led early peoples to revere women for their ability to bring forth life from their bodies.[305] In other words, because ancient peoples did not understand or recognize the role of men in the conception of children, these early communities considered women the head of the household and children traced their lineage through their mothers. This theory utilizes the anthropological writings of James Frazier, Margaret Mead and Jacquetta Hawkes, who opined that early peoples probably did not understand the biological processes of reproduction.[306]

Archaeological artifacts comprise the second line of evidence cited by supporters of the theory of ancient matriarchal cultures. Figurines called "dzulis," which were small female statues found in carved-out niches in the walls of homes and temples, suggested to these analysts that Paleolithic cultures worshipped a female ancestor deity who represented the origins of their people.[307] Allies of this theory argued that the figurines are the last remnants of rituals practices that had honored an ancient goddess.

The final line of reasoning in the argument that ancient matriarchal cultures existed also rests on archaeological evidence. While various female statues suggested that rituals for worshiping a goddess existed, they also led theorists to believe that this goddess devotion was widespread during the Upper Paleolithic Era. Supporters of the matriarchal theory note that these archaeological artifacts date back to 25,000 BCE and span a period of at least 10,000 years and several areas: Spain, France, Germany, Austria, Czechoslovakia, and Russia.[308] Thus, supporters claim that archaeological evidence corroborates their theory that a "great mother cult" existed in Paleolithic times.

Accordingly, Cynthia Eller posits that the myth of matriarchal prehistory functioned to offer hope for the status of women. The myth "takes a situation that invites despair—patriarchy is here, it's always been here, it's inevitable—and transforms it into a surprising optimism: patriarchy is recent and fallible, it was preceded by something much better, and it can be overthrown in the near future."[309] Eller suggests that women responded enthusiastically to this myth partly because it gave them a vision for the future, but also because it offered them an improved self-image. The myth stressed the divine within women, their innate goodness, their own natural majesty and it reframed their conceptions of 'femaleness.'[310]

Feminist scholars in this movement believed that after patriarchal societies dominated the ancient goddess cultures, male-centered institutional leadership deliberately lost or suppressed this female-centered past from the history books, although somehow it managed to survive.[311] They maintained that patriarchal leaders had changed the images of the goddesses, but did not erase them from mythologies, and that ritual practices secretly continued, passing from generation to generation. For instance, Charlene Spretnak argues in *Lost Goddesses of Early Greece*, that the goddess Athena had originally been the Cretan goddess who watched over the home and town. She was the patron of wisdom, arts, and skills, and she especially protected architects and artisans before she became the Grecian warrior goddess who defended the city of Athens.[312]

In formative Feminist Wicca, claims that their religion was recreating an ancient religion were important to adherents. Many asserted that their practices dated back to societies that existed before Christianity. Claims that Goddess worship had ancient roots and had been passed down through the centuries were an integral part of the developmental mythology; it gave potential members the impression that the new movement was part of a long-standing tradition. Gerald Gardner himself claimed that he was passing down ancient witchcraft practices that had been preserved in the small coven into which he was initiated. The claim of antiquity convinced many potential adherents of the legitimacy of this new religion because it instilled a sense of tradition.[313]

The question for many scholars might be whether Gardner's claims that he was passing down ancient traditions was important to members of formative Wicca. Aidan Kelly, founder of the New Reformed Orthodox Order of the Golden Dawn (NROOGD) was interested in discovering the origins of contemporary witchcraft in the 1970s. After years of research and study, he concluded that whether Gardner used ancient traditions or borrowed information, he "transformed [it] 'so thoroughly that he instituted a major religious reform—that is, as has happened so many times in history, he founded a new religion in the apparently sincere belief that he was merely reforming an old one."[314] For Kelly, it "really makes no difference whether or not Gardner was initiated into an older coven. He invented a new religion, a 'living system,' and modern covens have adopted a lot of it because it fulfills a need."[315]

Issac Bonewits, active in both Wicca and Druidism and a prolific writer on magic, described the ancient origins of witchcraft as "myth" in the early 1970s, when many others were still under the impression that they were "recreating" ancient goddess traditions.[316] When I asked Bonewits to paraphrase his early arguments against the ancient origins of Wicca for this project, he replied:

> There was never a single 'Old Religion,' but thousands; b) there was no evidence that anyone except the late medieval Church thought that witchcraft was a religion of any sort; c) underground religions don't stay intact very long (cf. the "Moranos"); d) there was nothing demonstrably older than a century or so in any of the early published materials about Wicca; e) ditto for the secret and personal notes about Wicca.[317]

Bonewits was convinced in the early years of Wicca in America that the myth of antiquity was a false history.

Canadian Naomi Goldenberg, of the University of Ottowa, believed that it mattered little whether or not the myth was true. She wrote in 1979 that:

> Although Witches do often speak of the times of the matriarchies, most are more concerned with that concept as a psychological and poetic force than as an historical verity. A popular aphorism among modern Witches is Monique Wittig's idea put forth in Les Guerilleres: 'There was a time when you were not a slave, remember…Or, failing that, invent.' Witches consider any thought or fantasy real to the degree that it influences actions

in the present. In this sense a remembered fact and an invented fantasy have identical psychological value. The matriarchies, i.e., the times when no woman was a slave to any man, create visions of the pride and power women are working to have in their present lives. Thus matriarchies are functioning in modern covens and in modern Witches' dreams whether or not societies ruled by females ever existed in past history.[318]

For Goldenberg, it did not matter if the ancient matriarchies were fact or fiction, the story itself held great psychological power for women.

Because Feminist Wiccans were interested in creating new forms of worship that were centered on a goddess and that celebrated women, they saw less need to prove the antiquity of their faith than did earlier adherents of Wicca. While drawing from visions of the past, they were more concerned with how to envision a more gender-equal society in contemporary America. However, while less worried about *proving* their claims of antiquity, Feminist Wiccans still affirmed ancient goddess worship as part of their religious heritage.

Ann Forfreedom, an early adherent of Feminist Wicca, in an unpublished paper entitled "Feminist Wicce Works," noted that "Modern witches claim these Europeans were members of 'the Old Religion' of Wicce (or Wicca), a religion that has been traced back to Neolithic and Paleolithic times. Certainly, many members of Wiccecraft (Craft of the Wise, the religion of witchcraft) hid their beliefs, since most Christian countries considered such beliefs to be both criminal and heretical until recently."[319]

Likewise, Carl Weschcke, the founder of Llewellyn Publications, said in 1976 "To believe in witchcraft is to believe in the 'Old Religion,' the pre-Christian religion."[320] When Carl Weschcke married Sandra Heggum in 1973, their wedding was covered by *The Sun*, which reported that "the marriage rite included rituals [Weschcke claimed were] passed down through centuries of the closely guarded practice of witchcraft." Thus, Weschcke believed that the rituals recorded by Gerald Gardner were authentically ancient. He thought that claiming Gardner's rituals were largely plagiarized from Aleister Crowley was an attempt by scholars to discredit Gardner and to detract from the historical continuity of witchcraft.[321]

Charlene Spretnak, a researcher of women's spirituality, explained that while antiquity gave Feminist Wicca some legitimacy, outsiders needed more convincing:

When I was traveling in the Middle East and Central Asia in 1969, the people I met, mostly peasants, would often ask about my home, my family, and my religion. Being a retired Catholic with an interest in Buddhist

meditation, I attempted to express my feeling about spirituality and nearly
always they would ask, "Do you have a book?" They felt that a holy book
of any sort—the Koran, the Upanishads, the Sutras, the Bible—would
signify legitimacy. Sometimes I sense that same reaction among
contemporary theologians and people in general toward Goddess
spirituality—to which I respond: We are older, so much older, than
books.[322]

The belief of adherents that they were resurrecting an ancient religion was
meaningful regardless of the details.

One might wonder why Feminist Wiccans chose the symbol of the
witch, if they were interested in being seen as forming a legitimate
religious tradition. After all, the witch had been a much maligned figure in
traditional religions. However, besides the romantic idea that they were
performing rituals that were centuries old, what appealed to many
Neopagan witches was the idea that their predecessors endured horrible
persecution and survived victorious. Said a priestess of the religion:
"Sexual equality, ecology, the belief in reincarnation, love, attunement and
magick are all part of the Old Religion, and despite a frightening and
gruesome history of persecution, bloodshed and misunderstanding, it has
survived for over 20 thousand years."[323] The claim that they were
continuing an ancient tradition that had survived centuries of persecution
gave practitioners a sense of pride and power. They believed that they
possessed religious truths that were impervious to authoritarian social
structures.

While Neopagan Wiccans claimed their rituals to be part of a
continuous hereditary line of practices and Feminist Wiccans believed
they were constructing a vision of a new world modeled on an imagined
past, antiquity was important to both of these witchcraft movements.
Asserting that their practices were centuries old endowed witches with a
sense of legitimacy. The sociologist Marcello Truzzi wrote:

> Basically, witchcraft constitutes a set of beliefs and techniques held in
> secret which the novice must obtain from someone familiar with them.
> The normal, traditional means for obtaining such information is through
> another witch who knows these secrets. Traditionally, this can be done
> through initiation into an existing witch coven or by being told the secrets
> of the Craft by an appropriate relative who is a witch. Any other means of
> obtaining the secrets of witchcraft, such as through the reading of books on
> the subject or obtaining a mail-order diploma, is not a traditional means
> and is not considered to be legitimate by traditional witches. Because most
> witches today have not been traditionally initiated into the Craft, they often
> create other links to the orthodox as a means of gaining legitimacy. Thus,

many of today's witches claim hereditary descent from some ancient witch
or claim to be the current reincarnations of past witches.

In general, ascertaining the source of legitimacy in witchcraft groups is
very difficult, especially since almost all claim ancient, traditional origins.
However, intense investigation usually reveals that the group's secret
sources are not as claimed.[324]

In Wicca, legitimacy was primarily a concern mostly for other practicing
witches. In order to be considered a legitimate witch, according to Truzzi,
one had to be initiated into a coven of witches who had been previously
initiated into the ancient secrets of witchcraft. For Pagan Wiccans and
Feminist Wiccans alike, claims of antiquity were important in order to
convince potential adherents of the truth of their magical status.

For Feminist Wicca, specifically, the vision of a past golden age of the
goddess was important because it gave hope for a potential future for
women in contemporary American society. Some Feminist Wiccans thus
became convinced that American society could improve the status of
women because there was a historical model.[325] Juliette Wood, in her
study of goddess cultures, states "If we look at the Goddess paradigm as
an exercise in creative history, then we are looking at a view of the past
which, however it may fail academic criteria, presents a powerful image of
feminine cultural identity."[326] Feminists in the 1970s looked at the past
and believed that they could do something to change their future. Temma
Kaplan, Feminist historian, states: "nostalgia is frequently more about
fantasies for the future than memories of the past."[327] This claim describes
the mindset of some feminists in the 1970s—visions of what the future
could be like were supported by visions of what the past may have been
like.

Armed with the matriarchal prehistoric myth, Feminist Wicca led some
women to re-envision the deities of their childhoods. Many began to feel
that it was debilitating for them to worship a male deity, headed by male
clergy, in patriarchal religious institutions such as Judaism and
Christianity. Feminist Wiccans determined that the male deity legitimated
the male power structure and the subjugation of women in the religion and
in society. Feminist Wiccans thus used the ancient goddess myth, with a
feminine divinity, to rally women to their cause of dismantling patriarchy
in America.

While the emerging Goddess movement took many forms in America
in the 1970s, all of them held that ancient Goddess worship offered
contemporary women hope. Women drawn to this myth believed that
ancient Goddess traditions had been peaceful and egalitarian societies.
They believed that these past cultures offered a model for contemporary

America. Women in Feminist Wicca asserted that this belief could compel their adherents into political action designed to bring about the end of the patriarchal power structures in America.

What Feminist Wicca Offered its Members

Feminist Wicca specifically drew in women from the feminist movement utilizing familiar feminist rhetoric and claims that it was resurrecting the worship of an ancient goddess. Members asserted that the worship of the ancient Goddess could bring about the end of patriarchy. While these claims attracted believers to its movement, ultimately what kept women in Feminist Wicca was the promise that an individual religious experience would enable women to make a real difference in the world. Feminist Wicca offered its potential members an authentic religious experience through a personal relationship with the Goddess. It thus offered to give potential members a practical religious avenue to seek an end to patriarchy.

Since many women in 1970s America felt that Judaism and Christianity had failed to create a better society for women and were complicit in their oppression, these traditions lost legitimacy for them. Feminist Wicca further elucidated the failings of their childhood faiths and promised to help women re-envision the deity through the lens of ancient Goddess worship, which would give them a personal religious experience and a special relationship with the deity. Most importantly, they believed that their new religious movement gave a model for a transformed America, one currently devoid of a patriarchal power structure. They believed that the combination of a personal relationship with the Goddess and a blueprint for a better society would empower women to overthrow a patriarchal America.

Explanation of Why Judeo-Christian Religions
Failed Women

One of the reasons that women were drawn into Feminist Wicca was that many of them felt the religions of their childhoods had lost legitimacy. For them, Christianity particularly, was complicit in the subjugation of women in America. They believed that the Christian church used scriptures and church traditions to justify the subservient roles women held in their institutions. Therefore Feminist Wiccans tended to distance themselves from Christian traditions. Feminist Wicca offered, instead, a religion with a female deity that legitimated leadership roles for women and offered them a religious means of attaining an egalitarian America society.   An article in the *Minneapolis Tribune* in 1972 explains, "Practitioners of the occult say that its popularity is part of a general spirit-searching in the world today, which stems from disenchantment with organized religion, especially among the young, and the fears and pressures of a nuclear age."[328] Women were searching for spiritual answers in an uncertain time. Many women did not feel they could find the answers they sought in the religions of their childhoods.

Feminist Wicca asserted that it offered the solutions to the problems of women in America.   This religion claimed to be older than Judaism or Christianity, and thus in possession of the "truths" withheld from women by these patriarchal traditions.

> Lady Sheba, high priestess of the American Order of the Brotherhood of the Wicca, claims Wicca is the oldest religion in the world...She goes beyond that and says many if not all of the basic tenets of all the worlds great religions are to be found in Wicca. Jesus the Christ, Lady Sheba claims, was himself a 'wise one' who studied in his youth with the Essenes, a group steeped in occult studies. He was in fact, she claims, a witch.[329]

Although most Feminist Wiccans would not have gone to the extreme of claiming that Jesus was a witch to prove their religions' antiquity, they did claim that their practices were ancient—inherited from ancient Goddess-worshiping cultures that pre-dated Judaism and Christianity.

While some feminist theologians, like Elizabeth Fiorenza, Carol Christ[330] and Mary Daly, originally tried to change existing religious institutions either to recognize women or envision the deity as feminine, other feminists were convinced that existing religious institutions were not likely to change in the near future.   Mary Daly, originally a Catholic theologian, was one feminist who eventually reached the latter conclusion. When she came to this realization, she asserted, "We cannot really belong to institutional religion as it exists. It isn't good enough to be token preachers...Singing sexist hymns, praying to a male God breaks our spirit, makes us less than human. The crushing weight of this tradition, of this power structure, tells us that we do not even exist."[331] Later, in her text *Beyond God the Father*, she suggests an alternative. She states that women could find:

> Sources of authentic hope... within Wild women—self-proclaimed Witches/Hags who choose the creation of our own space/time as a primal expression of intellectual/e-motional vitality, knowing that without this we will suffocate in the ranks of the living dead. Having learned from recent

> experience to understand more deeply than before that assimilation is
> deadly, deviant women can focus with renewed ferocity upon
> understanding the possibilities of our territory—the boundary—where/when
> we can Live the metaphorical journey of exorcism and ecstasy.

For Daly, witches offered women hope because, as outsiders to orthodoxy,
they could break new ground for all women.

In this context, Feminist Wicca offered the witch as a religious symbol;
this movement emerged as a response to the patriarchal institutions of
Judaism and Christianity. Judaism and Christianity portrayed God as
father, as the benevolent, removed male deity who loves His children.
However, the spiritual nature of humans and God were couched in
specifically male terms, while sexuality and sin were portrayed as
originating in the feminine. Casey Miller and Kate Swift, feminist editors,
explained in *Words and Women: New Language in New Times*, that
women were "the embodiment of sin, forever distracting men from
godliness: sons of God, but daughters of Eve, catalysts in a cosmic
struggle between evil as extremes of the sexuality men experience—whore
or virgin, agent of Satan or mother of God."[332] The language in these
traditional religions equated women with sin and evil, while men were
associated with virtue and holiness.

Consequently, potential adherents of Feminist Wicca felt not only
alienated from these religions, but oppressed and debilitated by them.
Goddess spirituality rejected several aspects of traditional religions,
particularly Christianity, in an effort to create a religious system in which
women were celebrated as spiritual individuals. Specifically, Feminist
Wiccans rejected what they understood to be the designation of the
Christian God as male, the subservience of the individual's will to God,
the hierarchical religious institution of Christianity, the dual nature of the
universe, the materialistic view of humanity, and negative views of
sexuality.

The most obvious aspect of Christianity that Feminist Wicca rejected
was the male gender of God, or the Fatherhood of God. While one could
argue that the Christian God was genderless, the male language utilized in
rituals spoke volumes to disenchanted women. Feminist Wiccan believers
claimed that the male gender of God inherently gave men a dominant
status and women a subordinate status in the religious community, based
solely on gender. For instance, Zsuzsanna Budapest, early Feminist Wicca
founder, denied the fatherhood of God: "Because Christianity says Father
God has no origin is to deny Motherhood. Obviously, to deny motherhood
is to deny wimmin (sic). Patriarchal religion is built on this denial, which
is its only original thought. The rest of their religious beliefs were ripped

off from Paganism."[333] Budapest felt that when Christianity denied any origins for their Father God, the institution denied the powerful, creative, magical experience of motherhood, of women. In doing so, Christianity denied women any meaningful religious experience.

Charlene Spretnak claimed that a society's culture decides whether gender determines a person's status. "Every person contains the entire range of options for thinking and behaving; s/he may be predisposed to some more than others, and cultural values will encourage or discourage the development of various options."[334] Accordingly, when Feminist Wiccans claimed that a religion such as Christianity offered theological justification for the oppression of women, they were arguing that Christianity discouraged women's potential in that society.

Another aspect of Christianity that Feminist Wiccans renounced was the notion that one's individual will is subordinate to God's will. In Wicca, identification with the Goddess placed value on one's own will. Carol Christ noted: "In a Goddess-centered context, in contrast, the will is valued. A woman is encouraged to know her will, to believe her will is valid, and to believe that her will can be achieved in this world, three powers traditionally denied to her in patriarchy...In the Goddess-centered framework, will can be achieved only when it is exercised in harmony with the energies and the wills of other beings."[335] The Feminist Witch did not consider her will to be subordinate to the Goddess; she worked *with* the Goddess. To prevent an individual from using her will irresponsibly, there were conditions that had to be met before she could work magic. She was expected to become aware of the conditions in nature and in the energies of those with whom she was working. The belief that whatever energy she sent out would be returned to her threefold was meant to encourage her to work for the benefit of others and the world around her. The Feminist Witch ideally worked to bring her will in harmony with Mother earth and Her inhabitants.

Feminist Wiccans also condemned the hierarchy of traditional religious institutions; they offered the consensus model instead. They believed hierarchal institutions to be the creations of patriarchy. They saw Christianity, particularly, as a corrupt hierarchy. While some Feminist Wiccan covens utilized a high priestess for a while, once everyone had been initiated, many of these covens would have members take turns leading rituals or performing different parts of the ceremony. If a group of women wanted to form a coven, they would start a "circle." Members would enter into an agreement of purpose and covenant with one another to effect change.[336] Members would meet before each ritual and vote on a course of action (what the ritual would accomplish) and the different elements that the ritual would include. Rejecting what they considered to be the hierarchical, male-dominated Christian church, Feminist Wiccans favored small groups run by consensus.

In addition, Feminist Wiccans repudiated what they understood to be the Christian idea that the universe consisted of dualities. Feminist Wiccans believed that dualities inferred a model of domination. Rather than think of the world in terms of man over woman, human over nature, spirit over matter, or God over Satan, Feminist Wiccans saw everything as interconnected. They thus believed that one's spiritual life should be integrated into one's whole worldview. They asserted that love of the Goddess should lead to love of self, others, nature, and world. As part of this rejection of dualities, Feminist witches rejected the concept of Satan as a purely Christian construct. Gerina Dunwich, a Wicca priestess said, "Witches today do not accept the concept of innate sin or absolute evil, and they do not worship the Devil as defined by the Christian tradition."[337] Since they believed they were reconstructing a pre-Christian belief, the idea of Satan was anathema. So, contrary to the beliefs of many Christians, modern witchcraft did not worship or even recognize the existence of Satan in opposition to God. Instead, they affirmed the wholeness and divinity of nature.

As part of this rejection of dualities, Feminist Wiccans also dismissed what they believed to be the Christian concept of the materialistic nature of humans. While some Christians saw soul and body to be separate elements, Feminist Wiccans did not recognize a distinction between the two. Feminist Wiccans identified the self with the Goddess; each person was the Goddess incarnate. This gave them a sense of self-love, self-respect, and self-empowerment. Part of this belief stemmed from the Neopagan concept that the divine is evident in all of nature including humanity. Z. Budapest explained: "there is no division between body and soul. One is not despised and the other glorified. There is no division of the sexes; both come from the same source, the Mother. There is no division of spiritual and profane; all is related to the universe, and none stands apart from nature. All is Nature...The Goddess within all."[338] Feminist Wiccans rejected what they understood as the Christian separation of humanity and divinity, or material versus spiritual, in favor of an idea of wholeness.

Finally, Feminist Wiccans, along with other Wiccans and Neopagans, viewed human sexuality as a positive experience. In this way, they rejected the negative beliefs about sexuality espoused by many Christians.[339] According to Starhawk:

> Pornography, rape, prostitution, sadomasochism simply bring out into the open the theme that underlies asceticism, celibacy, and Christian chastity—that sex is dirty and evil, and by extension, so are women. Under patriarchy, sexuality provides the rationale for violence against women—the stoning of adulteresses, the burning of Witches, the snickering probe into the conduct of rape victims. Goddess religion identifies sexuality as the expression of the creative life force of the universe. It is not dirty, nor is it merely "normal"; it is sacred, the manifestation of the Goddess. Fortunately, this does not mean you have to be ordained before you can do it. In feminist spirituality, a thing that is sacred can also be affectionate, joyful, pleasurable, passionate, funny, or purely animal. "All acts of love and pleasure are My rituals," says the Goddess. Sexuality is sacred because it is a sharing of energy, in passionate surrender to the power of the Goddess, immanent in our desire. In orgasm, we share in the force that moves the stars.[340]

Feminist Wiccans saw sexuality as an expression of the sacred life force and a gift from the Goddess. In witchcraft, it was believed that "all aspects of love and pleasure are my (the Goddess') rituals."[341] Feminist Wiccans rejected what they understood to be the Christian assertion that human sexuality is negative. Instead, they celebrated sexuality as an experience of the Goddess.

Many Feminist Wiccans claimed they never felt comfortable in the religions of their childhoods: they felt like outsiders or imposters. However, most people who joined Feminist Wicca in the 1970s did not feel that they had converted to a new religion. Instead, many described the experience as "coming home," or "finally being true to themselves." Wicca provided a reconciliation of what they believed with what they practiced. For instance, one woman in 1979 claimed: "At last I have a way to express what I have always felt—that there is no separation between religion and life."[342] The historical myth of a mother goddess offered Feminist Wiccans the sense that they were returning to their roots; that they were "coming home."

Feminist Wicca drew women who felt disenfranchised from their childhood religions. Since Christianity in particular was perceived by many of them to be part of the problem of patriarchy, it lost legitimacy for them. Rejecting these beliefs and creating a theology that uplifted women gave Feminist Wiccans a sense that they were outside the flawed patriarchal system called Christianity. In rejecting Christianity, Feminist Wiccans also affirmed the legitimacy of their new religion. While explaining why the religions of their childhoods had failed them, they demonstrated how their religion offered women something better. While this explanation drew potential devotees of the Goddess, Feminist Wicca also offered women a personal religious experience, a special relationship with the Goddess and the possibility of ending patriarchy in America in addition to maintaining religious authority for its adherents.

Personal Religious Experience and Special Relationship with the Goddess

Many women who joined Feminist Wiccan covens in the 1970s reported that they had been searching for a personal connection with a deity. Those who chose Wicca believed that they could not relate to the male deity in the traditional patriarchal religious institutions. Wiccan converts also believed that they had been oppressed by their childhood religious traditions. They therefore chose a new religion, one with a rich mythological past, and, not coincidentally, one that had existed in opposition to those rejected traditions. Feminist Wicca appealed to women in the 1970s because it offered them a legitimate religious experience and an intimate connection with an ancient goddess. Whatever their religious experience was, members of Feminist Wicca felt that this experience gave them a way to join their political concerns with their spiritual beliefs. Adherents considered the goddess to lend legitimacy to women claiming power in society. Also, the belief that the earth was a manifestation of a goddess gave them religious reasons for wanting to be actively engaged in advocating environmental reform.

Neopagan witchcraft in general envisioned the deity in dual form, both masculine and feminine, although the goddess held the greater power of the two. One of the unique contributions of Feminist Witchcraft was its insistence on the single power of a goddess as a political force for women. Cynthia Eller puts this well: "They wanted to worship a goddess—a big one, bigger than the god of patriarchy—and they wanted to worship themselves through her."[343] Some traditions of Feminist Wicca suggested that there was one goddess and that all goddesses were various aspects of Her. Others were content with the polytheistic idea of various goddesses, with different attributes. Feminist Wiccans rejected the male aspect of the Wiccan dual godhead, because it suggested the reliance of the Goddess on a male energy. They identified the Goddess with women: women became manifestations of the Goddess. For Feminists in the 1970s, this was an important tool for recovering a sense of control over their lives.

An example of this belief is seen in this observation by Cheri Lesh, an early 1980s student of Wicca in California, in an unpublished paper found in the Special Collections at the University of California Santa Barbara library:

> Women within this religion have a positive feminine principle to relate to, a mirror in which to find validation, self-worth and self-love. The Goddess possesses all the best aspects and attributes of femaleness...Wicca is the most Goddess-oriented of the pagan faiths, and places the most emphasis on developing the intuitional psychic side of the personality—the side that has to do with the craft of magic. Wicca emphasizes the power of the individual and in a society where women have been denied access to power, this is a crucial concept indeed.[344]

She notes that the identification of Wiccan women with a female divinity gives them a sense of self-worth and power.

Likewise, Sally McFague, a feminist theologian, argues in *Models of God*, that the most useful image of deity is the personal image. This is because "there is nothing we can say about God with the help of any other model that has the same credibility to us, because there is no other aspect of the universe that we know in the same way, with the privilege of the insider."[345] For McFague, when one identifies with the deity on a personal level, one can know the deity if one knows oneself. Feminist Wiccans, therefore, viewed the deity as mother, as goddess, as self. This self-examination gave women not only an insider view of the deity, as McFague argues, but self-empowerment: the self was divine.

Carol Christ, feminist spirituality author, agrees that the model of the divine was an important symbol for women. She states: "The symbols associated with these important rituals cannot fail to affect the deep or unconscious structures of the mind of even a person who has rejected these symbolisms on a conscious level...Symbol systems cannot simply be rejected, they must be replaced."[346] Therefore, women could not simply reject the male deity, but had to replace it with a female deity. "Religious symbol systems focused around exclusively male images of divinity create the impression that female power can never be fully legitimate or wholly beneficent."[347]

Carol Christ also notes that a Father God legitimates male authority in a society:

> If God in 'his' heaven is a father ruling his people, then it is the 'nature' of things and according to divine plan and the order of the universe that society be male dominated. Within this context, a mystification of roles takes place: The husband dominating his wife represents God 'himself.' The images and values of a given society have been projected into the realm of dogmas and 'Articles of Faith,' and these in turn justify the social structures which have given rise to them and which sustain their plausibility.[348]

Therefore, the gender image of the deity sends a deep-seated message to adherents. In worshiping the divine feminine, Feminist Wiccans wished to send the message of self-love to women.

Z. Budapest believed that all the goddesses of the world were but aspects of a single mother goddess:

> The Goddess has 10,000 names, shared by women around the world. Her name is Diana, Holy Mother. Her name is Tiamat, Her name is Hecate. Her name is Isis, Inanna, Belili; Her name is Sapasone, Belladonna, the Great Corn Mother; Her name is Alaskan Bear Mother, Artemis, Brigid, Io, Morrigan and Cerridwen; Her name is every woman's name—Carly, Doris, Lily, Catherine, Sharon, Susan. All of the personal names of women derive from Goddess names, as all women without exception are the expressions of the Mother—Goddess-on-Earth-Manifest.[349]

In this passage, Budapest equates all the manifestations of the Goddess with every woman. This is intended to give women a sense of personal power. In order to instill the power of the goddess within, women often chanted the many names of the goddess, as stated above, along with drumbeats as part of Feminist Wiccan rituals. The names of the goddess were chanted over and over again, and then the names of the participants were inserted as the ritual continued. This gave the participants a sense of their own divinity.

A portion of "The Charge of the Goddess," by Doreen Valiente, which Margo Adler reports was a much-recited passage by Feminist Wiccans, also asserts that the Goddess may be found within:

> I who am the beauty of the green earth and the white moon among the stars and the mysteries of the waters, I call upon your soul to arise and come unto me. For I am the soul of nature that gives life to the universe. From Me all things proceed and unto Me they must return. Let My worship be in the heart that rejoices, for behold—all acts of love and pleasure are My rituals. Let there be beauty and strength, power and compassion, honor and humility, mirth and reverence within you. And you who seek to know Me, know that your seeking and yearning will avail you not, unless you know the Mystery: for if that which you seek, you find not within yourself, you will never find it without. For behold, I have been with you from the beginning, and I am that which is attained at the end of desire. (Adapted by Starhawk from Doreen Valiente)[350]

In this passage, the Goddess can only be found by looking within oneself. Feminist Wiccans thus valued introspection as an avenue for seeking the Goddess.

For Starhawk, the goddess was part of the self and could be found in the world. For her, the idea that one could not believe in the Goddess was a strange notion. Her reply was: "Do you believe in rocks?" For her, the Goddess was manifest in the world:

> The phrase "believe *in*" itself implies that we cannot *know* the Goddess, that She is somehow intangible, incomprehensible. But we do not *believe* in rocks—we may see them, touch them, dig them out of our gardens, or stop small children from throwing them at each other. We know them—we connect with them. In the Craft, we do not *believe* in the Goddess—we connect with Her; through the moon, the stars, the ocean, the earth, through trees, animals, through other human beings, through ourselves. She is here. She is within us all. She is the full circle: earth, air, fire, water, and essence—body, mind, spirit, emotions, change.[351]

In this passage, it is clear that for believers, a connection with the Goddess was also a connection with the self, with others, and with the world around one.

The Goddess, for Feminist Wiccans, was a source of strength found within each person. Women were not required to envision or rely on a transcendental male deity. Instead, women could draw strength from an image of the deity that was her own likeness. The deity within was an important idea for feminists in the 1970s. Worshiping the Goddess was, in effect, worshipping womanhood, which made the worship of the Goddess an intensely personal religious experience.

In addition to worshiping the Goddess as self, Feminist Wiccans worshiped the Goddess as Mother Earth. Because Wicca was an earth-based religion, the earth itself was considered to be sacred. While most Neopagans would have said that one could worship different aspects of nature, Feminist Wiccans asserted that the earth itself was the Goddess. They understood connecting with nature as connecting with the Goddess herself. Note this poem, which appeared in Womanspirit in 1978:

> If you are separated
> From your Ceremonial Tools,
> Use a chunk of the Earth, a Stone.
> If you are separated
> From your Beloved Earth,
> Use your own body
> And blood (the Earth's children).[352]

This poem, written by a Wiccan adherent, shows the connectedness of every living thing with Mother Earth. Identifying with the earth identified one with the Goddess, which in turn, identified one with oneself.

While Wiccans found divinity in nature, they also saw magic composed of both male and female energies. Denise C. Brown, another Feminist Wiccan adherent writing in *Womanspirit* in 1979, addressed the concerns of the Neopagan community with regard to the masculine and feminine energy. She believed that envisioning the Goddess as self allowed women to "claim the wholeness and holiness of women."[353] She asserted that having both the male and female polarities physically represented in ritual was not necessary because these energies exist in each person. She insisted that because women could trust each other more than they could trust men, the all-female covens had more potential for closeness and raising energy.[354]

Another Feminist Wiccan contributor to *Womanspirit* in 1978, Seagull Mari, agreed that the Goddess was whole in and of Herself. However, she saw the Goddess mostly in natural forms, rather than identifying individually with Her:

> I am frustrated by a lot of goddess pictures 'in our image'—human. I have a picture of a white deer and a little snake, also several pictures of women. Though I see her in many aspects, I always see her as one—I don't feel polytheistic and can't relate to the concept of a horned god that is her consort or whatever, though I can see male-energy manifested/represented by Pan (whom I cannot see as a god). Just because a lot of earth creatures need two sexes for reproduction does not mean to me that Goddess has a mate—she should not have the limitations of mortals.[355]

Notice that this adherent, while not accepting the self-identification with the Goddess, still saw the Goddess as part of a unified whole of nature. She saw the Goddess as a monist would, as different aspects of nature all representing the Goddess.

An example of how ritual was used by Feminist Wiccans to give women a personal religious experience is described by Z. Budapest, celebrating Summer Solstice:

> ...this festival is sacred to the fire queen of love, Heartha, Vesta, Rhea, Artemis, Callisto, and Arianhod. On this day we celebrate the Goddess' power over men. Those witches who relate to men bring a lock of men's hair to be placed in the cauldron. Others take a strand from their own hair as a symbol of their personal homage to the fire Goddess. On the mountaintops in Europe, people still build roaring fires from old car tires to

Her. A wheel is placed in the circle, covered with flowers, symbolizing the turning of the year.

The circle is cast with stones. The cauldron plays the major role here, so it is decorated with flowers and placed at the southern part of the circle. All wearing summer flowers. Purify with water, consecrate with fire, admit in order of age, invoke the corners (using wands, not knives), mark the circle with the wand, and unify by humming:

High Priestess:

All ye assembled at my shrine,
Mother darksome and divine,
Mine is the scourge and mine the kiss,
Here I charge you in this sign.
All ye assembled in sight
Bow before my spirit bright.

The fire festival has begun. This is the day when the Goddess reigns supreme. At this time in particular, She has power over Her horned consort. In commemoration of this, I bid you honor Her by placing in Her sacred fire an oak branch that represents the male principle.

This is a great opportunity to cast spells over men who have bothered you this year. It can be anyone from political enemies to personal enemies. Rapists, for example, can be sacrificed with great success on this night. Each woman approaches the cauldron and places her oak branch in it, saying which man it represents. This may also be a blessing on sons and lovers, or just a love spell.

After this is done, the women begin dancing clockwise around the cauldron. Bring instruments or recorded music. We use ritual music from Africa.

When all are tired, gather again into a circle, and unify.

High Priestess:

Passionate sister of the living fire, accept our love. Great Rhea, Mother of all living, turn the wheel of fortune to the betterment of women and their liberation. You alone have power over patriarchy in this time of oppression. I invoke You and call upon You, O mighty Mother of us all, bringer of justice, fruitfulness! I invoke you by the vestal fires in our cauldron, by the passion in our hearts, by the intense flames of the pyres that burned Your witches not long ago. Descend upon our enemies in your fury. Avenge the wrongs, halt the rapes, illuminate the minds of our leaders and judges with your eternal fire. So mote it be!

All watch the burning fires for clues, pictures, or prophesies. After a while, bless all food and drink. Feast and praise the name Rhea, Vesta, Esmeralda, women passion. Dance. Party, Close circle as usual.[356]

This ritual exemplifies how women used gender imagery in order to engage in a personal religious experience. This particular ritual does utilize a symbolic token from men, a lock of male hair, but does not require males to be part of the ritual, nor does it require the practitioners to call on both male and female divinities. Women are to take a personal item to place in the fire, making the ritual meaningful to them. In addition, this particular ritual is performed in order to give women power to avenge wrongs done to them by men.

Margot Adler explained the need for feminist witches to identify with the Goddess as a desire for identification with positive images of female power:

> After all, if for thousands of years the image of woman has been tainted, we must either go back to when untainted images exist or create new images from within ourselves. Women are doing both. Whether the images exist in a kind of atavistic memory thousands of years old (as many women believe) or are simply powerful models that can be internalized, women are beginning to create ritual situations in which these images become real.[357]

For Feminist Wiccans, the goddess gave personal power and the strength to make needed societal changes. Carol Christ said the symbol of the Goddess was important for three reasons: "(1) The Goddess is divine female, a personification who can be invoked in prayer and ritual; (2) the Goddess is symbol of the life, death, and rebirth energy in nature and culture, in personal and communal life; and (3) the Goddess is symbol of the affirmation of the legitimacy and beauty of female power (made possible by the new becoming of women in the women's liberation movement)."[358] While these terms are not consistent with all Pagan Wiccans, the terms are quite typical for Feminist Wiccans' descriptions of the Goddess. In fact, for them, this would be a logical progression: *Because* the Goddess is divine female, she is the symbol of life, death and rebirth, and thus she is the symbol of the legitimacy of female power.

Thus, the Goddess, for Feminist Wiccans particularly, was a symbol of legitimate female power. When women identified personally with the Goddess, they internalized the strength, courage and power to enact change in their society. It gave them a sense of legitimate authority; they felt they had divine sanction to demand equality for women. In other words, the belief in the power of the Goddess in a woman's personal life gave her the strength to act on her political goals. The personal became political. The personal religious experience, then, was necessary for Feminist Wicca. The personal religious experience of Feminist Wiccans fuelled their ideology. They believed their actions could affect changes in the larger culture.

Starhawk, one of the early voices in Feminist Wicca, was one who became actively engaged in society because of her religious experience.

She learned about witchcraft while working on an anthropology project as an undergraduate student at UCLA in the late 1960s. Since she was raised in the Jewish tradition, the idea of a feminine god was a novel, but intriguing, idea for her. A few years later she encountered the feminist ideology through a reading of Kate Millett's book *Sexual Politics*. Soon thereafter she joined a consciousness raising group, got involved at a women's center and began to consider herself a feminist.[359] She felt that the Goddess had a lot to offer the feminist movement:

> I would say my major contribution has been articulating questions of the sacred from a feminist perspective, and maintaining that the issues and the questions that feminism deals with are questions of the sacred and questions of the spirit, as well as strictly political questions. In other words, I try to link the spiritual and the political in both directions. One of the great gifts is a spiritual connection, because without it, it's very hard to stay in political action for ten years, twenty years, thirty years, a lifetime. Political action tends to not be very rewarding in the sense that it's rare that you do something and immediately see a result that you want…And oftentimes you can only see the results many many years after it's over, so you have to do something to sustain yourself. And for me that comes out of the spiritual connection.[360]

For Starhawk, a spiritual connection with the Goddess gave the necessary energy, focus, and moral conscience to sustain her political activities.

Carol P. Christ, who came to the women's spirituality movement in the 1970s and continued to write about its theological claims well into the 1990s, described her experience of coming into the movement thus:

> For me and for many others, finding the Goddess has felt like coming home to a vision of life that we had always known deeply within ourselves: that we are part of nature and that our destiny is to participate fully in the cycles of birth, death, and renewal that characterize life on this earth. We find in the Goddess a compelling image of female power, a vision of the deep connection of all beings in the web of life, and a call to create peace on earth. The return of the Goddess inspires us to hope that we can heal the deep rifts between women and men, between 'man' and nature, and between 'God' and the world, that have shaped our western reality for so long.[361]

Christ, like other converts, believed that worship of the Goddess was part of a movement toward changing the world. She believed that the visions of ancient Goddess worship gave hope that women could "heal" the ailments of society.

Margot Adler grew up in the Jewish tradition and had an experience in grammar school with Greek mythology that left a lasting impression. While acting out the ancient myths, Adler dreamed that she became the goddesses in the plays. This experience gave her a sense of her own divinity. In 1971, she became involved in various economic and environmental reform movements. At that time, she came across a series of articles written by John McPhee entitled "Encounters with the Archdruid" in the *New Yorker*, which struck her deeply and began her search for a religious framework that supported her principles. She began to contact various Neopagan groups and one sent her a tape of a ritual that was very powerful for her because it invoked the ancient Greek and other European goddesses, which recalled her childhood experience. She records that:

> A feeling of power and emotion came over me. For, after all, how different was that ritual from the magical rituals of my childhood? The contents of the tape had simply given me permission to accept a part of my own psyche that I had denied for years—and then extend it. Like most Neo-Pagans, I never converted in the accepted sense—I never adopted any new beliefs. I simply accepted, reaffirmed, and extended a very old experience. I allowed certain kinds of feelings and ways of being back into my life.[362]

In Neopaganism, Adler believed that she had found a religion that resonated with her childhood experience of "becoming" a goddess. For her, this religion allowed her to engage in a special relationship with the divine.

When Adler interviewed contemporary witches for *Drawing Down the Moon*, published in 1979, she asked them "Why is this phenomenon (witchcraft revival) occurring?" and "Why are you involved?" While she did not break down the answers individually, members gave one or more of the following six reasons: Imagination (beauty, vision), Intellectual Satisfaction, Growth, Feminism, Environmentalism, and Freedom.[363] Feminist Wiccans in Adler's study said they were drawn to the religion because it gave a spiritual framework for their political beliefs.[364] While they had secular tools at their disposal, Goddess worship gave these women the spiritual means they sought in order to change the world. This put their political actions into a larger, more meaningful context.

Other women who had a personal religious experience with the Goddess in Wicca were those who were brought up with witchcraft as a family tradition. That is to say, many immigrant families brought healing and folk traditions with them to America that resonated with many Wicca beliefs. Their families instilled in them a relationship with the divine feminine. Adler gives Z. Budapest as an example of a "Family Tradition" witch in her Neopanganism survey. Z. Budapest explains:

> I was a Witch before I was a feminist. My family kept a book of who had lived and who had died, starting in 1270. There were quite a few herbalists in my family. At one point our family had a small pharmacy in a little town. My father was a doctor and many people in my family were healers. I observed my mother talking to the dead. I saw her go into trance and feel presences around her. She is an artist and her art often reflects Sumerian influences. She presents it as peasant, not Pagan, and so she gets away with it in Hungary. And in Hungarian, the word is the same. Many country folk buy my mother's ceramics. She uses ancient motifs, such as the tree of life, flower symbology, and the idea of the Goddess holding a child within a circle of rebirth. She does spontaneous magic and chants, and rhymes. She tells fortunes and can still the winds.[365]

After a difficult transition in her move to America, Budapest attempted suicide during which she had a vision that she had died. This experience drew her closer to the Goddess.

> After this vision, I regained my true perspective of a Witch, how a Witch looks at life—as a challenge. It is not going to last forever, and it's all right on the other side, so what are you going to do?...I began to talk to the Goddess. I knew a lot of Pagan customs that my country had preserved, but which had lost religious meaning—although not for me. I also began to read about Dianic Witchcraft, the English literature. A year later I began, with several other women, to have sabbats. In 1971, on the Winter Solstice, we named our coven the Susan B. Anthony Coven.[366]

Z. Budapest grew up in a family that encouraged her to form a relationship with the Goddess. She spoke to the Goddess and began to perform rituals that she remembered her mother performing when she was a child. She found that the religion in America closest to that of her upbringing was Wicca. She thus utilized some rituals and theology from Wicca to suit her needs as a feminist. As an early founder of Feminist Wicca, Budapest shared her own experiences with other women who were searching for a close relationship with a feminine deity.

While Feminist Wiccans were drawn into this religious movement because they found the claims of antiquity compelling, they stayed because of another type of legitimacy: personal experience. As noted in the introduction of this dissertation, personal authority is one of Max Weber's principles of legitimation.[367] When the adherent has a personal religious experience within a religious ritual, it gives legitimacy to that religious movement. When women participated in the religious rituals of

Feminist Wicca, they felt a meaningful connection with something greater than themselves. This authority was drawn from their personal experience; their religious experience and personal relationships with the Goddess made Wicca a legitimate religion for them. While tradition, or appeals of ancient origins, appealed to many women in Feminist Wicca, their personal religious experiences kept them there.

The Possibility of Ending Patriarchal Oppression in America

Feminist Wiccans believed that their new religion could result in a transformed America, with those changes extending to the world. With the motto "the personal is political" gained from the feminist movement, Feminist Wiccans asserted that women's personal religious experiences would translate into political action, transforming the American patriarchal power structures into egalitarianism.

Many women who discovered Feminist Wicca had previously been active in the feminist political movement. However, some, like Morgan McFarland, Feminist Wiccan Priestess, found that her new religion offered something broader than political action:

> I have begun to see a resurgence of women returning to the Goddess, seeing themselves as Her daughters, finding Paganism on their own within a very feminist context. Feminism implies equality, self-identification, and individual strength for women. Paganism has been, for all practical purposes, antiestablishment spirituality. Feminism and Pagans are both coming from the same source without realizing it, and heading toward the same goal without realizing it, and the two are now beginning to interlace.[368]

Women like McFarland in Feminist Wicca saw their spiritual lives giving strength to their political visions.

> We are each Virgin Huntresses, we are each Great Mothers, we are Death Dealers who hold out the promise of rebirth and regeneration. We are no longer afraid to see ourselves as her daughters, nor are we afraid to refuse to be victims of this subtle Burning Time. The Wicce is Revolutionary.[369]

What is perhaps more difficult to discern, is what Feminist Wiccans envisioned as the end result of their political actions. For the most part, it appears to be the end of patriarchal power and an equal status for women in society.

One can certainly see the goal of the transformed America in the manifesto of Z. Budapest's Susan B. Anthony Coven No. 1, shown earlier in this chapter. The members of this coven believed that their new religion could give women a sense of power over their destinies, the courage to fight patriarchal institutions and restore the "mythical golden age of matriarchy." They felt that during this matriarchy, the "Goddess-consciousness gave humanity a long-lasting, peaceful period" that they determined to reconstruct in the present age.[370] In "recovering" this ancient religious tradition, the women in Susan B. Anthony Coven No. 1 believed that they could defend the interests of women and they were "committed to winning, to surviving, to struggling against patriarchal oppression."[371] They saw themselves in a war against patriarchy that could only be won through spiritual means: "We believe that in order to fight and win a revolution that will stretch for generations into the future, we must find reliable ways to replenish our energies. We believe that without a secure grounding in womon's (sic) spiritual strength there will be no victory for us."[372] They believed that their religion could shape American culture into a "matriarchy" that would raise the status of women to be equal with men.

Z. Budapest believed that a woman-centered religion could change the world:

How we lost the Mother's Religion and why this continues to happen are not really the point. What counts is that it all has to do with a cycle—a Universal event—and that is related to the consciousness of a people. Whatever we think, we get. That is the very reason religions are all-important and all-political, and why they will always be that way…Just because the religions fed to us so far in the patriarchal scheme have been poison to us is no reason for women to totally reject their spirituality. The point is to be wise, to take our powers and think a way through—to find another way to feed our undernourished spirits. We must find a nourishing, healthy resource which will be the foundation of our spirituality, the basis for our rebellion against every kind of oppression, and our weapon for awakening and sustaining the Goddess within. And that's the future.[373]

For Budapest, political action came from a spiritual source. For her, a connection with the Goddess was necessary to "feed" her political actions on behalf of women in America. Her religious practices endowed her with the feeling that her actions in the secular world had a deeper meaning.

As discussed earlier, Starhawk's *Spiraldance* also greatly influenced the goals of Feminist Wicca. *Spiraldance* claimed that women in small covens could network together to transform society from disinterested institutions to integrated earth-savers.[374] In this text, she notes that women must be cautious in their actions toward changing the future, otherwise they might make mistakes similar to those of the patriarchy:

> Only when we understand the currents of the present can we clearly envision the future. If we accept the responsibility of claiming the future for life, than we must engage in the demanding task of re-creating culture. A deep and profound change is needed in our attitude toward the world and the life on it, toward each other, and in our conceptions of what is human. Somehow, we must win clear of the roles we have been taught, of strictures on mind and self that are learned before speech and are buried so deep that they cannot be seen. Today women are creating new myths, singing new liturgy, painting their own icons, and drawing strength from the new-old symbols of the Goddess, of the 'legitimacy and beneficence of female power.'

> A change in symbols is not enough, however. We must also change the context in which we respond to symbols and the ways in which they are used. If female images are merely plugged into old structures, they too will function as agents of oppression, and this prospect is doubly frightening because they would then be robbed of the liberating power with which they are imbued today.[375]

Starhawk was concerned that if women created a matriarchy, it would be just as oppressive as the patriarchy they wished to dismantle. She therefore called for the restructuring of society, calling for egalitarianism, in which everyone would be equal.

Another influential 1970s feminist writer, Riane Eisler, agreed, and called for a new form of power structure she called "the partnership model" in *The Chalice and the Blade*.

> Our reconnection with the earlier spiritual tradition of Goddess worship linked to the partnership model of society is more than a reaffirmation of the dignity and worth of half of humanity. Nor is it only a far more comforting and reassuring way of imaging the powers that rule the universe. It also offers us a positive replacement for the myths and images that have for so long blatantly falsified the most elementary principles of human relations by valuing killing and exploiting more than giving birth and nurturing.[376]

Eisler believed that the partnership model would ultimately diminish the need for war, would raise women's status in society to equal with men, and solve the problems of environmental pollution, energy shortages, poverty, and food shortages.[377] She saw all these issues linked with a domination/submission power model in societies. While Eisler may have been overly-optimistic, she clearly saw Goddess spirituality linked with the status of women, and as a solution for the problem of patriarchy.

While many American women read texts by Z. Budapest and Starhawk, ideas of Feminist Wicca were also spread through chants learned in workshops and camps, which women attended over weekends or during vacations. These chants were meant to be used in worship, and encapsulated the ideals of the movement in verse form. Some of the chants included Charlie Murphey's "The Burning Times," Starhawk's "She Changes Everything She Touches" and "Isis, Astarte, Diana," and Z. Budapest's "We All Come from the Goddess."[378]

> *We all come from the Goddess, and to her we shall return*
> *Like a drop of rain, flowing to the ocean.*[379]

Each of these songs was meant to spread the message of Feminist Wicca past the bookshelves and into the lives of women. Once learned in the rituals at workshops, these chants were sung at political rallies and protests, in drum circles, and in individual covens and homes.

> *Circle round for freedom, circle round for peace,*
> *For those of us imprisoned, circle for release.*
> *Circle round the planet, circle round each soul,*
> *For future generations, keep the planet whole.*[380]

Women who learned, and then taught, these chants believed that they were part of a global movement for change.[381]

Women came into contact with Feminist Wicca in several ways. Some attended consciousness-raising groups organized by radical feminists and met others involved in the movement. Some heard about Feminist Wicca through rape counseling, day care for working mothers, self-defense training, feminist bookstores, independent films about the plight of women, or battered women shelters in their neighborhoods. Other women read the rapidly-expanding goddess spirituality literature and began to look for religions that honored a goddess, which included Feminist Wicca.

While some women chose to practice the religion of Feminist Wicca alone, as sole practitioners, others chose to become members of covens. As they became more involved in the movement, women often went to workshops or camps to learn more about what they could do individually and as a member of a coven to enact change on behalf of women in American society. Many became active in grassroots movements in their neighborhoods or protest movements organized by feminist organizations. They came to believe that their personal religious experiences were a catalyst for their collaboration in shifting American culture to be more inclusive of women.

While guided by the image of their mythological golden age of matriarchy, Feminist Wiccans did not clearly agree on their goals for the future. They conceded that women needed more control over their own lives in American culture, but could not agree if that could be achieved through a matriarchal power structure or an egalitarian society. A member of the Ursa Major coven explained her ambivalence, "Right now I am pushing for women's power in any way I can, but I don't know whether my ultimate aim is a society where all human beings are equal, regardless of the bodies they were born into, or whether I would rather see a society where women had institutional authority."[382] While the precise goals may have differed, all agreed that the culprit of women's oppression lay in the existing patriarchal power structure in America. They meant for their religious practices to give women the courage to dismantle patriarchy and replace it with something that would improve the status of women in society.

Thus, Feminist Wiccans felt that their religion could give women in 1970s America the vision and the impetus to shape their world. While this religion offered women a vision of a future egalitarian American society, it was based on their beliefs about a "golden age of matriarchy" in which men and women worshipped an ancient goddess. Feminist Wiccans believed that this vision of a future America could be brought about by recreating the worship practices of ancient Goddess religions. They believed that when women encountered the Goddess in their own religious experiences, they would be moved to become active in bringing about a new age of the Goddess in America. Reading books by Budapest and Starhawk, becoming involved in regional workshops, and forming their own covens, brought women into contact with the ideals of Feminist Wicca. They believed that when women experienced the Goddess on the personal level, they would be moved to political action on behalf of women in American society.

Summary

In 1960s and 1970s America, Feminist Wicca utilized feminist rhetoric and claims of antiquity that attracted potential adherents. This movement also taught its adherents that a personal religious experience and a relationship with the divine would lead to political actions on behalf of women in American society. Since Feminist Wicca mostly drew in women who felt disenfranchised from the American male power structure, this religious movement also offered its members a meaningful path toward bringing an end to their oppression. Women believed their religious experiences propelled them into the political arena, giving their secular actions cosmic significance.

Most Feminist Wiccans believed they were practicing rituals passed down through the centuries. While many downplayed the questionable nature of their historical credentials, they nevertheless chose to romanticize their connections with ancient goddess traditions. They reclaimed the terms "witch" and "feminist" in order to give members a sense that they were part of a positive move toward change in America. Feminist Wicca employed these claims of antiquity, gaining new adherents and offering a vision of what American society could look like in a new age.

Many feminists found an ideology in Wicca that gave spiritual meaning to their political agenda. Most adherents came out of the feminist movement in the 1960s and 1970s, which they felt did not offer them the religious authority to effect change in American society. They took their cue from patriarchal institutions that claimed authority in Jewish and Christian scriptures. Feminist Wiccans also yearned for a personal connection with the divine, which they found in identifying with the Goddess. Wicca thus offered feminists a spiritual avenue to pursue their secular goals.

While they found the ideology of the Goddess particularly uplifting, feminists found that other aspects of Neopagan Wicca did not appeal to them. Feminists did not care for the dual godhead, and many did not want the presence of males in rituals. They also felt that the extant rites were limiting and not affirming for women. Thus, they created a new type of Neopaganism: Feminist Wicca. In this new movement, they were able to tailor the covens and rituals to meet their needs. Dianic covens strictly worshipped the Goddess and had female-only covens. Other Feminist Witchcraft covens allowed males in worship, but had a feminist agenda. Members tailored their rituals to allow for a focus on the political aims of the adherents.

In Feminist Witchcraft, and Goddess Spirituality in general, belief in the Goddess was particularly meaningful for many women. Women in these movements identified with the Goddess on a personal level, which they believed gave them power and legitimacy to act as their own authority. They believed this connection with the Goddess gave them a divine sanction to create a better society for women in America. They viewed the Christian church as one source of the oppression of women, and they explained many of their beliefs in contrast to their understanding of Christianity: the female nature of God, the rejection of duality, and the rejection of negative beliefs about the human body and sexuality. Feminist Wicca celebrated the female self as divine, had a holistic view of the world, and celebrated the body and sexuality as gifts from the Goddess.

The mythological history of the Goddess drew new members and gave them a model for the future. Claims of antiquity distanced them somewhat from many other New Age movements. They offered themselves as a known category: witches. Because "witch" was a controversial term, they chose to reclaim this title and revise it. Instead of an evil figure, witches became strong, independent women outside of traditional society. For Feminist Wiccans, witches were healers, wise women, and nature-worshippers, and witches had always worshipped the Goddess. Because Feminist Wiccans revised a known category, they offered "witch" as a more acceptable figure in society. Since they believed that witches had historically been powerful and independent women who worshipped the Goddess, Feminist Wiccans used them as a model.

Thus, using Wicca, Feminists connected the idea of the witch with worship of the ancient Goddess. They utilized the myth of the golden age of the Goddess, which painted a romantic picture of an ancient, peaceful world, where there was equality of the sexes, cultural prowess, and justice for everyone. Feminist Witches offered the past golden age as a model for the future. They reasoned that since worship of the goddess caused the ancient societies to be pacifistic, this same religious practice could bring about a more peaceful contemporary America. This romantic view of ancient goddess religions ignored goddess-worshipping traditions that did not allow social equality for women. Their version of a past golden age of the Goddess held a meaningful place in the belief system of Feminist Wicca—for them, it was proof that women had, and could again, change society for the better.

In an early essay on Goddess spirituality, Carol Christ noted: "As women struggle to create a new culture in which women's power, bodies, will, and bonds are celebrated, it seems natural that the Goddess would reemerge as symbol of the newfound beauty, strength and power of women."[383] She cites Clifford Geertz's definition of religion as a cultural system.[384] Christ explains that in order to change a culture, one must change meaning systems. If religion is a system of symbols that act to produce powerful motivations of people in a culture, it would follow that feminists were drawn to a symbol of feminine power found in the ancient goddess religions.

The use of the past as a model for the future is a common American phenomenon. Ancient heritage gives new religious movements a sense of legitimacy, because members base their faith on an established historical tradition. For instance, the American justice system is based on the English justice system, because the colonists believed that the older model worked. The colonists revised the older model to work for the new world, but they did not try to invent something entirely new. Likewise, while the Puritans wanted to create a "City on a Hill" as a model for the Church of England, they based their new church in America on what they believed the original Christian church to have been. While the conservative movement wanted to create a more moral, family-oriented, Christian society, they based their new model on what they believed earlier American society had been like. In other words, it is a common practice in American culture for a new group to base its movement on a model taken from the historical past. Like the Unification Church, Feminist Wiccans in the 1970s offered American women hope for a future that was based on an idyllic past. In their version of the past, men and women worshipped the Goddess in a gender-equal society. Their religion offered the opportunity to create a contemporary version of this ancient mythological culture.

CHAPTER THREE

NATION OF YAHWEH,
A BLACK HEBREW-ISRAELITE RELIGION

You have to admit you are being punished in America. You are being punished by your oppressor...The reason you are being oppressed and discriminated against is because all nations in this country know who you are and that you should be submitting to your God Yahweh, and they'll all fall down at your feet and worship you when you do.
—Yahweh ben Yahweh[385]

Like Feminist Wicca, the Nation of Yahweh attracted those frustrated with their subordinate status in America. While Feminist Wicca appealed to women specifically, the Nation of Yahweh drew black Americans. Both religions offered a plan based in religious ideals intended to enable otherwise disempowered people to be personally involved in improving their society. Like the Unification Church and Feminist Wicca, the Nation of Yahweh promised their members spiritual rewards for their tireless efforts to reform America: a personal relationship with their deity and a religious experience that would equip members with the tools they needed to transform their world.

Also like the Unification Church and Feminist Wicca, the public has been critical of the Nation of Yahweh. Law enforcement officials indicted and later convicted the Nation's founder, Yahweh ben Yahweh, and several members on racketeering charges based on their participation in criminal activities in the 1980s. Many believed the movement was involved in assaults, murder, financial mishandling, and at least one bombing incident. Perhaps understandably, the media was more concerned with showing Yahweh ben Yahweh to be a charlatan, rather than a legitimate religious leader. While I do not wish to ignore the Nation of Yahweh's involvement in these criminal activities, I think it is important to ask why members were drawn to this movement. After these convictions, the movement continued to expand and teach its message and is still a small religious movement today. In this chapter, I argue that the Nation of Yahweh continued to grow after these problems because

Yahweh ben Yahweh offered the members of his movement a vision of a more inclusive America and a way for each of them to be personally involved in nurturing that goal to fruition.

Patricia Lynn Albert was twelve years old when she first encountered "Brother Love's" teachings in the late 1970s. She was a part of the Mitchell family's Holiness Pentecostal Church in Enid, Oklahoma. Hulon Mitchell, Jr. (a.k.a. "Brother Love" and later, "Yahweh ben Yahweh"), the founder of the Nation of Yahweh, had returned to Enid before going to Miami in order to convince some of his family members to join his Hebrew Israelite religion. As a friend of the Mitchell family, Patricia read through the leaflets that Mitchell handed out and attended classes at Mitchell's sister Jean's house. The teachings "made her feel special, unique, maybe even a little better than anyone else. 'We believed in a black heaven and earth,' she reflected many years later. After reading the tracts and attending meetings, she tried to persuade her stepfather, Jeffrey Glover, that the *Book of Job* says white people are lower than dogs."[386] Although it took Glover awhile, he too was persuaded that there was something distinctive about Mitchell's new religion. In 1980, Patricia, along with her family and many other Oklahomans, moved to Miami with Brother Love to create a "sacred community" later called the Nation of Yahweh.

Like Patricia Albert, Yahweh ben Yahweh drew others away from their childhood religions and into the Nation of Yahweh because this new religious movement offered them the promise of a better life. Incorporating Black Power and Hebrew identity rhetoric into its message, the Nation of Yahweh offered its members an explanation of why Christianity had failed black Americans and how ancient Judaism could save them. In addition, the new religion promised prospective members a personal religious experience, a special relationship with God, and the possibility of transforming their world. Since many potential recruits to the Nation of Yahweh believed that Christianity was complicit in the oppression of black Americans, the church lost legitimacy for them. The Nation of Yahweh gained authority because it offered potential members explanations and possibilities in the framework of the ancient religion of Judaism.

Members of the Nation of Yahweh claimed that black Americans descended from one of the tribes of Israel. Asserting their ancient Jewish origins allowed them to identify with an oppressed people, which, in turn, gave them a special status. In other words, their oppression as Jews made them feel morally superior.[387] Members of the Nation of Yahweh believed that the historical suffering that Jews endured proved they were chosen by

God for a special purpose. Other American religious movements such as the Church of Jesus Christ of Latter-Day Saints, African Hebrew Israelites of Jerusalem, and the Worldwide Church of God, also claim to be descendants of the lost tribes of Israel. These groups adhere to at least some of the religious laws from the Hebrew Bible including dietary laws, grooming requirements, holy days, and moral prescriptions. In addition, they claim they are the rightful heirs of the covenant made with the Hebrew God, and that other practicing Jews are not.

The Nation of Yahweh emerged in America in the late 1970s and early 1980s as part of the Black Power movement of that era. Members believed that blacks should create their own self-supporting communities, rather than relying on the white establishment in America. They utilized Black Power ideology and rhetoric, combined with the moral prescriptions of the Hebrew Bible, in order to create a model for a virtuous black community. The Nation of Yahweh is the focus of this chapter because this movement developed in 1970s America and integrated an ancient religious tradition with a new religious movement in order to improve their world. In this case, they hoped to dismantle the white power structure in America in order to create a more equitable society for African Americans.

Existing Scholarship on the Nation of Yahweh

Not many scholars have documented the Nation of Yahweh as a new religious movement. There are some short entries in encyclopedias of religion and unpublished papers, but for the most part, this religion has been largely ignored by the academic community.[388] Some scholars are aware of the Nation of Yahweh and its beliefs, but a scholarly treatment of this movement's belief system is lacking.

Sydney P. Freedberg, a newspaper reporter for the *Miami Herald*, has written the most comprehensive study of the Nation of Yahweh. Freedberg's articles were compiled into a full book entitled *Brother Love: Murder, Money and a Messiah*.[389] While this book was not a scholarly study, information from it was drawn from witness testimony, court transcripts, and police interrogation transcripts. The thesis of the book is that Hulon Mitchell, Jr., the founder of the Nation of Yahweh, had illusions as a child that he was special, and spent his life in search of his religious mission. Freedberg believes that, after trying several religious movements, Mitchell found his calling in the Nation of Yahweh, claiming to be the son of God. As her title indicates, Freedberg is less than objective in her treatment of this new religious movement. She asserts that Yahweh ben Yahweh used his self-proclaimed divinity to control his followers, who obeyed his instructions even to commit murder and amass money for the movement.

In addition, other reporters from the *Miami Herald*, such as Emilia Askari, Patricia Andrews, and Donna Gehrke, contributed articles about the development of this new religious movement in the early 1980s. Anticult group websites and Court TV transcripts also contain other available information about the Nation of Yahweh. Since the state convicted Hulon Mitchell, Jr. and 15 members of this movement of various crimes in 1992, the court trials had extensive coverage in the *New York Times*, *The Washington Post*, *The Miami Herald*, and other national newspapers. Just before Yahweh ben Yahweh was released from prison in 2001, the Discovery Channel aired a documentary about the movement drawn from these same sources. Reporters writing these articles paid most attention to the charges against the defendants and secondarily, to the claims the group made that they were Hebrews.

The beliefs and motivations of this new religious movement deserve to be explored in a scholarly study. Because this group was so controversial, most of the coverage has been of the criminal proceedings against members of the Nation of Yahweh. While not ignoring this controversy, this chapter explores why people were attracted to this movement. Because they focused on controversial aspects of this religion, reporters all but ignored the personal religious experience of its members. In addition, Yahweh ben Yahweh utilized Black Power and Hebrew identity rhetoric to draw in potential adherents. This chapter argues that the Nation of Yahweh's claims of being descendants of the Hebrews were important for its survival as a new religious movement in America. The Nation of Yahweh asserted these ancient origins in order to engender in its adherents a model of a moral, self-sufficient community chosen by God. Since this movement has directly and indirectly impacted many in the black American community, it should be of interest to American religion scholars.

The research for this chapter utilizes not only the secondary sources mentioned above and court transcripts when available, but also primary sources from the Nation of Yahweh. While Hulon Mitchell, Jr., as Yahweh ben Yahweh, composed many texts for his adherents, this study focuses mainly on those written at the inception of the movement, since they include the origin myths containing historical claims. The two writings to which I refer the most are *You are Not a Nigger! Our True History, The World's Best Kept Secret* and *Yahweh Judges America*. In order to demonstrate the influence of the cultural context, I also reference scholarly texts about the Black Power Movement and about black Hebrew Israelites.

Unfortunately, the only available interviews containing members' voices come from court transcripts, flyers distributed by members, and newspaper articles. For this reason, they tend to either defend the religious experiences of members, or explain what attracted persons to the movement. While this data is limited, it nevertheless offers a glimpse into the religious lives and the worlds of meanings of the Nation of Yahweh's adherents in the early years of the religion.

This chapter gives a brief history of the Nation of Yahweh and then demonstrates that its use of Black Power and Hebrew identity rhetoric attracted new members. While important for drawing in new adherents, claims of antiquity not only gave members a religious identity, they offered a model for a holy community. Thus, this chapter argues that the Nation of Yahweh offered its new converts an explanation for Christianity's failure of American blacks, a personal religious experience because of their special relationship with God, and the possibility of ending racism and oppression of American blacks in order to retain new members.

History of the Nation of Yahweh

The Nation of Yahweh was founded by Hulon Mitchell, Jr. Mitchell's religious ideas were largely influenced by his Pentecostal upbringing and his involvement in the Civil Rights Movement, Rosicrucianism, and the Nation of Islam. His spiritual journey led him to reject Christianity as the religion of the oppressor and claim a Jewish identity. He believed that the revelations he received from God would help him free black Americans from their oppression by the white establishment.

Hulon Mitchell, Jr., the founder of the Nation of Yahweh, was born in Kingfisher, Oklahoma on October 27, 1935. He was the son of a Holiness Pentecostal minister, Hulon Mitchell and his wife, Pearl Olive Mitchell.[390] During his life he was deeply affected by Jim Crow laws and the Civil Rights movement, as is evident in his later writings. After High School, he attended Texas College in Tyler, Oklahoma for about a year before being drafted into the military in 1954. He enlisted in the Air Force and married a friend from his home town, Nodie Mae Chiles, before accepting his first military assignment in California at Parks Air Force Base.[391]

Mitchell and his wife Nodie had four children and traveled from California to Texas while Mitchell was in the Air Force. Mitchell, choosing to leave the religion of his youth, began looking for other religious paths. The first of these religions was Rosicrucianism, a mystical tradition that claimed secret wisdom about the nature of the relationship between God and humans. Mitchell learned the idea that each person had a spark of the divine from this religion. His wife, Nodie, was not interested in his new religious ideas and was unhappy as a military wife. Mitchell received an honorable discharge from the Air Force and they moved back to Enid, Oklahoma, where Mitchell filed for a divorce.[392]

In 1958, Mitchell took advantage of the GI Bill to study American Government at Phillips University. He took a job as a library assistant at the college. Along with two of his high school friends, he attended NAACP youth rallies, calling for an end to the oppression of blacks in America. He studied non-violence strategies with his friends and participated in protests and sit-ins against racist practices. His divorce from Nodie was finalized in 1959 and he was granted custody of his four children. He continued to study at Phillips University, receiving his Bachelor of Arts with a concentration in Psychology in 1960. He then decided to pursue a career in law; he began his graduate studies at Oklahoma Law School in 1960. He was the only black student in his law classes.[393] He met his second wife, Chloe, in graduate school, and left school after one year to move with his family to Georgia, where Chloe took a teaching job at Albany State.

Although the Civil Rights Movement was active in Albany, Georgia, Mitchell chose not to participate. Talking about this several years later, he said:

> The civil rights movement was not about becoming free from the oppressor. The civil rights movement was about fighting and dying to get inside of oppression, to be better oppressed. The civil rights movement was about being able to go and stay in a hotel that you couldn't afford to pay one night's rent in. The civil rights movement was about being able to stop giving your money to your Black brother and give it all to your oppressor. That's what the civil rights movement was all about. You wanted to sleep in the white hotel and eat in the white restaurant, so you wouldn't have to eat in the Black restaurant no more. The civil rights movement was not about owning a hotel.[394]

Mitchell became disillusioned with the Civil Rights Movement, because he felt the movement's leaders made too many compromises with white lawmakers. He was thus next drawn to a separatist movement, the Nation of Islam.

In 1961, he began to study the teachings of Elijah Muhammad with the Nation of Islam. He became Hulon X. He and his family moved to Atlanta, where Hulon X became more involved in the movement. He was taken under the wing of Elijah Muhammad and became friends with Malcolm X. While in Atlanta, Mitchell enrolled in Atlanta University, finishing his Master's degree in economics in 1965. That same year, he became a minister in the Nation of Islam, so Hulon X became known as "Minister Shah." He helped his parishioners find jobs, counseled former prisoners, helped congregation members manage their businesses and taught Elijah Muhammad's message of the superiority of the Black race. From the Nation of Islam, he learned separatist ideas and the notion that the black community should become self-sufficient. He later brought these ideas with him to the Nation of Yahweh.

In 1967, Mitchell left the Nation of Islam due to possible discovery of some questionable financial practices on his part. The specifics about the altercation are unclear, however, Mitchell told members of his family that he feared an assassination attempt by members of Elijah Muhammad's bodyguards for some time afterward.[395]

In 1968, Mitchell partnered with a friend, Billy Steven Jones, to start a ministry in Atlanta called the Modern Christian Church. Mitchell went by the name "Father Michél" and Jones went by the name "Father Joné." They became popular gospel radio evangelists known as "the prophets."[396] After the movement had been going for some time, Mitchell's partner Father Joné was shot to death in their church building. Mitchell was convinced that the Nation of Islam had attempted to assassinate him. The Modern Christian Church survived the loss of one of their leaders and went on to become somewhat successful. Mitchell preached a message of self-help and social uplift. However, he left the church sometime in late 1977, and in 1978 was sued by his congregation for possible financial mishandling. He moved to Florida, leaving his church and his wife Chloe.[397]

Around 1977-1978, Mitchell became a new religious personality in Orlando, Florida, known as "Brother Love." He found a new partner, Linda Merthie Gaines, to help with his religious calling. He reported to potential members of his new church that he had received a revelation from God (Yahweh) sometime in 1978 that he was to move to Miami to begin a new black Hebrew religious movement. This eventually became the Nation of Yahweh. Some of his friends tried to dissuade him from starting a new congregation in Miami, explaining that black Americans there were more impoverished and divided than any other group. To this, he replied, "To take them and do something with them proves that I am the divine."[398]

Mitchell preached that God revealed His true name, the four Hebrew letters Yod Heh Vav Heh, or YHWH, pronounced "Yahweh" in English to Mitchell in a revelation. This name was so sacred that it was not to be spoken. Instead, other titles for God were inserted in the Hebrew

Scriptures, such as Lord, the Most High, Elohim, and Adonai. In his revelation, Brother Love learned that God's name was kept secret because it revealed that God was black.[399]   Brother Love preached that he was called to lead black Americans from their years of oppression to the promised land of Israel. This new religion, like earlier American black Hebrew groups, believed that blacks were the true Jews, and that God and Jesus were black. Members of the new religious movement observed traditional Hebrew practices, changed their last names to "Israel," and followed the teachings of Brother Love, who then changed his name to Moses Israel. Before officially starting this group in Orlando, Mitchell went home to Enid, Oklahoma to recruit family members and friends from his home town to join his new religion. Many of them moved with him to Orlando.

In 1979, the Black Hebrews, as Mitchell's new religion was originally known, moved into the Joseph Caleb Center in Liberty City, Miami, Florida. The building had a 1000 seat auditorium, a library, a black archives history room, a food-stamps office, and classrooms. Moses Israel gave "the World's Best Kept Secret" lectures every Wednesday night and Saturday morning. Many of the members rented houses and created small communities together. Mitchell, as Moses Israel, taught his members the need to separate themselves from the "evil ways" of white people. He insisted that to rise above their oppression, the community must unite, because disunity would destroy their cause. Interpreting from the Book of Acts, he insisted, "We move like one! We look like one! We love like one! We are one! We get rich as one! We rise up as one! We are high above all nations as one! We rule the world as one!"[400]

In 1980, the Black Hebrews moved to a new home, 2766 NW 62nd Street in Liberty City, naming their new building the Temple of Love. Moses Israel asked many members to move into the Temple to serve Yahweh full-time. The building housed an auditorium, a cafeteria, a laundry room, a barber shop, a sewing room and a printing shop. Sometime in 1981, Moses Israel revealed to his congregation that his true name was Yahweh ben Yahweh, or God, son of God.[401]

"Who am I? How many of you know who I am? Ock Moshe [Moses Israel] is not my real name. My name is Yahshua! I'm here! I told you I was coming. I said after you served the enemy four hundred years, I'll come and judge!"[402]

Yahshua was the name of the deliverer, the lord of salvation. Mitchell was claiming to be the messiah, the son of God. At this point, the group's name officially became the Nation of Yahweh and Mitchell became Yahweh ben Yahweh, the savior of American blacks.

Yahweh ben Yahweh intended to build a self-sufficient Hebrew community. Hence, he established a school that taught the Hebrew language to both children and adult members. Children also learned basic math and English skills, but the curriculum focused primarily on the Hebrew Scriptures and teachings of Yahweh ben Yahweh. Members followed a strict vegetarian diet and wore white tunics and turbans. While they followed the Jewish holy days enumerated in the Hebrew Scriptures, they adhered to the solar rather than the lunar calendar.

Like Mitchell's earlier Modern Christian Church, the Nation of Yahweh taught a message of self-help and uplift. Yahweh ben Yahweh preached against crime, complained about the waste of welfare, and stressed the need for Blacks to work hard and save their money.[403] The Nation helped black Miamians find employment, food stamps, education, and job training. The Temple of Love bought grocery stores, apartments, and hotels and staffed them with Temple members. Members sold groceries, lotions, shampoos, fruit drinks, T-shirts, and books that the Temple published in-house.[404] Some members lived at the Temple and worked full-time for the movement, while others held outside jobs and donated part of their income. Full-time members of the Temple spent much of their time fundraising for the movement, with daily quotas, according to later court testimony. The Temple claimed that it helped clean up the neighborhoods around buildings owned by the movement. Once purchased by the Temple, all their buildings were painted white. The crime rate around their buildings reportedly dropped as well, since they had their own security patrols. The Nation of Yahweh trained Elders to preach its message and sent them out to other cities to form new branches for the faith.

Yahweh ben Yahweh encouraged members who did not live at the Temple to share housing in order to remain separate from the white community. Beginning in the early 1980s, several of these members became concerned with the pressure placed on them by Yahweh ben Yahweh. Many felt anxious if they did not give enough time or resources to the Nation that they would be punished severely. Members of Yahweh ben Yahweh's closer advisors threatened Temple members who questioned the faith with bodily harm. Some of these members reported their fears to the police and to radio stations, which propelled the Nation of Yahweh into the public eye.

Unfortunately for the Nation of Yahweh, police began investigating Yahweh ben Yahweh's special security forces starting in the early 1980s, due to some unsolved violent crimes associated with the Temple. The Circle of Ten, named after a group in II Kings, were Yahweh ben Yahweh's personal body guards. The Circle of Ten surrounded Yahweh ben Yahweh during his lectures and accompanied him when he left the temple. According to a former member, Robert Rozier, in addition to the Circle of Ten, there was a group of approximately 25 men called the "brotherhood" who carried out orders from Yahweh ben Yahweh that may have included bombing, arson, murder, physical assault and intimidation.[405] To become a member of the brotherhood, one reportedly was required to kill a white person and bring Yahweh ben Yahweh proof in the form of an ear, a head, or some other body part.[406] People began to "disappear" on the streets around the Temple, and one man, Leonard Dupree, was reportedly beaten within the compound. In addition, renters in one of the apartments owned by the Temple were beaten and one was killed for refusing to evacuate.[407] While the Nation of Yahweh was prospering financially, the actions of the Brotherhood were alienating outsiders. At the same time, these select members of Yahweh ben Yahweh's movement believed they were fulfilling a higher calling, punishing defectors and bringing on the apocalypse. They later said they felt they were doing what Yahweh ben Yahweh expected of them.[408]

Part of the eschatological vision of Yahweh ben Yahweh was the prediction of a war between blacks and whites, in which white people would be driven from the earth. Yahweh ben Yahweh described Yahweh as a "Terrible Black God" of war and violence who wished for his "death angels" to destroy those not of the tribes of Israel.[409] Some of these slayings allegedly took place by Yahweh's "brotherhood" members in 1986 in retribution for four hundred years of oppression of black Americans. Some of those murders are as yet unsolved, although police have connected them with the movement.[410] While members of his Nation were being questioned by police, Yahweh ben Yahweh denied the claim that his members had committed crimes. Instead, he asserted that they were attempting to rehabilitate the ghetto areas in Miami and restore pride and self-sufficiency to blacks.[411]

Members of the business and political society in Miami believed that the Nation of Yahweh existed to improve the lives of Miami Blacks. Because Yahweh ben Yahweh owned a number of businesses and became financially powerful in the Miami area, he attracted the attention of the mayor and other business leaders. His business and charity efforts earned him a certain amount of respect in Miami, and the mayor even declared October 7, 1990 "Yahweh ben Yahweh Day."

Subsequently, law enforcement officials became aware of the darker aspects of Yahweh ben Yahweh's power among his Hebrew community. Some members of Yahweh ben Yahweh's "Brotherhood" were arrested in 1990 and convicted in 1992 for various crimes perpetuated in the name of their movement. Simultaneously, law enforcement officers arrested twelve members of the Nation of Yahweh in four cities. Seventeen members total were indicted on charges of racketeering in a scheme the FBI called "patterns of terrorism."[412] Yahweh ben Yahweh and fifteen members of his Nation were charged with ordering the murders of fourteen people, the attempted killings of two others and the firebombing of a neighborhood in a town 50 miles north of Miami.[413] According to a 1996 opinion by the 11th US Circuit Court of Appeals upholding the convictions, "Between April and October 1986, Yahweh sent his death angels into the Miami community on multiple occasions to kill white people randomly and to commit acts of retribution against blacks who interfered with the Yahweh's sales of products and collection of donations."[414] Yahweh ben Yahweh was incarcerated, along with several other members. He was released from prison in December of 2001, on the condition that he not contact members of his movement.[415]

In the meantime, the Nation of Yahweh continued to function in Miami and elsewhere. Membership, which was approximately 2000 in the early 1990s,[416] has dwindled, but the movement is still active. They have a website, a television series that airs in some cities, and their publishing house continues to produce manuscripts for interested members. The group is no longer concentrated in Miami; its membership is spread throughout the United States. The PEES Foundation, with locations in San Antonio, Texas and Quebec, Canada produce the Nation of Yahweh's radio and television shows and publishes their religious tracts. Their present literature downplays racist tendencies, though they continue to assert their identity as the descendants of the tribe of Judah. They maintain that they are the chosen people of God, and that Yahweh ben Yahweh is the anointed one who will lead them to their salvation.

In October of 2006, lawyers for Yahweh ben Yahweh filed a motion with the courts asking to be released from the conditions of his 2001 parole. Dying of advanced prostate cancer, he asked the court that he be able to "die with dignity," surrounded by his faithful followers.[417] One of the conditions of his parole was that he not communicate with members of the religion that he founded. His five years of parole were completed, but he died soon thereafter.[418]

Black Power Rhetoric

While the Nation of Yahweh emerged in America in the late 1970s and early 1980s, its founder, Hulon Mitchell, Jr. was influenced by the Black Power Movement. Mitchell utilized rhetoric from the Black Power Movement of that time and rhetoric about Hebrew identity in order to draw in new members. Mitchell had grown up the son of a Pentecostal minister and later became involved in the Black Power Movement in the 1960s and 1970s. As Yahweh ben Yahweh, he taught that blacks needed to stop relying on the white establishment in America and create their own self-supporting communities. In addition, he taught that Christianity had failed blacks because its clergy used Christian scriptures to justify their oppression. He claimed to have received a vision that black Americans were deceived by whites about their true identity as descendants of the ancient Hebrews. He felt that blacks needed to reclaim their Hebrew identity and begin living the moral life prescribed in the Hebrew Bible. He thus utilized Black Power ideology and rhetoric, combined with the moral prescriptions of the Hebrew Bible, in order to draw members into his new religious community.

Yahweh ben Yahweh utilized Black Power rhetoric to appeal to disillusioned blacks in American society. He hoped to create a black religious community free from oppression. He thus taught his members about self-help, black pride and separation from whites. His use of Black Power rhetoric was successful because it appealed to that part of American society most likely to resonate with his religious message. He appealed to those who felt disenfranchised from American society by the white establishment.

The ideology of Black Power was an important force for change during the 1960s and 1970s. While the ideologies of Black Power were somewhat consistent, the goals and methods differed throughout the movement. Most proponents of Black Power agreed that blacks needed to have some control over the issues that affected their communities. They agreed that blacks were still oppressed by white society, long after slavery had been abolished. They agreed that something needed to be done to change this situation for black Americans. However, some felt this could be done through existing power structures, others through non-violent demonstrations, others through legislation handing authority over to blacks, and others through violent demonstrations. Many of these methods overlapped and intersected. What held each of these ideas and methods together was the slogan "Black Power."

The Black Power Movement in America was a product of the Civil Rights Movement. The phrase "Black Power" had been around for some time, probably used first by Richard Wright.[419] However, the slogan was originally adopted by members of the Civil Rights Movement in Greenwood, South Carolina during the Mississippi Freedom March in 1966. During one of the speaker rallies, Stokely Carmichael, then a member of SNCC (Student Nonviolent Coordinating Committee), shouted from the platform, "What we need is Black Power!" Willie Parks then repeatedly asked the crowd, "What do you want?" to the response, "Black Power!"[420] What the term meant, however, was a source of contention for many leaders of the movement.

According to John T. McCartney, author of *Black Power Ideologies: An Essay in African-American Political Thought*, characteristics that members of the Black Power Movement shared included: the use of power in relation to blacks as a group, self-determination for blacks, a realistic approach to politics, the black community's need to take the lead in alleviating racism, and the confidence that strategies emphasizing "blackness" can succeed.[421] While each group had different approaches to these goals, all of them felt that these were important aspects of Black Power.

Members of SNCC were the first to use the phrase "Black Power" during the Civil Rights Movement. Many SNCC members were influenced by the ideas of Malcolm X, former minister for the Nation of Islam and the founder of the OAAU (Organization of African-American Unity).[422] In 1964, Malcolm X and the OAAU planned to submit to the United Nations a list of human rights violations and acts of genocide against blacks committed by the United States. They called for black Americans to reclaim their rights, including: election of individual black Americans for public offices, voter registration drives, rent strikes to promote better housing conditions for blacks, building of all-black community schools, creation of black cultural centers, and black committees for community and neighborhood self-defense.[423] Malcolm X declared:

> The Negro holds the balance of power and if the Negro in this country were given what the constitution says he is supposed to have, the added power of the Negro in this country would sweep all of the racists and the segregationists out of office. It would change the entire political structure of the country.[424]

In short, Malcolm X charged the United States with the oppression of blacks and called black citizens to claim their rightful place in American society.

The ideas of Malcolm X influenced many SNCC members, including Stokely Carmichael. The SNCC Freedom Singers attended an OAAU meeting in Harlem in 1964. In 1965 Malcolm X was asked by SNCC to speak to black students and workers in Selma, Alabama. This exposure to ideas more radical than those espoused by the Civil Rights Movement gave the already "radical nationalist tendencies within SNCC another boost."[425] After the Mississippi Freedom March in 1966, many members of SNCC broke away from the Civil Rights Movement altogether in favor of Black Power. By 1967 and early 1968, Black Power had become the dominant ideological concept among a majority of black youth and a significant number of working class and middle class black Americans.[426]

Stokely Carmichael was the chairman of SNCC in 1966. He helped steer the organization from its original stance of nonviolence toward Black Power. He called black Americans to become self-reliant and to be empowered by their "blackness." He joined the Black Panther Party in 1967. In 1973, he changed his name to Kwame Toure, moved to Ghana and became a spokesperson for Pan-Africanism.[427]

Carmichael believed that Black Power meant for black Americans to consolidate their political and economic resources to achieve power. "Power," he said, "is the only thing respected in this world, and we must get it at any cost."[428] In 1966, Stokely Carmichael explained to a black audience in Detroit that the time for nonviolent resistance was over:

> We don't have to move to white schools to get a better education. We don't have to move into white suburbs to get a better house. All they need to do is stop exploiting and oppressing our communities...It's time to say to our Black brothers that success is going to mean coming back into your community and using your skills to help develop your people... we want to talk about nonviolence. We want to say that nonviolence has to begin to be taught in our neighborhoods. We have to teach ourselves to love and respect each other. Because the psychology of the man has worked on us, and we're trying to destroy each other every Friday and Saturday night. That's where we're going to preach nonviolence and no where else.[429]

Stokely Carmichael was a vocal proponent of Black Power. He co-authored a text on the subject entitled *Black Power: the Politics of Liberation in America* with Charles Hamilton, a professor at Roosevelt University in Chicago in 1967. He was against integration because he felt that it was a process of assimilating the black community into the white community. He felt that black culture and pride in black identity would be lost in the process. He argued that Black Power was a means for the black community to take control over issues that directly affected their lives.

For Carmichael, there were three major implications of Black Power: personal pride in being black, responsibility to other black Americans, and power as a group to deal with outsiders. Most importantly, though, was that black Americans, as a matter of personal pride, must be able to assume the right to define their own identity, their relationship to the total society, and the meaning of such important terms as Black Power.[430]

Charles V. Hamilton, who co-authored the book on Black Power with Stokely Carmichael, felt that Black Power needed to organize black rage toward constructive goals. According to Hamilton, "Black Power must (1) deal with the obviously growing alienation of Black people and their distrust of the institutions of this society; (2) work to create new values and to build a new sense of community and belonging; and (3) work to establish legitimate new institutions that make participants, not recipients, out of a people traditionally excluded from the fundamentally racist processes of this country."[431]   Mitchell incorporated exactly these sentiments into his formation of the Nation of Yahweh. Like Hamilton, he felt that if black rage were channeled, it could result in a black community that had legitimate authority over its own people.

Hoping to capture the presidency by pulling in votes from the black community, Richard Nixon utilized a seemingly pro-Black Power stance in his 1968 bid for the presidency of the United States. He said that Black Power was "the power that people should have over their own destinies, the power to affect their own communities, the power that comes from participation in the political and economic processes of society."[432] He continued, stating that the federal approach "ought to be oriented toward more Black ownership, for from this can flow the rest—Black pride, Black jobs, Black opportunity, and yes, Black power."[433] To have their goals delineated by a presidential candidate was a sign for the black community that Black Power speakers were being heard.

Part of the Black Power Movement was a move toward black nationalism. This led to a renewed interest in African culture and history. Many activists read books by African theorists and leaders and drew inspiration for their work in the United States. Maulana Ron Karenga, an author and activist, developed cultural programs such as a black catechism he called "nguzo saba" and a black holiday called "kwanza" in 1966. These were meant to honor black heritage and reinforce family and community connections and values.

One of the groups that called for Black Nationalism was the Nation of Islam. While the Nation of Islam was founded much earlier than the Black

Power Movement, some of its ideals influenced Black Power. Malcolm X had been a prominent minister in the Nation of Islam before he left it to form his OAAU group, and the ideas of Malcolm X influenced members of SNCC responsible for the call to Black Power. Mitchell (Yahweh ben Yahweh) had also been a minister for the Nation of Islam, known as Minister Shah. As a member of this movement, Mitchell learned many of the strategies of community building and a distrust for Christianity that he later incorporated into the Nation of Yahweh.

The Nation of Islam called its members to form their own black communities without the assistance of whites. Elijah Muhammad argued that blacks were the original humans on earth, and that they were Muslims. He also taught that white people were the result of a biological experiment gone wrong. The Nation of Islam believed that God had sent the prophet Muhammad to convert whites to the Muslim religion, but that his ideas were rejected. Members of the Nation of Islam also believed that Wallace D. Fard came to earth to recruit Elijah Muhammad to preach that the 6,000 year domination of blacks by the white race was nearly at an end. In the meantime, Muhammad taught that blacks needed to recognize their true identity as members of the Shabazz tribe, part of the original black Muslim nation. Muhammad taught that this tribe had discovered Mecca and the Nile River valley.[434]

Like the Nation of Yahweh taught their members later, the Nation of Islam professed that although whites had denied blacks the knowledge of their true identity, the Nation of Islam was established to reveal it, so that they might be freed from oppression by whites. Members shed their last names, rejecting their slavery origins, and took "X" as their new last name. Muhammad's teachings gave believers a sense of pride in their black identity and a sense of purpose in revealing to other blacks this empowering information.

The common goal of the different groups in the Black Power Movement was to give black Americans a sense of identity and community, some independence from the white power structure, and the ability to affect change for themselves. While the goals were consistent, the methods of achieving them differed. Many of these ideas and various methods greatly influenced the founder of the Nation of Yahweh.

Yahweh ben Yahweh, as Hulon Mitchell, Jr., was personally affected by the Civil Rights and Black Power movements of the 1960s and 1970s. He participated in non-violent demonstrations as a college student, and, feeling that they were ineffective, became involved as a minister for the Nation of Islam. Later, as the founder of the Nation of Yahweh, he preached a message of self-help and separatism from the white community.

He taught that Christianity was a part of the white power structure and that black Christian ministers were pawns of the white establishment and were therefore ineffective leaders in their communities. He was disdainful of blacks who worked together with whites to enact change. He often made use of the term "Uncle Toms" to refer to blacks who cooperated with white oppressors and compromised the needs of the black community.

While Harriet Beecher Stow may have portrayed her character Uncle Tom as a kind, humble and big-hearted slave in her book *Uncle Tom's Cabin*,[435] some black separatists felt that Uncle Tom symbolized compromise and betrayal. An example of this rhetoric, as used by Yahweh ben Yahweh, follows:

> Our Great, Good, and Terrible God (Yahweh), is angry with America and Black Uncle Toms. "THUS SAITH THE LORD GOD, (YAHWEH): WOE (serious trouble) UNTO THE FOOLISH PROPHETS (wicked leaders), WHO FOLLOW THEIR OWN SPIRIT, AND HAVE SEEN NOTHING (from our God) YAHWEH!" (Ezekiel 13:3).[436]

In another example, Yahweh ben Yahweh states:

> It is our oppressors' nature to deceive and destroy us all the days of their life. "THEY ALSO THAT SEEK AFTER MY LIFE LAY SNARES FOR ME (the so-called Negroes); AND THEY THAT SEEK MY HURT SPEAK MISCHIEVOUS THINGS, AND IMAGINE DECEITS ALL THE DAY LONG" (Psalm 38:12). This truth about our oppressors will set you free from them and false (Tom) Black leaders.[437]

For Yahweh ben Yahweh, blacks who preached the message of non-violence as a means to enact change for their community, were doing the bidding of the white power structure. According to him, these black leaders, such as Martin Luther King, Jr., were "Uncle Toms" in that they were "false prophets," betraying the trust of black Americans.

Like other leaders of black communities in the 1970s, Yahweh ben Yahweh utilized Black Power rhetoric in order to get across his message that blacks should stand against the white oppressor. Part of Black Power rhetoric pointed out the inequities of the American justice system, which seemed to inherently favor whites. Sometimes Black Power rhetoric called for violence as a solution to change the existing inequities. This idea is reflected in the following message from Yahweh ben Yahweh:

> Our oppressors are very skilled at twisting THEIR LAW. The law of the land never has and never will bring JUSTICE to our people in America. Our oppressors are INTERNATIONAL CRIMINALS, running from

> justice. They are "FUGITIVES AND A VAGABONDS IN THE EARTH"
> (Genesis 4:12). Cain's seed is "MARKED." ... THUS WITH VIOLENCE
> SHALL THAT GREAT CITY BABYLON (America) BE THROWN
> DOWN, AND SHALL BE FOUND NO MORE AT ALL" (Revelation
> 18:21).[438]

While he pointed out that there were inequities, Yahweh ben Yahweh did
not delineate what those inequities were, nor how specifically they could
be remedied. Instead, he called the white oppressor evil and in need of
violent punishment from God. Here, he refers to America as Babylon, in
need of being overthrown.

Like some in the Black Power movement, Yahweh ben Yahweh felt
that the only way to enact change was through instrumental acts of
violence. However, he couched these calls for violence in terms that made
them appear to be acts of vengeance by God.

> We, Hebrew Israelites, are praying for the destruction of our enemies:
> "LET THEM BE CONFOUNDED THAT PERSECUTE ME, BUT LET
> NOT ME BE CONFOUNDED: LET THEM (the wicked) BE
> DISMAYED, BUT LET NOT ME BE DISMAYED: BRING UPON
> THEM THE DAY OF EVIL AND DESTROY THEM WITH DOUBLE
> DESTRUCTION" (Jeremiah 17:18).[439]

> YAHWEH AT THE RIGHT HAND SHALL STRIKE THROUGH (and
> destroy) KINGS IN THE DAY OF HIS WRATH. HE SHALL JUDGE
> AMONG THE HEATHEN, HE SHALL FILL THE PLACES WITH THE
> DEAD BODIES; HE SHALL WOUND THE HEADS (and break the
> leaders) OVER MANY COUNTRIES (Psalm 110:5-6).

Yahweh ben Yahweh painted a picture of a world that was about to be
turned on its head. God would avenge the violence toward blacks by
bringing whites to justice. The violence toward white oppressors would be
an act of God and a sign of the apocalypse: the end of this world and the
beginning of the time for black rule. Also, Yahweh ben Yahweh named
himself as the avenging angel, as the son of God.[440] As the one who spoke
for God, Yahweh ben Yahweh yielded a certain amount of power in his
movement.

In addition to utilizing the Black Power rhetoric of groups who
advocated calculated acts of violence, Yahweh ben Yahweh also sought to
instill a pride in his congregants' black heritage. While claiming their
ancestry as a lost tribe of Israel went a long way toward instilling this
black pride, he also wanted to uplift their spirits in other ways. He wanted
them to "ACCEPT THE TRUTH. It is time for us to stop destroying

ourselves by trying to be like our oppressors [whites] and patterning ourselves after a DOOMED group."[441] This is similar to Carmichael calling for blacks to stop "trying to destroy each other every Friday and Saturday night."[442] Likewise, Yahweh ben Yahweh called for his congregation to "shake off the mentally dead, dumb, and blind shackles that have beset us for generations of evil rule and MOVE TOWARD UNITY OF OUR BLACK PEOPLE. THIS IS THE TRUTH."[443]

Yahweh ben Yahweh taught that in order for blacks to take their proper place as the chosen people of God, they had to be proud of their "blackness." Claiming that God, Jesus, and all the Hebrew heroes of the Bible were black was one tactic that accomplished this pride in their black heritage. Calling for unity under a common identity with a common goal was another way to give blacks a sense of pride. He also brought a sense of outrage against the treatment of blacks:

> They seek to destroy Hebrew Israelites today and you tomorrow...How long are we going to sit down and allow white people to kill us one by one? How long are we going to stand around allowing white people to kill every model of Black excellence? All Black people must now stand up in unity against lies and falsehood.[444]

This was a way for Yahweh ben Yahweh to unite his religious community. Their outrage could bring them together, and together they could be a powerful force for change. Many members of the movement were attracted by this theme.

Ernest Lee James, Jr., also known as Ahinidab Israel, was an adherent of the Nation of Yahweh who felt that the Black Power message gave hope for a brighter future in America. Although he earned a decent living at the Maimi-Dade Water and Sewer Department, Ahinidab felt "economically trapped and politically and socially disenfranchised."[445] His lawyer said that the Nation of Yahweh "provided some solace for him."[446] Like other blacks in the 1970s and 1980s, the Black Power message of Yahweh ben Yahweh gave James a sense of pride and belonging.

Yahweh ben Yahweh utilized Black Power rhetoric to bring black Americans together to change their world. One of the ways he did this was to utilize Hamilton's call to give people an answer for the growing alienation from the white power institutions, to create a sense of community and belonging, and to establish a new legitimate institution that made members participants in a force for societal improvement.[447] Yahweh ben Yahweh dealt with the alienation of black Americans by giving them a sense of a superior identity. He worked to create new values and a sense of community through his Nation of Yahweh live-in Temple and instilling a sense of duty toward Hebrew laws. Finally, he worked to establish a legitimate new religious institution that made each person a participant in a positive force for change. Although using many other methods Hamilton identified as Black Power, Yahweh ben Yahweh also incorporated calculated acts of violence, which he taught were signs that Yahweh had begun punishing whites.

Members were often attracted to the movement because of its Black Power rhetoric. Carlton Carey was one such member. Carey had been an accountant who wanted to make a difference in Miami's black neighborhoods. He was drawn into the movement by Yahweh ben Yahweh's teachings about Black Pride and self-help. He joined the movement and took the name Mishael Israel. He became a leader in the movement, contributing more than $5,000 of his own money. He studied the scriptures and became an authority for other members. He did some minor bookkeeping for the temple as well.[448] He believed that he was a part of a new black religious community working toward improving the situation for blacks in America, starting with the immediate community in Miami.

Likewise, Aston Green was attracted by the Black Power rhetoric used by Yahweh ben Yahweh. Green studied at the Temple of Love in Liberty City and became convinced of Yahweh ben Yahweh's message. He believed that whites had kept the true Hebrew identity of blacks a secret in order to oppress them. As a member of the movement, he became a strict vegetarian in keeping with his religious beliefs and wanted his parents to join the movement. "Mama, he's a man of God for the black race. Come and look. See what me talkin' about."[449] Although his parents declined to join, Aston became a member. He took the name Elijah Israel and moved in with other members of the movement. In November, 1981 he started to question the motives behind some of Yahweh ben Yahweh's teachings. Some in the movement feared that he would pull others members away. He was killed that month, the first of three murders tied to the "Circle of Ten" or the "Brotherhood" members of the Temple of Love.[450] What had attracted Green most to the movement, were the teachings couched in Black Pride rhetoric. However, he disagreed with the unquestioning devotion of the movement's members to Yahweh ben Yahweh.

Likewise, Lloyd Clark joined the Nation of Yahweh, at the Temple of Love, in response to the race riots following the May 1980 acquittal of the white police men charged with the beating death of a black insurance agent named McDuffie.[451] The rhetoric of Yahweh ben Yahweh convinced Clark that blacks had to fight back. He was convinced that there was a white conspiracy against blacks. Yahweh ben Yahweh's message that the Hebrew identity of American blacks had been withheld by whites fit into his belief system.

During the trials against some members of the Nation of Yahweh in Miami, others in the community kept their printing presses running, producing flyers in their leader's defense. Many of the flyers, such as the following, utilized the Black Power rhetoric of their movement:

> We are tired of being attacked by racist movements! We are tired of our people mysteriously found dead across America! We are tired of being hung on trees! We are tired of fighting wars in other countries and coming back home to be faced with race wars here in America! We are tired of being overworked and under paid! We are tired of being trapped in the ghetto in government-sponsored slums! We are tired of this criminal injustice system only showing fairness to white people! We are tired of our oppressors and their Uncle Tom agents subverting the minds of our people and neutralizing all efforts to unite Moral people in America to be contributors to society instead of burdens on society![452]

The Black Power rhetoric utilized by Yahweh ben Yahweh clearly struck a chord with the members of his community.

Yahweh ben Yahweh utilized Black Power rhetoric in order to establish a moral black community that would combat the white power structure in America. He wished for his religious community to be financially self-sufficient and kept apart from the corrupt influences found in white culture. While he invoked some separatist tactics learned from the Nation of Islam, Yahweh ben Yahweh was not adverse to promoting violent solutions for the problems of racism. He believed that black Americans were the chosen people of God and thus their suffering would be avenged.

Hebrew Identity Rhetoric

In addition to Black Power rhetoric, Yahweh ben Yahweh utilized discourse about Hebrew identity to attract members to the Nation of Yahweh. The new religious movements in America that claim a Hebrew identity tend to be successful in part because they appeal to those who are oppressed or disenfranchised and are searching for religious meanings for their social status. In many cases, a powerless group claims an ancient heritage and/or knowledge that propels them into action meant to change the world. The Nation of Yahweh claimed to have knowledge that the "true" Hebrew identity of American blacks had been kept from them by the white establishment. Yahweh ben Yahweh asserted that if blacks were to affirm their Hebrew identity, God would topple the white establishment. This message appealed to black Americans who felt disenfranchised by the white governmental structure and powerless to change their situation.

The concept that some lost tribes of Israel survive into the present day has appealed to many new religious movements. This is especially true in American history; several groups in America claim to be descendants of the lost tribes. African Americans in particular have historically had a complex relationship with the Jewish faith. Members of these religions believed that identifying themselves as "true" Jews revealed the hidden value of their black heritage. Religions other than the Nation of Yahweh have advanced the theory that the blacks are the lost tribes of Israel, such as the Church of the Living God, the Pillar Ground of Truth for All Nations, the Church of God and Saints of Christ, and Ben Ami's Black Hebrew Israelites. These groups rejected Christianity as the religion of their white American slave masters and often preached a militant black supremacy doctrine.[453] Their oppressed status endowed them with a "morally superior status over their oppressors."[454]

African-Americans have historically identified with the Jewish story: "a lowly people is chosen by God, suffers slavery and exile, and is ultimately redeemed and returned to the Promised Land. This story resonated profoundly with the African slaves and their descendants who cried by the rivers of their own Babylon—America—during centuries of oppression and exile."[455] Black slaves sang songs of oppression that used symbols of the Hebrew slaves in Egypt. In addition, Albert Raboteau, author of *Slave Religion*, notes that black preachers often offered their own exegesis of Hebrew Biblical tradition by emphasizing the chosen-ness of African-Americans and the promise of delivery from their oppression.[456]

Biblical themes that particularly attracted the attention of African-Americans included the Hebrews in bondage and their escape from bondage in Egypt, the devastation of the Assyrian invasions, and the deportation into Babylonian captivity.[457] Vincent L. Wimbush, professor of New Testament and Christian Origins at Union Theological Seminary, states "African-Americans interpreted the Bible in light of their experiences."[458] They saw their own slavery and oppression as analogous to the slavery and suffering of the Hebrews. The Back-to-Africa movements also had an effect on the development of these groups. Africa was believed to be the "Zion," or the promised land, for African-Americans, and it was a dream for many to have a national center to give them a sense of pride and belonging. In the meantime, America was "Babylon," or the nation of exile.

The Nation of Yahweh is not the first group to claim to be black descendants of the lost tribes of Israel. The first was the Church of the Living God, the Pillar Ground of Truth for All Nations founded by F.S. Cherry in 1886 in Chattanooga, Tennessee.[459]   Cherry preached that Adam, Eve, and Jesus were black and that African Americans lost their Hebrew identity during slavery.[460] Later, William S. Crowdy founded the Church of God and Saints of Christ in 1896 in Lawrence, Kansas. Crowdy taught that blacks were heirs of the lost tribes of Israel, while white Jews were descendants of inter-racial marriages between Israelites and white Christians.[461] His group practiced several Jewish rituals and observed the Jewish calendar. Jewish practices included circumcision, wearing yarmulkes, observance of Saturday as the Sabbath, and celebration of Passover. These were blended with Christian practices, however, such as baptism, communion, and foot washing.[462]

One of the most significant groups prior to the Nation of Yahweh to identify themselves as black descendants of the lost tribes of Israel, was the Black Hebrew Israelites. This group was led by the Abeta Hebrew Israel Cultural Center of Chicago in the early 1960s. The Black Hebrew Israelites believed in African repatriation. They intended to leave Babylon (America), purchase land in Zion (Africa), and relocate as a group. The Black Hebrew Israelites found a sympathizer in Liberia who was willing to purchase land for the group. Members determined to find as many people as possible to migrate to Africa and join their effort to repatriate their homeland.[463] Unfortunately, the settlement in Liberia was a disappointment; hardships frustrated the members' efforts there.

When the settlement in Africa was unsuccessful, the group decided to emigrate from Africa to Israel. Ben Ammi, a leader in the group, claimed he had received a revelation that the Israelites were to make offerings of themselves to God by their strict obedience of the laws of the Hebrew Bible. Ben Ammi was instrumental in the group's emigration to Israel. He taught, like Crowdy, that blacks were the true descendants of Israel, and that whites could not be genuine Israelites because Moses and Abraham were black. Over time, he became a messiah-figure for the group.[464]   According to Ben Ammi, Jesus Christ was the Greco-Roman name for the messiah. Because a militant black man would have never accepted a name given by his oppressor, the Hebrew messiah's name was Yeshua, which was in keeping with the Hebrew tradition.[465]

Ammi made a distinction between the tribes of Israel and the Jews. He stated: "The descendants of the tribe of Judah were called Jews, or those who resided in Judea. Portions of other tribes such as Levi, Benjamin, were also in Palestine, but the majority that had returned from exile and who took on all the positions of power and authority were Jews, descendants of the tribe of Judah....When I am referring to national Israel let it be perfectly clear that a significant number of the great slave trade of North and South America were in fact descendants of the biblical Israelites."[466] In other words, Ammi taught that the Jews of today are descendants of the wealthy and powerful Hebrews who were taken into captivity in Babylon. American blacks were considered to be descendants of the other tribes of Israel, those who were left behind due to their poverty and political unimportance.

The Nation of Yahweh inherited the tradition of previous Black Hebrew groups in America. They were closest to Ben Ammi's Black Hebrew Israelites. They borrowed the name "Black Hebrew Israelites" in Miami before changing their name to the Nation of Yahweh. Like the Black Hebrew movements before them, members of the Nation of Yahweh believed that they were the true descendants of the tribes of Israel. They asserted that white Jews could not claim true Jewish identity. Yahweh ben Yahweh taught that members must follow the laws of God laid down in the Hebrew Bible and that God would uphold His covenant with His true chosen people. The Nation claimed that the prophets, Jesus, and God were black, and that this information had been withheld intentionally from them by their white slave owners. Members sought to learn Hebrew, in order to read the Hebrew Bible in its original language. Yahweh ben Yahweh also insisted that members observe modified kosher dietary and hygiene laws and other community precepts from the Hebrew Bible. Members of the Nation of Yahweh saw themselves as the true chosen people of the God, Yahweh.

In this way, the Nation of Yahweh is part of a long tradition of groups claiming to be descendants of one of the twelve tribes of Israel. Yahweh ben Yahweh employed the rhetoric of Hebrew identity in order to attract new followers. This claim of Hebrew identity accomplished three things: it offered a religion to replace Christianity, the religion of white oppressors; it allowed a special status for the disenfranchised; and it gave the followers a legitimate ancient religion as a model for a moral community.

Eric Burke was an early member of the movement in Miami who was attracted by the claim that American blacks were the true descendants of the Hebrews. He was a self-employed mechanic who specialized in air conditioner repairs. He studied with the Nation of Yahweh for two years and believed that they traced the lineage of black Americans back to the biblical tribe of Judah. Freedberg says of Burke in her text: "They discussed the world situation together and called the big white building where they met the Yahweh temple, or the Temple of Love...He found the people warm and caring, not like some blindly ignorant Christians swaying in their seats and bursting into hallelujahs. They didn't believe the meek would inherit the earth. They thought that by standing up for themselves, they would."[467]   What Burke liked about the group was the sense of community and empowerment he found there. He changed his name to Yakim Israel, told people that he worshiped the God Yahweh, and that he was a member of the "true Hebrew Israelites of a Tribe of Judah."[468]   He felt that he found his cultural roots in this new religious movement.[469]

Often, disenfranchised groups claim to be one of the lost tribes of Israel. Historically, the idea that there were lost tribes comes from a passage in II Esdras, which states that after the Israelites had been given into the hands of King Nebuchadnezzar and held captive in Babylon, there was a season of suffering. This passage explains that when the Lord saw that the Israelites began to repent of their evil doings, he liberated the children of Judah and permitted them to go home and rebuild. However, the ten tribes left in Samaria were invaded and carried away out of their own land to Assyria in 721 BCE. The passage reads:

> Those are the ten tribes, which were carried away prisoners out of their own land in the time of Osea the king, whom Salmanasar the king of Assyria led away captive, and he carried them over the waters, and so came they into another land. But they took this council among themselves, that they would leave the multitude of the heathen, and go forth into a further country, where never mankind dwelt, that they might there keep their statutes, which they never kept in their own land. And they entered into Euphrates by the narrow places of the river. For the most High then shewed signs for them, and held still the flood, till they were passed over. For through that country there was a great way to go, namely, a year and a half: and the same region is called Arsareth. Then dwelt they there until the latter time; and now when they shall begin to come, the Highest shall stay the springs of the stream again, that they might go through: therefore sawest thou the multitude with peace. (2 Esdras 13:40-47)[470]

Since these tribes were "carried over the waters" into a new land and were not heard from again in Hebrew Scriptures, myths about their possible whereabouts abounded. What happened to these ten tribes is a mystery that has intrigued many groups. Those who identified themselves with a lost tribe of Israel did so in order to give themselves a sense of chosen-ness in the "new world." In fact, some early American settlers identified the Native Americans as lost tribes of Israel. This helped the colonists to put an "unknown" group, the Native Americans, into a known category.

Claiming to be descended from one of the twelve tribes of Israel gave the Nation of Yahweh a Jewish identity. Thus, they believed that there was one God, Yahweh. They claimed to follow the Hebrew Bible and Yahweh ben Yahweh as their rule and guide for the practice of the "laws, statutes, judgments, and commandments of Yahweh."[471] In addition, adherents were required to practice charity and benevolence, to respect the ties of blood and friendship, open the eyes of the blind and the ears of the deaf, raise up the oppressed, be industrious, and support the government of Yahweh.[472] They believed that during the rule of the Romans in Jerusalem, the Hebrews were forced to leave their homeland and move to the west coast of Africa.[473]

In this way, the group claims that African-Americans are descended from the tribes of Israel.[474] However, unlike other groups who claim the lost tribe of Israel identity, the Nation of Yahweh claims to be descendants of the tribe of Judah, which is not traditionally considered to be one of the lost tribes.[475] The tribe of Judah is the group that was led into captivity in Babylon and whose descendants came back to Israel to rebuild the city. They are not one of the lost tribes that were dispersed according to II Esdras. Instead, the Nation of Yahweh considered the tribe of Judah to have been "lost" because it had forgotten the knowledge of its identity. According to Nation of Yahweh members, when blacks were enslaved, their Hebrew identity was withheld from them as a measure of control by their slavemasters.

The claim of Hebrew identity assumes blood ties with the ancient Israelites. As such, members of the Nation of Yahweh believed they were required to abide by the laws of their ancestors. The group therefore encouraged its members to retreat from the material world as much as possible, because it was considered to be immoral, in order to live a holy life at the Temple.[476] They were to separate themselves from the world of their white oppressors. They were to be circumcised as a sign of their covenant with God and they were to observe the laws of the Hebrew Bible. They also agreed to give up their given names (slave names), adopt first names found in the Hebrew Bible, and take the last name of Israel.

The claim of Hebrew identity was based on Yahweh ben Yahweh's assertion that the ancient Hebrews were black. To support this declaration, Yahweh ben Yahweh pointed to Lamentations 4:8, "THEIR VISAGE (meaning their faces) IS BLACKER THAN COAL."[477] In addition, he offered Joel 2:6, "The day will come when 'ALL' FACES SHALL GATHER BLACKNESS," as proof that whites fear that one day all people will one day become black. He gives various scriptures to prove that

Abraham was black, that Job and Moses were black, and that Egyptians were black.[478]

After establishing that black Americans have a Jewish heritage, Yahweh ben Yahweh exhorted that they must affirm their nationality. This text was titled *You Are Not A Nigger* because he rejected "African" as the nationality of blacks, since slaves came from many places other than Nigeria (one of the derivations of the term "Nigger") and because he claimed that American blacks came from Israel. "It is clear that as so-called Negroes of America, we are LOST and cut off from the knowledge of our NATIONALITY; we are cut off from the knowledge of our LANGUAGE; we are cut off from the knowledge of our NAME; we are cut off from the knowledge of our LAND. Why? Because we are cut off from the knowledge of our God Yahweh, the only true and living God, our Creator, the Creator of all things seen and unseen."[479] He argued that blacks can claim the Nationality of Hebrews:

> Acts 7:6 says, "AND GOD (YAHWEH) SPAKE ON THIS WISE, THAT HIS SEED SHOULD SOJOURN IN A STRANGE LAND; AND THAT THEY SHOULD BRING THEM INTO BONDAGE, AND ENTREAT THEM EVIL FOUR HUNDRED YEARS"; also Genesis 15:13 says, "AND HE SAID UNTO ABRAM, KNOW OF A SURETY THAT THY SEED (your children) SHALL BE A STRANGER IN A LAND THAT IS NOT THEIRS, AND THEY SHALL SERVE THEM (their oppressors); AND THEY (their oppressors) SHALL AFFLICT THEM FOUR HUNDRED YEARS."

Yahweh ben Yahweh reasoned that since blacks were the only race to have been in bondage 400 years, and since the Hebrew Bible describes the children of Abraham (Hebrews) enduring 400 years in slavery, then American blacks must be Hebrews.[480]

Like Ben Ami's Black Hebrew Israelites, Yahweh ben Yahweh claimed that others who assert their Jewish heritage are "false Jews." He professed that others have usurped the Hebrew identity rightfully belonging to blacks, because black Americans were kept from knowing their "true identity." He quoted Hosea 4:6 "My People are destroyed for lack of knowledge: because thou hast rejected knowledge, I will also reject thee, that thou shalt be priest to me: seeing thou hast forgotten the law of thy God, I will also forget thy children."[481] According to Yahweh ben Yahweh, since blacks have been denied the truth of their identity, others have claimed their heritage. He called blacks to correct this injustice by affirming their rightful Hebrew heritage and following the laws of God.

Yahweh ben Yahweh called his followers to observe the laws of the Hebrew Bible, because he taught that the Bible was their "true" history, and the laws found therein were meant to apply to them.[482] Jewish practices observed by members of the Nation of Yahweh included celebrating the Sabbath on Saturday, observing other holy days including the Feast of the Tabernacle,[483] following a kosher diet, learning the Hebrew language in order to read the Torah, following the Jewish calendar, and following other laws from the Hebrew Bible. In addition, they were to take the last name of "Israel," put their children in the Nation's Hebrew school, and live in close community with one another. Their diet consisted of beans, rice, and salad. Meat was prohibited.[484]

Part of the Nation of Yahweh's beliefs about their chosen-ness included the idea that after the apocalypse, blacks would rule the earth forever. They believed that Yahweh ben Yahweh, as God's son, was sent to deliver the Hebrews out of their bondage in America. As the Black Hebrew Israelites, they believed that God would deliver them to their homeland in Israel.[485] The Nation of Yahweh asserted that it had the divine right to lead all blacks out of bondage to their freedom and to their legitimate place as rulers.

Like their Black Hebrew predecessors, the Nation of Yahweh, while claiming a Jewish identity, also utilized some aspects of Christianity. The Christian references lent some legitimacy to Yahweh ben Yahweh's assertion that he was the messiah. While the Messiah is arguably a Jewish theme that was realized in Christianity, Yahweh ben Yahweh took on this role in the Nation of Yahweh religion. Rather than utilize strictly Hebrew scriptures for his claims, he borrowed liberally from the Christian scriptures when it came to "revealing" his messianic nature:

O My people, the hour is come that Yahweh ben Yahweh should be glorified. We must give up all immoral leaders and stop following and listening to them. All of them have failed us and have not profited us at all... IF ANY MAN SERVE ME, LET HIM FOLLOW ME; AND WHERE I AM, THERE SHALL ALSO MY SERVANT BE: IF ANY MAN SERVE ME, HIM WILL MY FATHER, YAHWEH, HONOR (John 12:23-26).[486]

BLESSED BE THE LORD YAHWEH, GOD OF ISRAEL; FOR HE HATH VISITED AND REDEEMED HIS PEOPLE, THE SO-CALLED BLACKS OF AMERICA, AND HATH RAISED UP YAHWEH BEN YAHWEH, A HORN OF SALVATION, A STRONG PROVIDER FOR US IN THE HOUSE OF HIS SERVANT DAVID...AND THOU, CHILD OF YAHWEH, SHALL BE CALLED THE PROPHET OF THE

HIGHEST...TO GUIDE OUR FEET INTO THE WAY OF PEACE (St. Luke 1:68-79).[487]

Yahweh ben Yahweh, the messiah figure for the Nation of Yahweh, chose a Christian view of a messiah, rather than the traditional Jewish view of messiah.

While the Nation of Yahweh identified itself as the inheritor of the ancient religious tradition of the Hebrews, it couched this identity within the Black Power rhetoric of 1970s America. The Nation asserted that the true Hebrews had been black and that members of the Nation of Yahweh could reclaim this nationality by observing the laws of the Hebrew Bible. The realization of Yahweh ben Yahweh as the messiah empowered adherents and was legitimated by using Christian scriptures. The use of this rhetoric gave members the hope and the tools they needed to improve their society.

What the Nation of Yahweh Offered its Members

One of the reasons that The Nation of Yahweh appeared legitimate to potential members was that it offered prospective followers an explanation of why Christianity had failed black Americans. More importantly, this religion professed to offer a solution to this problem. The Nation of Yahweh claimed that the ancient religion of Judaism was the original religion of American blacks and that this tradition offered much for the disenfranchised. Potential members were promised a personal religious experience and a special relationship with a God who looked like them. Additionally, the Nation of Yahweh promised to make members active participants in changing American society. They claimed that if American blacks "returned" to their ancient religion, that Yahweh would enable them to end racism and oppression of blacks in America.

Explanation of Why Christianity Failed Blacks

Due to his own experiences and revelations about Judaism, Yahweh ben Yahweh rejected Christianity as the religion of American white oppressors. He taught members of the Nation of Yahweh that Christianity had been complicit in the domination of black slaves in early American history and that black Christian preachers continued to preach the religion of subjugation. Yahweh ben Yahweh taught that blacks who remained in the Christian faith aided the white establishment in further abusing their brothers and sisters.

Hulon Mitchell, Jr. had been raised in the Pentecostal Holiness religious tradition, but rejected it early in his adult life. When Mitchell founded the Modern Christian Church in Atlanta, his ideology was a mixture of Christianity, Islam, Rosicrusianism and New Age prosperity theology.[488] "God wants you to be rich. The Bible says 'Riches and wealth is the gift of God.'"[489] He performed miracle cures, blessed his parishioners, and gave inspirational talks. "The Lame Walk! The Blind See! The Deaf Hear! Disorders Disappear! Operations are Cancelled!" read the brochures for the church, citing many satisfied parishioners.[490] After this failed attempt at a "Christian" church, Mitchell left the church to form the Nation of Yahweh, a Jewish tradition.

This rejection of Christianity had to do with Mitchell's belief that many black Christian ministers, including his (biological) father and three brothers, were willing to compromise with the white "establishment" when it came to the welfare of their black communities. As Yahweh ben Yahweh, he claimed that other religions, such as Christianity, failed blacks. These pastors were "false prophets," and "dumb dog preachers" who opposed "all true efforts of freedom, justice, and equality" for blacks and acted in their own interests.[491] According to him, black Christian pastors were "false leaders" and "false prophets."[492]

> FALSE LEADERS MUST GO. The words of THE MOST HIGH are against them. "HIS WATCHMEN (the false leaders) ARE BLIND: THEY ARE ALL IGNORANT, THEY ARE ALL DUMB DOGS, THEY CANNOT BARK (warn you about God's plans); SLEEPING (dreaming or talking in their sleep, thus, now knowing what they are talking about), LYING DOWN, LOVING TO SLUMBER. YEA, THEY ARE GREEDY DOGS WHICH CAN NEVER HAVE ENOUGH, AND THEY ARE SHEPHERDS THAT CANNOT UNDERSTAND: THEY ALL LOOK TO THEIR OWN WAY, EVERY ONE FOR HIS GAIN, FROM HIS QUARTER (slice of the pie of false leadership)" (Isaiah 56:10-11).[493]

Yahweh ben Yahweh saw black Christian ministers as co-conspirators with the white establishment, and therefore encouraged his congregation to separate themselves from these "unbelievers" and "false prophets."

Yahweh ben Yahweh taught that the Christian church had failed blacks. Not only did black preachers compromise with whites, but Christianity was the religion of the white oppressors.

> If the Christian God is so great, then why does he inflict Black people with evil? Turn to Acts 7:6 in your King James Bible. Read! 'And God spake on this wise, That his seed should sojourn in a strange land, and that they should bring them into bondage, and entreat them evil for 400 years.'

Genesis 15:13: 'And he said unto Abram, Know of a surety that thy seed shall be a stranger in a land that is not theirs, and shall serve them; and they shall afflict them for four hundred years.' The message interpreted: the afflicters are white people and false Christian prophets. The afflicted are so-called Negroes, brought to America on slave ships in the year 1555, serving in a strange land in bondage for more than four hundred years. We have served our time, according to the Bible.[494]

Yahweh ben Yahweh interprets this passage about the descendants of Abraham to be American blacks. He saw the white establishment as synonymous with Christianity, and thus entreated blacks to turn to the Hebrew God Yahweh and observe His laws found in the Hebrew Bible.

While Yahweh ben Yahweh claimed to be teaching a Jewish tradition, in reality it was a mixture of Jewish and Christian beliefs. Although he claimed to reject the Christianity of the white oppressors, he accepted the Christian scriptures and relied on them for references to himself as the long-awaited messiah. For instance, while Matthew 12:18 describes the baptism of Jesus, Yahweh ben Yahweh cites this scripture to show that God has sent him as his son.[495] His claims to be the son of God, the long awaited messiah, included the promise that under his guidance, American blacks would be led out of the "wilderness of white domination."[496]

In addition, Yahweh ben Yahweh taught that God, Jesus, Moses, and Job were black, although the Jewish religion would not have been concerned with the race of Jesus, a Christian figure. Although he taught that Jesus was black, Yahweh ben Yahweh also taught that there could not have been such a person in history because there was no letter "J" nineteen hundred years ago.

Nobody by the name Jesus ever walked the earth nineteen hundred years ago. No such name existed because there had never been a letter J until six hundred years ago. Go to your dictionary! Go to your encyclopedia! Look up the letter J. There is no Jah, no J, no Jesus. So just shut up that stuff. Go to the dictionary. THERE IS NO J!" So how could a man living almost two thousand years ago have the name Jehovah or Jesus? No, he said, it was the white man, the trickster of technology, who changed the color of the son of God into a lie. It was the white man who changed the name of Yahweh. The white man handed out pictures of a white savior so the Black man wouldn't recognize the true messiah when he made his appearance.[497]

According to Yahweh ben Yahweh, while the lineage of black biblical heroes includes Jesus, there was never a historical Jesus.

These inconsistencies show that Hulon Mitchell, Jr., as Yahweh ben Yahweh, was conflicted about his Christian upbringing. He borrowed from it at times and rejected it others. Claiming a Hebrew identity for the Nation of Yahweh lent the movement credibility as an ancient religious tradition. The imagery of a Christian savior lent credibility to the founder, Yahweh ben Yahweh. While he originally took the name Moses Israel, he later took on the name Yahweh ben Yahweh, God, son of God. Several years later, during his incarceration in the 1990s, Yahweh ben Yahweh used the imagery of the crucified savior to describe his "persecuted" situation.[498]

Personal Religious Experience and a Special Relationship with God

Yahweh ben Yahweh promised members of the Nation of Yahweh that they would have a special relationship with Yahweh, the God of the ancient Hebrews and they would experience his love and acceptance on a personal level. He assured members that they shared the same skin color as God, who chose them for a special purpose. In addition, many members reported that they noticed a feeling of belonging and purpose due to their involvement in this religious group.

Part of Yahweh ben Yahweh's religious claims revolved around the idea that the God of the Hebrews was black. While this claim partly involved giving black Americans a sense of pride in their racial heritage, an important function of this claim was also to introduce a deity with whom individuals could personally identify. When he offered his second "proof" of God's ethnicity found in the Hebrew Bible in the Book of Daniel 7:22, Yahweh ben Yahweh interpreted the scripture to say that God's hair was like wool. After he cited this, he asked his listeners to "reach up and feel your own head or look at the nappy heads of our people, the so-called Negroes, the so-called Blacks, and you have to admit that we are the only people on earth who have hair like the pure wool."[499] This was intended to give people a sense that they had something uniquely in common with God.

Additionally, the message from Yahweh ben Yahweh to potential members of his movement involved convincing them that black Americans were descended from the ancient Hebrews and thus were the chosen people of God. After explaining that the Hebrew Patriarch Abraham was black, Yahweh ben Yahweh pointed to the promise made by God to Abraham that He would make of his descendants a "great nation, and I will bless thee, and make thy name great and thou shall be a blessing" (Genesis 12:2).[500] In his teachings, he tried to persuade his followers that all of the promises made in the Hebrew Bible to God's chosen people were indeed meant for American blacks. According to him, the slaves transported to America from Africa had originally been Hebrews who had migrated there from Israel. In order to convince the disenfranchised in his black community, Yahweh ben Yahweh also claimed that the reason American blacks were unaware of their ancient heritage was due to intentional deception by the white power structure in America. This point was particularly convincing to many converts.

Like many other members, Amtulla Raheem of Chicago became a member after reading *You Are Not A Nigger!*, which had been given to her by a door-to-door missionary from the Nation of Yahweh in 1983. She said that an hour after reading the book, "I was shouting, I was crying, I was asking him to forgive me for being so stupid."[501] After reading the tract, Raheem felt that she had been deceived for too long. At the time, she was seventy-five years old. She packed all her belongings and traveled to Miami to become a full-time member at the Temple of Love. After a few days, Yahweh ben Yahweh saw Amtulla standing behind a door and called her over to bless her. He gave her the name "Amtulla Bat Yahweh," mother of Yahweh's kingdom. She responded by saying, "You can see I'm in love! Everybody can look at me and see I'm in love! Look at him! He's smiling at me!" She felt a sense of belonging; she determined she had found her spiritual home.

Louis Mack was also attracted to Yahweh ben Yahweh's message of a special relationship with God. He had left home in 1968 as an idealistic recruit for the Vietnam Police Action. While there, Mack took enemy rounds in his right leg and right arm and was shipped back to the United States. He spent six months in the hospital recovering, and still had a limp. Mack went on permanent disability. "He had lived and almost died for his country, and all he could see was how badly the black man was treated in America," his lawyer said.[502] He got married, but led a troubled life. He took much of his anger out on his wife, and at one point police were called to calm a domestic abuse situation. He became angry any time he saw black men stopped for no apparent reason by police. One day, he was outside a movie theater and Yahweh ben Yahweh approached him and talked about his Hebrew heritage. He was attracted by the idea that American blacks were the chosen people of God. "Yahweh ben Yahweh preached forgiveness. He gave him something to love," explained his lawyer, Ellen Leesfield.[503] While he left the group in 1988, he claimed that his experience in the Nation of Yahweh had changed his life and made him a moral person. When Mack left the group, he became a maintenance man and began paying child support for his children.

The Nation of Yahweh offered acceptance for blacks who felt disenfranchised and lost in American society. Brian Lewis was one of these people. Lewis had been an alto-saxophone player in his high school band and had been an active student government leader in college. One of his goals had been to improve race relations in Miami. But in his senior year at St. Augustine College in Raleigh, North Carolina, he felt lost. "He wasn't quite sure where he was going or what he wanted to do with his life. He began asking. 'Who am I?' And he started getting a lot less active with student government. He kind of dropped out in a way…I guess he gave everything to this group as part of his acceptance," said his political science advisor, Allan Cooper.[504] In 1982, Lewis became Hezion Israel, an active member of the Nation of Yahweh. He felt that belonging to this group could help him be a part of changing the negative racial climate in Miami.

For some, the Nation of Yahweh offered acceptance by God and the feeling they belonged to a special group. A former athlete, who was attracted by Yahweh ben Yahweh's teachings, was Michael Mathis. He had previously been an all-star linebacker at South Miami High School. He grew up in a working-class poor family as one of nine children. In 1983, Mathis enrolled in a program called "Upward Bound," a federal program designed to improve his grades so that he could get into college. However, he dropped out of school in 1984. A friend told him about the Nation of Yahweh, so he went to the Temple to learn more. He "wanted something to believe in more than himself," said his lawyer, Ron Polk.[505] He found the Bible teachings interesting and stayed. For Mathis, the Nation of Yahweh seemed to "address many of the problems that so many black people in America feel," said the lawyer of one of his fellow sect members.[506] Mathis was attracted to the Nation of Yahweh because it addressed his concerns and made him feel a part of something "bigger than himself."

When Yahweh ben Yahweh referred to God in his writings, he tended to describe Him as "Our Great, Good and Terrible God, Yahweh."[507] The term "Great" was intended to give members a sense of awe at the power of God. The term "Good" was meant to let members know that God was just and kind. But the term "Terrible" was reserved for the vengeance that Yahweh ben Yahweh claimed that God would wreak on the white power structure in America. The first two terms were so that members could identify with God and feel a closer connection with him; the last term was intended as a pledge that this same God would avenge the injustices that members faced in American society.

One of the reasons people joined the Nation of Yahweh, was the promise that they would have a personal religious experience and a special relationship with God. They felt they were the chosen people of God, which gave them a sense of belonging and a belief that they could identify in a unique way with God. While potential adherents were attracted by the Black Power rhetoric, this movement offered them something more than a secular political group. The Nation of Yahweh also promised members that they were a part of God's plan to end the oppression of Blacks in America. Their participation in this holy community could effect change. This gave their efforts a level of meaning that was absent from other such movements.

Possibility of Ending White Oppression in America

Like the other new religious movements discussed in this study, the Nation of Yahweh appealed to the disenfranchised in America by offering them a way to be active participants in changing their situation. While Yahweh ben Yahweh claimed that blacks in America had been enslaved and deprived of the knowledge of their "true" Hebrew identity, he also promised that simply reclaiming this identity would begin their journey toward changing their social status. He explained that accepting and practicing the ancient religion of the Hebrews was a way for American blacks to rise above their oppression and end the racism that had disabled their progress in an unjust American society.

Yahweh ben Yahweh identified American blacks as descendants of the ancient Biblical Hebrews. He claimed that the Hebrew Scriptures had prophesied about the suffering of the American slaves. He revealed the Jewish identity of black Americans as part of his "World's Best Kept Secret" sermons preached from the beginnings of the movement. According to Yahweh ben Yahweh, blacks had been intentionally denied the knowledge of their true identity by the white establishment. Whites had oppressed and demeaned blacks in America, who were God's chosen people. He claimed that God would avenge these wrongs. Thus, he condemned America for the treatment of blacks, and called on his followers to reject their oppression by whites.

Yahweh ben Yahweh taught his followers that black Americans were descendants of the Hebrew tribe of Judah. He claimed that this tribe was forced to move from Jerusalem during the reign of the Romans, and they then settled on the west coast of Africa. His story continues that while the Hebrews were in Africa, they encountered an English trader named Sir John Hawkins. Hawkins had allegedly sailed his ship "The Good Ship Jesus" along the west coast of Africa in search of "the Black Hebrews who were prophesied to be brought into slavery as the seed of Abraham."[508] Yahweh ben Yahweh claimed that Queen Elizabeth commissioned Sir

John Hawkins to go to Africa to kidnap the Black Hebrews with the help of the "Ishmaelites" (Arabs) and the "Hamites" (Africans) and bring them to the new world to make them slaves.[509] He then says that Sir John Hawkins tricked many of the black Hebrews into following him to the new world, where he promised that they would make more money for their labor than they had made in their homeland of Israel.

According to Yahweh ben Yahweh, after the black Hebrews were on the ship, Sir Hawkins and his crew overwhelmed them and put them into chains. They broke their will, robbed them of their dignity, raped their women and "bred fear into them from the womb."[510] They brought the black Hebrews to Jamestown, Virginia, in 1555, "[r]obbed of the knowledge of self, kind, and others."[511] Yahweh ben Yahweh explained: "Instead of finding gold as we were promised, we found a land that was a wilderness, an uncultivated, hostile land. Instead of payment, we were placed on slave blocks and auctioned off like cattle."[512] In this way, he "traced" the journey of black Hebrews from Jerusalem, to Africa, to America.

Instead of freedom from slavery, Yahweh ben Yahweh described the emancipation of Blacks in America as a farce:

> After 310 years of this inhuman treatment, an ex-slave master turned President named Abraham Lincoln, began having trouble in The White House. He was faced with the problem of keeping America united. In this crisis were the Black HEBREW slaves, who were but pawns in the whole transaction. Lincoln was forced by the turn of events in his administration to PRETEND TO FREE US, the so-called Negro/Blacks. He did it with great apprehension and fear. Even while PRETENDING TO FREE US, he was heard to say, "AS FOR THE SUPERIOR POSITION, I AS MUCH AS ANY WHITE MAN, WANT IT ALWAYS TO BE IN THE HANDS OF THE WHITE MAN."
>
> Actually, this freedom was not genuine freedom, for we were not given back OUR HEBREW KNOWLEDGE of our God Yahweh, our history, culture, language, our HEBREW names, nor were we returned to our HOMELAND, called ISRAEL today.[513]

Since this was a "fictional" emancipation, Yahweh ben Yahweh figured that the black Hebrew Israelites had been in bondage for more than 400 years. While most black rhetoric described oppression by the white establishment to be composed of economic, legislative, and racist elements, Yahweh ben Yahweh additionally described the subjugation by whites to include the deprivation of knowledge of their "true" identity. Because whites supposedly held the knowledge of blacks' true identity, they felt they had the right to deprive blacks of economic security, equal rights, and the right to govern themselves.

However, Yahweh ben Yahweh promised his followers hope. Black Hebrew Israelites would rule America one day and there would be doom in store for the American white oppressors. According to him, God would bless the Nation of Yahweh.

> Although we must stay in America for a little while, Yahweh is with us, and will bless us; for unto us and our children, Yahweh will give us all the countries on Earth to rule, and our God, Yahweh, will perform the oath which HE sware unto Abraham, our father. WHY WILL YAHWEH DO ALL THIS FOR US? Because we obey the voice of Yahweh and keep HIS charge, HIS commandments, HIS statutes, and HIS laws (Genesis 26:3-5).[514]

As the inheritors of the covenant with Abraham, Yahweh ben Yahweh claimed that God would bless blacks who recognized their true identity and kept their part of the covenant.

While Yahweh ben Yahweh claimed God's promises for His people, the Nation's leader reassured his followers that God would punish America for her sins against the black Hebrews.

> AMERICA, WHAT HAST THOU DONE? The voice of thy Black slaves' blood crieth unto Yahweh from the ground. And now, America, thou art cursed from the Earth, which hath opened her mouth to receive thy Black slaves' blood from thy hand. THE TIME WILL SOON COME THAT EVERY ONE THAT FINDETH YOU SHALL SLAY YOU. Your sin is very bad! (Genesis 4:8-12)[515]

In this passage cited by Yahweh ben Yahweh, he asserts that America is Cain, who has slain her black brothers and sisters. He believed that the scripture cited God condemning Cain to death. As in his other teachings, Yahweh ben Yahweh interpreted these biblical passages to refer to contemporary situations of his religion.

Likewise, in the following passage, Yahweh ben Yahweh explains that God has warned America that she will be destroyed because of her treatment of blacks:

> America has a serious problem concerning her ex-slaves, a terrible burden to bear. Because of her mistreatment of our people, she is facing absolute destruction from Almighty Yahweh, as recorded in the Bible. Because she is an opponent of Yahweh, she goes against HIS word. Although the servants of Yahweh give her clear warning, yet will she continue her evil ways (Isaiah 13:1-2).[516]

In this passage, Isaiah says that God will raise a signal when the "Day of the Lord" will come, and yet people will still be destroyed. Yahweh ben Yahweh mentioned this signal as "clear warning" that America ignored. Thus, he claims that God will destroy America because she ignored His signal and continued oppressing His people.

Yahweh ben Yahweh saw America as the place where the black Hebrews were held in bondage. Like other American black Hebrews, he believed that America was Babylon, the land of exile. He held America accountable for persecuting the people of Yahweh, black Americans, as well as keeping their "true" identity a secret from them. While he taught that God would punish America severely, Yahweh ben Yahweh also promised that God would bless His chosen people for their faithfulness to Him.

Yahweh ben Yahweh asserted that members of the Nation of Yahweh could be active participants in ending their oppression by recognizing their "true" identity as Hebrews and following God's laws found in the Hebrew Bible. In addition, they were to be faithful to their religious community and to its leader, Yahweh ben Yahweh. They believed that their allegiance would be rewarded when God avenged the evils done to them by destroying the white power structure of America.

Carter Cornelius, Mitchell's cousin, was one such believer. He was a former recording artist who hoped to make a comeback through his association with the Nation of Yahweh. Several years earlier, he had been the lead singer of Cornelius Brothers and Sister Rose, with recorded hits such as "Too Late to Turn Back Now," and "Treat Her Like a Lady." When he converted to the Nation of Yahweh, he said that modern music "set black people back thousands of years." He became Elder Gideon, who later released a divinely-inspired album, *Love Train*. His more religious tunes included titles like "Can I Get a Witness?" "I Want to Be Connected to the Mighty God," and "Going Back to Miami, Going Back to the City of God."[517] On this album, he sang and played drums, piano, organ and guitar. He recorded this new album in a studio set up for him by Yahweh ben Yahweh. He said about his new religion, "I left Broadway and went the straight and narrow way. I left all the bright lights to lead the simple life. But the world is going to change real soon, to bend toward Yahweh. Then all those bright lights will be shining for Yahweh ben Yahweh."[518] He became an Elder in the new religion and led a group in a small temple in South Broward.[519] He saw his music and his leadership as an Elder in the Nation of Yahweh as his part in a larger change that the movement would bring about in America, starting in Florida.

Another member who wanted to be an active participant in changing what he perceived as a racially unjust American society was Bobby Rozier. Rozier, a former football player, became Neariah Israel in the Nation of Yahweh. He happened upon the Hebrew Israelites when he was walking by the Temple of Love in 1981 just before serving time in prison. Bobby saw a bearded man in a white turban outside the building and approached him. "What's this all about?" he asked, "I'm looking for the truth."[520]   He resonated with the message that there was a conspiracy against blacks and liked the people he met in the Temple. He stayed in the Temple until he had to start his prison term. He read the *Bible* and *You Are Not A Nigger!* in prison and was visited by members of the movement. After serving his time, Neariah Israel returned to the Temple and became a full-time member. He became part of the "Brotherhood" members who felt they were seeking vengeance for God. He was involved in the death of a tenant in one of the Apartment Complexes purchased by the Temple. Later, in 1988, he made a deal with the State of Florida and testified against Yahweh ben Yahweh and members of the Nation. Rozier wanted to change the world—he wanted to create a level playing-field for African-Americans. He believed that this involved being faithful to Yahweh ben Yahweh, which he understood as being faithful to God.

Carl Douglas Perry was also attracted to the Nation of Yahweh's message of black pride and wanted to be a participant in changing American society. He had grown up in a Methodist Church and served the Army in Korea. After his discharge, Perry "grew dissatisfied with a religion [Christianity] that tended to view blacks as 'rootless slaves.'"[521] Eventually, he followed two of his brothers into the Nation of Yahweh. His brother Alfred explained that the group "built moral and ethical teachings among people who may not hold such values."[522]   After becoming a member, Carl felt that he was called to bring about justice for blacks. The court accused him in 1990 of shooting two Yahweh dissenters, stabbing two "white devils," and slicing off ears as trophies for Yahweh ben Yahweh.[523] He believed that he was an instrument of Yahweh's wrath. These actions were a result of his understanding of how Yahweh would punish the injustices toward blacks. Eventually, the allure of the group wore off for Perry. He disassociated from the group in 1987.[524]

Many members who joined the Nation of Yahweh were drawn to this movement because it offered them a way to actively change their society for the better. They felt disenfranchised by the white power structure in America and needed to feel that theirs was a religious solution to this problem. While some Nation of Yahweh adherents became full-time members, working in the shops owned by the Temple, peddling Temple wares, "punishing whites" through violence, or cleaning Temple properties, others worked outside jobs and donated a large percentage of their income to the Temple.

In any of these cases, members felt that they were working toward a time when American whites would be punished by God for their unjust treatment of blacks. In accepting their "true identity," they could help bring about a better world, one in which their identity was recognized and respected by whites. In their ideal world, whites would be subjugated by God and blacks would rule the promised land.[525] Whether members believed this or not, they identified the conspiracy of a white nation oppressing blacks with the oppression and suffering of the ancient Hebrews. As the chosen people of God, they believed they were part of God's plan to throw off this subjugation and enjoy their much-deserved freedom.

Summary

Because the legacy of the Nation of Yahweh has been one of terrorism, many have overlooked the religious claims that originally drew members into this movement. Hulon Mitchell, Jr., or Yahweh ben Yahweh, created the Nation of Yahweh in the 1970s and early 1980s America in response to the Black Power movement of that era. He claimed that blacks were descendents of the lost tribes of Israel. He preached that black Americans needed to stop relying on the white establishment in America and create their own self-supporting communities. He utilized Black Power ideology and rhetoric, combined with the moral prescriptions derived from the Hebrew Bible in order to create a model for a moral black community. This was more than a secular Black Power movement; this movement claimed that its members could experience God through their ancient Hebrew identity. Members were drawn to this movement because they believed it made them an integral part of God's plan for ending the oppression of blacks in America.

Yahweh ben Yahweh utilized Black Power rhetoric because it was meaningful to potential adherents. He also asserted that God, Moses, Job, and Jesus were black. He claimed that whites had kept these secrets from them in order to oppress and demean their race. He addressed blacks who felt powerless and betrayed by the white power structure in America. He called blacks to unite and create their own self-sufficient communities. One of the ways that he addressed Black Pride, was to assert black Americans' inheritance of God's promise to the Hebrews. As descendents of the Hebrews, American blacks were a chosen people. This gave the members of his movement a sense of pride in their "blackness." He also claimed their suffering would soon end. God would punish whites and elevate blacks to their rightful place as leaders in America.

The claim of an ancient identity served another purpose as well; it gave his movement authenticity for its members. Yahweh ben Yahweh quoted verses from the Hebrew and Christian Bibles to legitimate his religious claims in his texts *You Are Not a Nigger!*, *Yahweh Judges America*, and other brochures and tracts. Since these scriptures were authoritative for most of his potential adherents, this lent his teachings some credibility. Black Christian preachers had been using the plight of the ancient Hebrews for a long time, since blacks could identify with the suffering of the biblical people. Yahweh ben Yahweh took this one step further and claimed that they were not *like* the ancient Hebrews; they *were* the ancient Hebrews. Using canonical scriptures and claiming a known religious tradition lent Yahweh ben Yahweh's teachings some authority for potential adherents.

As part of their religious beliefs, the Nation of Yahweh rejected the oppression of blacks in America. Christianity, as the mouthpiece of the conqueror, was cast aside. Members consciously chose to reject Christianity in favor of a Jewish identity. Converts also believed that God would punish America for its oppression of blacks since the time of slavery. Because America used Christian justification for slavery, she was to be subject to punishment by God. These beliefs fit into their self-identification as chosen people. They asserted that blacks had endured their adversity long enough and that according to biblical prophesy, the end of their suffering was near. This promised a triumph for blacks and a blessing from God.

While members accepted the teachings of Yahweh ben Yahweh as authoritative, they formed another type of legitimacy with their own religious experience. This gave members a sense that their participation in this movement was authentic. Members of the movement reported that they felt a sense of chosen-ness. They felt they belonged to a religion with an ancient past and a long tradition. They celebrated their newfound identities by observing biblical practices and holy days. These practices set them apart and made them feel special. They believed they had a special connection to God that others did not experience. They felt loved by God, by one another, and by Yahweh ben Yahweh. Their relationship with this self-proclaimed son of God gave them a personal connection with their divine. They also felt that they were a part of a movement that would change their world, starting with America. Their acceptance of their ancient identity assured them that God would visit vengeance on the white power structure and would bless them, as His chosen people, with freedom from oppression.

Although at first, Yahweh ben Yahweh was not interested in the movement being accepted as legitimate by the larger society, it became an issue in the later 1980s and early 1990s. Early members who had children in the movement did not register the births of those children with the United States government. They did not wish to participate in the larger American society. However, in 1986, members got birth certificates for their children, went to work in the traditional workplace, and became more of a visible presence in Miami. As part of this wider public acceptance, Yahweh ben Yahweh began to mix with important people in town: hoteliers, restaurateurs, big business, and members of the Chamber of Commerce. In 1987, the Urban League of Greater Miami awarded him a Whitney M. Young, Jr. humanitarian award for economic development. His business and charity efforts earned him a certain amount of respect in Miami, and the mayor even declared October 7, 1990 "Yahweh ben Yahweh Day." In 1990, Louis Farrakhan appeared with Yahweh ben Yahweh in the Miami Arena in front of 9000 people to shake hands and pledge an alliance between the movements. This shows a paradox between his wide-spread appeal in Miami and his religious rejection of that same society.

The rhetoric of the Black Power movement and the assertions of ancient Hebrew identity helped Yahweh ben Yahweh claim converts to his religion. The political and social sensibilities of new members resonated with Black Power rhetoric, and they believed the biblical interpretations claiming they were God's chosen people. Most importantly, this religion offered adherents a special relationship with God, which allowed them to be personally involved in transforming their world. They believed that Yahweh ben Yahweh could help them end racism and oppression of blacks in America. While the incarceration of Yahweh ben Yahweh and other members of the Nation of Yahweh brought unwanted public criticism, this religion continued to practice their beliefs and spread their message of black empowerment in America.

CONCLUSION

Imagine an America where all citizens are members of one big happy family obedient to the same father God. Picture an America where citizens are legally and economically equal, regardless of gender, under the guidance of a mother Goddess. Envision an America free of racial oppression under the care of a black Hebrew patriarch. The new religious movements examined in this dissertation developed these grand dreams of reinventing American society in the 1960s and 1970s. They sought to improve their nation, not through direct legal or governmental reform, but by influencing American cultural values, perceptions and beliefs.

Although the Unification Church, Feminist Wicca and the Nation of Yahweh each had its share of tension with the larger American culture, each of these movements believed that it had a viable vision for an improved America. While it might be easy to dismiss any one of these new religious movements as a passing ideological fad, the fact that they have all survived into the twenty-first century should persuade us to give them a second look. These religions offered their potential members a way to be personally involved in changing the world through religious means interwoven with social goals.

While limited to three new religious movements that emerged in 1960s and 1970s America, this text sheds light on larger questions in the study of religion and American culture. It uncovers some factors in recent American society that led people to form new religious movements. It reveals that claims of tradition and novel personal experience gave authority to new religions and their leaders. This project answers, in part, why young people in the 1960s and 1970s chose new religious movements and rejected already-established religions. In addition, it suggests a different strategy for grouping new religious movements by their claims of ancient origins in order to assist scholars in understanding more about how these groups view themselves.

This research demonstrates that certain new religious movements arose in the 1960s and 1970s in response to the perceived failure of secular social movements and established religions. During this time period, America experienced the Vietnam War, the Civil Rights movement, radical protest movements, the Roe v. Wade abortion rights case, and the Watergate scandal that took down the President of the United States. For some, existing secular and spiritual institutions seemed incapable of dealing with the death, discrimination and moral dilemmas symbolized by these events. New religions formed because persons sought religious explanations—and solutions—outside of those offered by traditional religions. In this tumultuous time, people had new revelations, such as the Reverend Sun Myung Moon's vision of what the "real" message of Jesus was for Christianity, or Yahweh ben Yahweh's proclamation that black Americans were descended from the ancient Hebrews. Feminist Wicca arose in response to new interpretations of archaeological evidence that gave religious expression to feminist ideas. I have argued in this text that these three religions formed because their leaders and membership felt powerless in American society, yet desired to make a meaningful difference in the world.

This study shows that important new religious movements formed in America as the result of novel ideas espoused by charismatic persons or small groups. These movements, instead of claiming inspiration from unknown deities that offered unique ideas, tied themselves to the past. Prospective members were more inclined toward these connections with ancient religious traditions. Thus, Sun Myung Moon claimed to have had a revelation from Jesus. Supposedly blessed by Christ, the theology of Moon's Unification Church was at once fresh but non-threatening to interested converts. Feminist Wiccans chose to work within an existing Neo-pagan tradition that, while less familiar than Christianity, was still reasonably well-known to those who joined. Feminist Wiccans practiced their interpretation of ancient Goddess worship, rather than creating a religion with unknown ties. Likewise, Yahweh ben Yahweh asserted that black Americans were descended from the ancient Hebrews, marrying the recognizable religious tradition of Judaism to an ethnic membership that he hoped to empower.

While these connections with ancient religions bestowed some semblance of legitimacy, the links only formed a framework on which to build new ideas. As Max Weber explained, emerging religious movements claim authority by professing new revelations drawn from old traditions or by claiming that a recently-formed religious tradition is actually an obscured ancient truth that members are restoring to its rightful place.[526] Claims of antiquity give new movements the advantage of familiar categories and habits of thought without restricting their license to bring innovative ideas into their religious visions. This means that new religions, while drawing inspiration from ancient traditions, in fact recreate distinct histories in line with their new religious ideas.

In the late 1960s and early 1970s America, many of the nation's young people turned their back on their Christian and Jewish faiths because they believed that these traditions had failed to create a better American society. They saw the Vietnam War, the Watergate scandal, the pollution of the earth, the moral decline of society, and other cultural issues as failures of the American establishment. They were convinced that their Judeo-Christian traditions "had sanctioned both racial discrimination and American involvement in the Vietnam War. Further, they often charged that the Christian doctrine of creation had legitimized the destruction of the environment."[527]   Responding to what seemed a spiritual betrayal, many turned their backs on established traditions and looked toward new religious movements in their quest to create a better society. Fresh interpretations of established religious doctrines answered two problems for the converts of new religious movements. These new religions explained why traditional religions had failed American society, and gave young people a religious method for correcting societal ills. In other words, they restored the bedrock of religion: faith.

New religious movements taught their converts that personal daily religious practices could revitalize America.   Hence, converts to the Unification Church believed that their individual sacrifices could collectively heal a corrupt American society. New adherents of Wicca believed that resurrecting ancient goddess religions could help implement an egalitarian American society. Members of The Nation of Yahweh asserted that their participation in a holy community that already enjoyed some measure of respect and success would create a more equitable society for black Americans.

Meanwhile, as converts to new religious movements fled the religions of their childhoods, some shared the ultimate goals of the old institutions: changing the world. Certainly the old faiths wanted the world to be more "God-centered" and morally upright. Several denominations participated in the struggles to obtain equal rights under the law for women and African Americans. However, caught in turbulent times and craving better results, Americans who chose to follow alternative religious paths felt that traditional religions, such as Christianity, were actually responsible for many of the societal problems in their nation. Some believed that the old faiths were inherently corrupt or immoral; some thought that they were inherently patriarchal; others believed that they legitimized racism in America. For this small percentage of believers the only option was to choose new movements that offered what seemed to be a theological fit, but also gave them a religious path to be personally involved in improving their society.

A common objection to new religions in the 1960s and 1970s was the belief that they were "cults" that "brainwashed" young people. Many parents believed that their children were not voluntarily defecting from their families' religions. Numerous parents could not understand how their children could believe the doctrines taught by the new religions. These parents claimed that their children must have been psychologically manipulated and held against their will. While many parents certainly felt this way, their children disagreed. New converts believed they had legitimate religious experiences that gave them spiritual tools to build a better world. The converts were convinced that they operated on higher moral ground than adherents of other faiths, and thus, believed that membership in new religious movements was an essential part of their quest for a better American society.

Some adherents of new religions had previously engaged in secular movements to change society. While many of these movements made great strides in their efforts to improve America, the subjects of this study keenly felt their limitations and noticed their failures. Protest movements and progressive politics focused attention on Vietnam, political scandals and gender and racial inequalities, but the idealistic wanted more. These young Americans argued that the Vietnam War continued to take lives, that society was in moral decline and that gender and racial discrimination still permeated American culture. They needed to abandon secular strategies and engage spiritual tactics. New religions, they felt, would allow them to make an impact on a cosmic scale.

While discontented with the motivations of the secular movements, converts of new religious movements did not hesitate to borrow their strategies and rhetoric. These methods helped gather and organize like-minded people. Strategies such as non-violent protests, consciousness-raising groups, volunteer-based organization, and media alerts raised awareness about new religious ideas. The lessons learned from secular social movements went toward a higher calling. This was much more than politics.

Appealing to idealistic young people, new religious movements offered a way to answer why traditional religions had failed them. The new religions promised an authentic personal relationship with the divine, which in turn, lent these religions authority for new members. When a member experienced what they believed to be an encounter with the divine, they became convinced the new religious movement must be authentic. This experience varied from person to person, but examples could include a Unification Church member identifying feelings of sadness with the disappointment God has with his creation. This personal connection with God energized members to be a part of the solution for a more moral America. Thus, fueled by their new religious visions of a better world, members believed that their individual actions took on cosmic implications.

In addition to personal religious experience, Weber stressed that the charisma of a religious leader could lend a certain amount of authority to a new religious movement. Both Sun Myung Moon and Yahweh ben Yahweh were charismatic leaders, and their new religious movements attracted many followers. However, in the case of the Unification Church, the Reverend Sun Myung Moon was not a significant factor in attracting new members during the formative years in the United States. Moon's messianic claims were still understated, and he was not a forceful presence in America until the mid-1970s. His charisma grew over the years and is arguably what currently holds the movement together. Yahweh ben Yahweh, on the other hand, relied heavily on personal charisma in order to attract new members during the Nation's formation, but his movement did not splinter with his incarceration in 1990. Instead, members continued to spread his message and interpret his teachings.

As James Lewis argues, "no matter how much personal charisma a prophet might have, his or her message must always address the concerns of the community in a satisfactory manner."[528] For this reason, I have focused largely on the societal concerns of members of new religious movements in this study, even though charisma is important. Alongside the charisma of their leaders and historical claims, societal concerns were crucial in drawing members to these new religious movements. Prospective members were attracted by the new religions' grand dreams for an improved American society. Once persons were converted, their personal religious experiences gave the movements authenticity for believers.

In addition to answering why some people chose to join certain movements, in this study, I offer a new strategy for categorizing emerging religions. Since many new religious movements choose connections with antiquity, they can be classified by the ancient tradition they claim. Doing so will give scholars new insight into these religions' worldviews and beliefs. This method will allow scholars to interpret new religious movements that believe they have roots in ancient eastern traditions such as Hinduism, Buddhism, Judaism, formative Christianity, Gnosticism, Mystery Religions, or Celtic traditions.

Gordon Melton, a prominent scholar of American new religious movements, believes that new religions resemble their "parent" religion more than they resemble one another.[529] While new religious movements go through similar stages in their development, it is difficult to point to traits they share in common. Instead, new religions begin with religious beliefs held by an ancient religious tradition and branch out into new ideas. Thus, scholars can also learn about new religions by beginning with the ancient religion with which the new religious movement claims connections. Although they profess to be ancient, new religious movements can be considered "new" because they adapt or change the ancient tradition through revelation or interpretation.

Aligning themselves with ancient religious traditions is a statement of identity for these new religious groups. Thus, new religious movements offer revolutionary revelations in the context of already existing religions, or they profess to be reclaiming ancient religions. This presents scholars with a paradox: in order to appeal to potential members, new religions use terms, worldviews, and language of ancient religions because these are easily identifiable, while at the same time, new religions reject these same ancient traditions.

The new religious movements in this study asserted that they had new revelations or interpretations of an ancient religion. The Unification Church put forth a new revelation they believed would bring Christians back into the plan God originally intended for his creation. Feminist Wiccans utilized their beliefs about ancient Goddess worship and new rituals and practices in order to bring about a more egalitarian American society. The Nation of Yahweh offered new revelations about the Hebrew Scriptures intended to raise the social status of black Americans.

For scholars to better understand new religions, then, they must understand how these movements incorporate an ancient religion. For instance, the Unification Church included the creation myth of ancient Christianity in the core of its new revelation, which convinced adherents that the church would restore Christianity to the form originally intended by God. Since most scholars are aware of the major tenets of Christianity, placing the Unification Church in this context helps in understanding this new religious movement. Beginning research of the Unification Church with their claims of Christian identity, for instance, can equip the scholar with specific knowledge about the church. He or she would know immediately that Jesus plays a role in the ideology of the church and could understand some of the values and the worldviews that undergird Unification teachings. Scholars may also compare and contrast the new tradition with the known beliefs and practices of Christianity. This gives scholars a starting point in better understanding the Unification Church.

Knowing that Feminist Wicca claims to be a resurrection of ancient Goddess worship also explains much about this new religion. While Wicca in general claims connections with ancient Celtic religions, Feminist Wicca focuses on Paleolithic worship of the Goddess. In this case, it would help to have familiarity with the archaeological evidence and the accompanying scholarship involved with the study of ancient goddess religions. Knowledge of these historical claims gives scholars a window on these worldviews that might otherwise be lacking. Again, if one considers the goddess religions that Feminist Wicca accepts and those it ignores, one can gain insight into the goals and mindset of adherents. In addition, because Feminist Wiccans identify themselves as "witches," one can use this category in comparisons of Wicca with other religions using this term.

Placing the Nation of Yahweh into the category of religions that claim to be descendants of the ancient Hebrew faith, and more specifically, the tribes of Israel, will help scholars better understand members' worldview. Judaism is an ancient faith with which many are familiar. Hence, the new religious movement making these claims tends to take an interest in the Hebrew language and following the laws of the Hebrew Bible. Scholars can compare known Jewish rituals and practices with those of the Nation of Yahweh. In order to understand what motivates members of new religions such as the Nation of Yahweh, one must view the religion through the perspective of its members. Adherents of the Nation of Yahweh believed that they were inheritors of the promises God made to the ancient Israelites. Thus, beginning with these claims gives the scholar a better understanding of the significance members gave their actions. In each of these cases, some knowledge of the ancient religion would help scholars to understand the visions of an improved society that motivated members of these new religious movements. In the case of the Nation of Yahweh, we would be able to place their violent acts into some semblance of historical context.

While the categorization of new religious movements based on the ancient religions with which they claim does not explain what is new about the religions, it gives scholars insight into their worldviews and their goals. Classifying new religious movements in this way gives scholars a "starting point" toward a better comprehension of the belief systems and practices of the religions. Since new religious movements assert connections with ancient religions, scholars can place them in known categories. Thus, the religions are not required to explain who their deity is, where their scriptures originated, or what comprises the basic worldview from which they draw inspiration. While claims of antiquity primarily lend the movement authority for potential adherents, it can also benefit scholars interested in studying these movements.

Classifying new religious movements based on the ancient connections they claim would benefit scholars investigating several new religions, not just those included in this book. For instance, if one were to begin to research Sylvia Browne's movement *Novus Spiritus* with her claimed Gnostic roots, one could gain insight into the ideals this church values. While it might be easy to dismiss her Gnostic claims, one could learn that Browne stresses the mystical nature of Gnosticism and secret knowledge. It would be important to compare and contrast Browne's understanding of Gnostic beliefs with what Biblical scholars know about this group. The analysis of this comparison would have to take into account those aspects of Gnosticism Browne accepts and those she rejects. A study of *Novus Spiritus* based on its claimed Gnostic connections would lead a scholar toward an understanding of the ideals that motivate members of this religion.

Since many new religious movements, including those in this study, are surrounded by controversy, information about their members often has been shrouded in convenient media claims of brainwashing or stress. In order to understand why people joined new religious movements, scholars should seek the answers from the subjects themselves within their historical context. In this text, I tried to let the voices of believers tell how they created worlds of meaning within their new religious movements and within their various cultural contexts. However, I do not rely on members' points of view alone for an interpretation of the religions' worldviews. Rather, I compare and contrast these voices with the beliefs as espoused by the founders and writers of these traditions and, when possible, with their ritual practices. As Robert A. LeVine, a Harvard University anthropologist, explains:

> Culture cannot be reduced to its explicit or implicit dimensions. It would be fallacious to take what is given by informants at face value and assume that the rest of behavior and belief is untouched by culture. It is equally fallacious to discount explicit rules, beliefs, and labels as lacking social or psychological reality or as mere reflections of, or disguises for, implicit cultural orientations. In culture, as an organization of shared meanings, some meanings are more explicit than others, for reasons having to do with the pragmatics of social life and their history for a given society.[530]

I have thus tried in this study to approximate a "thick description" (to borrow Clifford Geertz's term) of the new religious movements and their shared values and beliefs. The use of witness testimony, primary and secondary sources, descriptions of rituals and practices, and consultation of historical writings bearing on this time period allow the scholar to paint a broader picture of the religion as the adherents understand it.

Historical perspective is crucial in the study of new religious movements. Because these religions have formed in the recent past, their earliest documents and their founders are often still available for study. Scholars need only research the archives and local repositories of new religions for diaries, membership directories, flyers and pamphlets, educational material, devotional literature, scriptures and other primary sources. Cultural historians should take advantage of this material while it is still available, since the passage of time makes it more and more difficult to compile complete histories. In some cases, it was difficult for me to compile histories of the movements contained in this study, even though only 20-35 years had passed, due to limited or unavailable material. Conversion stories recorded in the appropriate timeframe were limited to those taken by other authors or newspaper reporters. Information was restricted because I could not control the questions asked of the witnesses. Fortunately, in most cases, there were many other primary and secondary sources containing necessary information.

This study utilized primary and secondary documents and witness testimonies in order to understand why young people in the 1960s and 1970s left their childhood religions and joined new religious movements. The available documents led to the conclusion that these young people were disillusioned with their religious traditions and sought new religious movements that would help them realize their dreams of changing the world. They chose religious movements that offered them personal religious experiences and gave their actions toward changing American society cosmic significance.

Each of the new religious movements presented in this book interacted with the larger American culture in different ways. The Unification Church, while forming its own family culture, wished to bring all of America into its "morally superior" family. Church members sought to improve the moral fiber of America by creating the perfect family and expanding their clan one member at a time. Feminist Wicca, on the other hand, created its own culture as a source of strength for members. The movement believed it could empower members to go out into the larger American culture and make changes at the grassroots level. The Nation of Yahweh chose to set its culture apart from the larger American culture associated with the oppression of blacks. Members meant for their separatist religion to wage a war against the white establishment in the United States, one action at a time, dismantling the power structure of the persecutors of African-Americans.

The new religious movements in this study did not incorporate claims of originations in antiquity uniformly; instead, those claims fell on a spectrum between intentional and convenient use. Claimed connections with historical religions functioned differently in each of these movements. For the Unification Church, claims of ancient origins were in the form of revelations Sun Myung Moon believed he had received from God. Because these visions occurred within the context of the existing Judeo-Christian creation myth, members did not initially have to reject their Christian faith. Thus, the claims of antiquity conveniently offered the Unification Church the legitimacy of ancient origins for its prospective members. Feminist Wiccans, on the other hand, intentionally manipulated ancient truths to suit their ideological agendas. In choosing matriarchal traditions that supported their theories that Goddess-worshipping cultures were peaceful and egalitarian, Feminist Wiccans were able to support their conclusions that Goddess religions offered a blueprint for contemporary society. Feminist Wiccans thus ignored counter examples or historical theories that did not support their assertions. The Nation of Yahweh's use of the Hebrew tradition falls somewhere in between the other two movements on the spectrum. While claiming a revelation that American blacks descended from the ancient Hebrews gave the Nation of Yahweh historical roots, Yahweh ben Yahweh also selected only those scriptures that supported his conclusions. For members of the Nation of Yahweh, the claims of antiquity directly supported their Hebrew identity and were thus integral to their belief system.

These new religions had expansive dreams of recreating America. One might wonder if they were successful in their goals of changing America. Since these movements still are extant, albeit greatly changed from their formative years, one can say they successfully survived into the twenty-first century. However, these movements are still working toward their goals. All three groups have moved past their grassroots approach of worldview change into a broader political arena as they have matured. They have each been instrumental in shaping the cultures created by them and have had limited success in the larger American culture. The Unification Church, while its numbers have reduced, has found a niche in the political arena of the Christian Right. Feminist Wicca has forever changed the structure of Wicca and has propelled many believers into political action on behalf of women in America. The Nation of Yahweh lost many members locally in Miami but was able to distribute its temples throughout the United States, where it continues to spread its leader's message through books and television shows. The adherents of these movements persist in their efforts to redefine American culture through their own religious visions of what America can become.

AFTERWORD

While there are a number of approaches for studying new religious movements, this study combines historical and ethnographic methods. The blending of methods allows for a thick description of these religions. Studies like this one offer a glimpse into the mindsets of those who join new religious movements. Scholars should look for ways to situate their analysis of alternative religions within the historical context of their foundation, taking into consideration the perspectives of adherents, founders, formative literature, and conversations with the surrounding culture.

Since scholars of new religious movements are re-examining approaches for the study of these religions, the approach offered here is particularly timely. Sociological studies are necessary for understanding how religions function in society and answering questions about relationships between religions and society. In addition, however, historical research methods contribute cultural context, and ethnographic data shed light on the motivations of adherents. The approach described in this study thus offers another way to understand the appeal of new religious movements.

In the future, scholars might further explore the relationship between social reform movements and religious ideologies. Does the desire for social reform drive the need for a new religious ideology that supports a similar vision? Is it possible that the ideologies of new religious movements drive the need for social reform? What is the connection between religion and social reform in the minds of potential adherents? This study suggests that young people, desiring social reform in the 1960s and 1970s, sought new religious movements that closely resonated with their goals. However, there is much room for future exploration of the relationship between religious and social ideologies.

One challenge encountered during the research for this book was problematic data. Part of this was due to missing or fragmentary witness accounts that had a mediating source. Also, because this study considered three very different religions, the sources of information varied a great deal. While data was somewhat limited, it reasonably suggested that the religious experience of the adherents of these new religious movements and a resonance with their ideologies propelled individuals into social action. In the future, scholars might find more reliable data with other new religious movements and use the methods offered in this paper. In fact, obtaining reliable data while it is still reliable and relevant is crucial for drawing conclusions about the development of new religious movements.

Now that some new religious movements have been in existence for thirty or forty years, scholars are beginning to discover how the religions change and develop over time. Scholars are beginning to interview children and grandchildren of the converts of some new religious movements. Historical methods such as the one utilized in this paper are necessary in order to historically situate analysis of these new religious movements. A historical approach is essential for giving cultural context for the social interaction and motivations of adherents in any given historical moment. Thus, the historical method could contribute much in the contemporary scholarly discussion about how new religious movements are changing and adapting to the modern American cultural environment.

NOTES

[1] Todd Gitlin. *The 60s: Years of Hope, Days of Rage* (Toronto, NY: Bantam Books, 1987), 18.

[2] Charles Hirshman, "America's Melting Pot Reconsidered, *Annual Review of Sociology*, 1983.(9:397-423), 398.

[3] Gitlin, 18.

[4] Teresa Brush, in a brochure entitled "Unification Church: Only if you discover things for yourself." Published by the Unification Church, 4 West 43rd Street, NY, NY 10036, (212) 730-5782, no date.

[5] Aidan A. Kelly in the introduction for *Cults and New Religions: Sources for Study of Nonconventional Religious Groups in Nineteenth and Twentieth Century America/Neo-Pagan Witchcraft I and II;* J. Gordon Melton, ed. (NY and London: Garland Publishing, 1990), i.

[6] Elijah Siegler, *New Religious Movements*, Religions of the World Series (Upper Saddle River, NJ: Prentice Hall, 2007), 8.

[7] For example, Melton, J. Gordon, *New Age Encyclopedia: A Guide to the Beliefs, Concepts, Terms, People and Organizations that Make Up the New Global Movement Toward Spiritual Development, Health and Healing, Higher Consciousness, and Related Subjects.* Detroit, MI: Gale Research, 1990. Lewis, James R. *Cults in America: A Reference Handbook.* Santa Barbara, CA: ABC-CLIO, 1998. Lewis, James R. *The Encyclopedia of Cults, Sects, and New Religions.* Amherst, NY: Prometheus Books, 1998. Lewis, James R. *The Oxford Handbook of New Religious Movements* (Oxford University Press, 2003). Chryssides, George D. *Historical Dictionary of New Religious Movements* (Lanham, MD: Scarecrow Press, 2001). Ronald Enroth, ed. *A Guide to New Religious Movements* (Downers Grove, Ill: InterVarsity Press, 2005). Christopher Partridge, ed. *New Religions, A Guide: New Religious Movements, Sects, and Alternative Spiritualities* (NY: Oxford Press, 2004). Ellwood, Robert S. *Alternative Altars: Unconventional and Eastern Spirituality in America* (University of Chicago Press, 1979). Ellwood, Robert S. *Religious and Spiritual Groups in Modern America* (Englewood Cliffs, NJ: Prentice Hall, 1973). John A. Saliba, *Understanding New Religious Movements*, 2nd ed. (Walnut Creek, CA: AltaMira Press, 2003).

[8] For example, Lorne L. Dawson. *Comprehending Cults: The Sociology of New Religious Movements* (Oxford, NY: Oxford University Press, 1998), 11. Stephen Hunt, *Alternative Religions: A Sociological Introduction* (Aldershot, Hampshire, England; Burlington, VT: Ashgate, 2003). Louis Richard Binder, *Modern Religious Cults and Society: A Sociological Interpretation of a Modern Religious Phenomenon* (NY: AMS Press, 1970). William Sims Bainbridge, *The Sociology of New Religious Movements* (NY: Routledge, 1997).

[9] James Beckford. *Cult Controversies: the Societal Response to New Religious Movements* (London, NY: Tavistock Publications, 1985), and James Beckford, ed. for Research Committee 22 of the International Sociological Association. *New Religious Movements and Rapid Social Change* (London, Beverly Hills, CA: Sage Publications, 1986). Jeffrey Kaplan and Helene Loon, eds. *The Cultic Milieu: Oppositional Subcultures in an Age of Globalization* (Walnut Creek: AltaMisa Press, 2002). Brian Wilson and Jamie Cresswell, eds. *New Religious Movements: Challenge and Response* (London and NY: Routledge, 1999). Phillip Charles Lucas and Thomas Robbins, eds. *New religious movements in the Twenty-First Century: Legal, Political and Social Challenges in Global Perspective* (NY: Routledge Press, 2004).

[10] James A. Beckford, *Cult Controversies: The Societal Response to New Religious Movements* (London and New York: Tavistock Publications, 1985), 1.

[11] Beckford, 5.

[12] John A. Saliba, *Understanding New Religious Movements* (Grand Rapids, MI: W.B. Eerdmans, 1996).

[13] Benjamin Zablocki and Thomas Robbins, eds. *Misunderstanding Cults: Searching for Objectivity in a Controversial Field* (Toronto, Buffalo, London: University of Toronto Press, 2001).

[14] James R. Lewis, "The Scholarship of 'Cults' and the 'Cult' of Scholarship," *Journal of Dharma* (12 Ap-Je, 1987, p. 96-107).

[15] James Lewis, *Legitimating New Religions* (New Brunswick, NJ and London: Rutgers University Press, 2003), 31.

[16] Clifford Geertz defines culture as "an historically transmitted pattern of meanings embodied in symbols, a system of inherited conceptions expressed in symbolic form by means of which men can communicate, perpetuate and develop their knowledge about and attitudes towards life." Clifford Geertz, "Religion as a Cultural System," *The Interpretation of Cultures* (NY: Basic Books, 1973), 89.

[17] Clifford Geertz, 5 and 14.

[18] Martha Banta, *Imaging American Women: Idea and Ideals in Cultural History* (NY: Columbia University Press, 1987), 13. She cites Josiah Royce, Charles Saunders Peirce, William James and John Dewey here, but one might also mention similar theories by Michele Foucault.

[19] James Davidson Hunter, *Culture Wars: The Struggle to Define America* (New York: Basic Books, Harper Collins Publishers, 1991), 54-55.

[20] Rhys H. Williams, "Religion as Political Resource: Culture or Ideology?" *Journal for the Scientific Study of Religion* (Vol. 35, No. 4, December, 1996, pages 368-378).

[21] Williams, 377.

[22] James Lewis, 13 and 14.

[23] This list is loosely based on Weber's explanation of 3 types of legitimate authority, rational grounds, traditional grounds (established beliefs), and charismatic grounds (devotion to the exemplary character of a person). Max Weber, *Basic Concepts in Sociology*, translation by H. P. Secher (NY: Citadel Press, 1968), 328.

[24] Max Weber, 81.

[25] Max Weber, 82.

[26] R. Laurence Moore, *Religious Outsiders and the Making of Americans* (NY and Oxford: Oxford University Press, 1986).

[27] Moore, xi.

[28] Moore, 208.

[29] Stephen A. Kent, *From Slogans to Mantras: Social Protest and Religious Conversion in the Late Vietnam War Era* (Syracuse, NY: Syracuse University Press, 2001), xi.

[30] Kent, 5.

[31] Beatriz Gonzales, Unification Church brochure entitled "Unification Church: Only if you discover things for yourself." Unification Church, 4 West 43rd Street, NY, NY 10036 (212) 730-5782. Beatriz became a student at Unification Theological Seminary. Located in the American Religions Collection, Department of Special Collections, Donald C. Davidson Library, the University of California, Santa Barbara.

[32] John T. Biermans, *The Odyssey of New Religious Movements: Persecution, Struggle, Legitimation: A Case Study of the Unification Church* (Lewiston, NY: E. Mellen Press, 1986).

[33] Michael L. Mickler, *A History of the Unification Church in America 1959-1974: Emergence of a National Movement* (NewYork : Garland, 1993).

[34] Introvigne, Massimo. *The Unification Church: Studies in Contemporary Religion* (Salt Lake City, UT: Signature Books; Torino, Italy : CESNUR, c2000).

[35] George D. Chryssides, *The Advent of Sun Myung Moon: The Origins, Beliefs and Practices of the Unification Church* (New York : St. Martin's Press, 1991).

[36] Roger Allen Dean, *Moonies: A Psychological Analysis of the Unification Church.* Cults and Nonconventional Religious Groups: A Collection of Outstanding Dissertations (New York : Garland, 1992).

[37] James H. Grace, *Sex and Marriage in the Unification Movement: A Sociological Study.* Studies in Religion and Society, Vol 13 (New York: E. Mellen Press, c1985).

[38] Irving Louis Horowitz, *Science, Sin, and Scholarship: The Politics of Reverend Moon and the Unification Church* (Cambridge: MIT Press, c1978).

[39] Kathleen S. Lowney, *Passport to Heaven: Gender Roles in the Unification Church.* Cults and Nonconventional Religious Groups (New York : Garland, 1992).

[40] John Lofland and Rodney Stark, "Becoming a World-Saver: A Theory of Conversion to a Deviant Perspective," in *American Sociological Review* (Vol. 30, No. 6, December, 1965, pages 862-875).

[41] Eileen Barker, *The Making of a Moonie: Choice or Brainwashing?* (NY, Oxford: Blackwell, 1984), 38.

[42] Barker, 38.

[43] Barker, 38.

[44] Barker, 38.

[45] Michael Mickler, *A History of the Unification Church in America, 1959-1974: Emergence of a National Movement* (NY and London: Garland Publishing, 1993), 3.

[46] Mary Farrel Bednarowski. *New Religions and the Theological Imagination in America.* (Bloomington and Indianapolis: Indiana State University Press, 1989), 10.

[47] J. Gordon Melton, *Encyclopedic Handbook of Cults in America*, revised (NY and London: Garland Publishing, Inc., 1992), 296.

[48] Sun Myung Moon, *The Divine Principle* (published by The Holy Spirit Association for the Unification of World Christianity, NY, 1973), Introduction, 16. This will be the edition cited in the rest of this dissertation.

[49] Barker, 43.

[50] Melton, 297.

[51] Barker, 44.

[52] Mickler, 4.

[53] Mickler, 6.

[54] Mickler, chapter 5 "A National Movement Attempts to Emerge," 133.

[55] Barker, 54.

[56] Melton, 297.

[57] Barker, 60.

[58] Melton, 298.

[59] Melton, 298-299.

[60] Barker, 63.

[61] Barker, 63.

[62] Mickler, 209.

[63] Barker, 64.

[64] Barker, 3. She also cites Albert Somit, 'Brainwashing' in David Sills (ed) International Encyclopedia of the Social Sciences, vol. 3, New York, Macmillan, 1968, p. 138. Along with works by Robert J. Lifton, Edgar H. Schein, and Denise Winn.

[65] Beckford, 95.

[66] John T. Biermans. *The Odyssey of New Religions Movements—Persecution, Struggle and Legitimation: A Case Study of the Unification Church.* Symposium Series, Vol. 19, The Edwin Mellen Press (Lewiston/Queenston, 1986), 27-28.

[67] Biermans, 28.

[68] Beckford, 6.

[69] Mickler, 210.

[70] David Bromley, Bruce C. Busching, and Anson D. Shupe, Jr. "The Unification Church and the American Family: Strain, Conflict and Control," in *New Religious Movements: A Perspective for Understanding Society*, ed. Eileen Barker (NY and Toronto: Edwin Mellen Press, 1982), 309.

[71] Sarah Lewis, "The Family Federation for World Peace and Unification (Unification Church) in Christopher Partridge's *New Religions: A Guide* (NY: Oxford University Press, 2004), 74.

[72] Moon, *Divine Principle,* 536.

[73] Sontag, "Marriage and the Family," 91.

[74] Gregory L. Schneider. *Conservatism in America Since 1930: A Reader* (NY, London: New York University Press, 2003), 3.
[75] Ibid.
[76] Schneider, 93.
[77] Schneider, 247.
[78] Schneider, 247.
[79] Ann Burlein, "Counter-memory on the Right: The Case of Focus on the Family," in *Acts of Memory: Cultural Recall in the Present,* Mieke Bal, Jonathan Crewe, and Leo Spitzer, eds. (Hanover and London: Dartmouth College, 1999), 298.
[80] David Farber and Jeff Roche, eds. *The Conservative Sixties* introduction (NY: Peter Lang, 2003), 1.
[81] Farber and Roche, 2.
[82] N.A., Building Democracy Initiative, "Shell Games: the 'Minutemen' and Vigilante Anti-Immigration Politics," Center for New Community, Special Report, Chicago, Illinois 60647, (312) 266-0319, October 2005, page 2. Found: http://www.buildingdemocracy.org/shellgames.pdf.
[83] Farber and Roche, 2.
[84] Robert Welch, "Americanism versus Amorality," in Robert A. Rosestone's *Protest from the Right* (Beverly Hills, Glencoe Press, 1968), 16.
[85] William C. Berman, *America's Right Turn: from Nixon to Bush* (Baltimore, MD: John Hopkins University Press, 1994), 1.
[86] Berman, 3.
[87] Eileen Barker, *The Making of a Moonie: Choice or Brainwashing?* (NY: Basil Blackwell, 1984), 44.
[88] Barker, 53.
[89] Schneider, 277.
[90] Joseph Fichter, "Family and Religion Among the Moonies: A Descriptive Analysis," in *Families and Religion: Conflict and Change in Modern Society*, William V. D'Antonio and Joan Aldous, eds. (Beverly Hills, London, New Delhi: Sage Publications, 1983), 294.
[91] Sun Myung Moon, "November 12th Could Be Your Re-Birthday," speech given by Moon on October 21, 1973 and reprinted in the *Chicago Tribune*, Thursday, November 7, 1974, Section 3, 21.
[92] Barker, 63.
[93] Jenkins, 5.
[94] Jenkins, 18.
[95] James H. Grace, *Sex and Marriage in the Unification Church* (NY and Toronto: Edwin Mellen Press, 1985), 2.
[96] Barbara W. Hargrove, "Some Thoughts About the Unification Movement and the Churches," found in Irving Louis Horowitz, ed. *Science, Sin and Scholarship: The Politics of Reverend Moon and the Unification Church* (Cambridge, MA and London: The MIT Press, 1978), 90.

[97] John T. Biermans, *The Odyssey of New Religious Movements—Persecution, Struggle, and Legitimation: A Case Study of the Unification Church*. Symposium Series, Volume 19 (Lewiston, Queenston: The Edwin Mellen Press, 1986), 173

[98] Neil Albert Salonen, President of the Unification Church of America, "The Truth About the Reverend Sun Myung Moon," *Los Angeles Times*, Sunday, January 25, 1976, 6 Part VIII.

[99] Sun Myung Moon, translated by Mrs. Won Pok Choi, "The True Pattern of Family Life," (Barrytown, NY, March 7, 1975). Located in the American Religions Collection, Department of Special Collections, Donald C. Davidson Library, the University of California, Santa Barbara. Moon also explains filial piety in the *Divine Principle*, 49.

[100] Biermans, 172.

[101] Fichter, "Family and Religion," 295.

[102] Stephen A. Kent, *From Slogans to Mantras: Social Protest and Religious Conversion in the Late Vietnam War Era* (Syracuse, NY: Syracuse University Press, 2001), 115-116.

[103] Moon, *Divine Principle*, (NY: Holy Spirit Association for the Unification of World Christianity, 1973), 11, 109, 125.

[104] Moon, *Divine Principle*, 10.

[105] Moon, *Divine Principle*, 14.

[106] Moon, *Divine Principle*, 532-535.

[107] Moon, *Divine Principle,* 123.

[108] Sun Myung Moon, *Divine Principle.* 7.

[109] Agnes Cunningham, J. Robert Nelson, William L. Hendricks, and Jorge Lara-Braud, "Critique of the Theology of the Unification Church as Set Forth in Divine Principle," in Horowitz, Irving Louis. *Science, Sin, and Scholarship: The Politics of Reverend Moon and the Unification Church.* (Cambridge: MIT Press, c1978), 111. They also cite *Divine Principle*, page 123.

[110] Cunningham, Nelson, Hendricks, Lara-Braud, 112.

[111] Sun Myung Moon, "New Hope for America: Christianity in Crisis." Excerpts from "New Hope: 12 Talks by Sun Myung Moon," 1973. Located in the American Religions Collection, Department of Special Collections, Donald C. Davidson Library, the University of California, Santa Barbara.

[112] Barker, 57.

[113] "Charles," in Joseph Fichter's *Autobiographies of Conversion*, Studies in Religion and Society, Vol. 17. (Lewiston/Queenston: The Edwin Mellen Press, 1987), 35.

[114] Ibid.

[115] "Eugenia," in Joseph Fichter's *Autobiographies of Conversion*, Studies in Religion and Society, Vol. 17. (Lewiston/Queenston: The Edwin Mellen Press, 1987), 124.

[116] "Andrew," in Joseph Fichter's *Autobiographies of Conversion*, Studies in Religion and Society, Vol. 17. (Lewiston/Queenston: The Edwin Mellen Press, 1987), 166.

[117] "Patricia," in Joseph Fichter's *Autobiographies of Conversion*, Studies in Religion and Society, Vol. 17. (Lewiston/Queenston: The Edwin Mellen Press, 1987), 173-174.

[118] Cunningham, Nelson, Hendricks, Lara-Braud, 109.

[119] Frederick Sontag, "Sun Myung Moon and the Unification Church: Charges and Responses," *in Science, Sin and Scholarship: The Politics of Reverend Moon and the Unification Church*, edited by Irving Louis Horowitz. (Cambridge, MA and London: The MIT Press, 1978), 35.

[120] Sontag, 36.

[121] Sontag, 38.

[122] Cunningham, Nelson, Hendricks, Lara-Braud, 118.

[123] "New Life" lecture pamphlet. Distributed by the Unification Church of America, National Headquarters, Washington D.C., 1611 Upshur Street, NW 20011, n.d. Located in the American Religions Collection, Department of Special Collections, Donald C. Davidson Library, the University of California, Santa Barbara.

[124] Moon, "God's Hope for America."

[125] Ken Sudo, Director of Training at Barrytown Unification Seminary, "The Meaning of Brothers and Sisters," Student Training Manual, 1975, page 164.

[126] Sun Myung Moon, "One God, One World Religion," Lecture given at Goucher College, Towson, Maryland, February 11, 1972. Located in the American Religions Collection, Department of Special Collections, Donald C. Davidson Library, the University of California, Santa Barbara.

[127] "Divine Principle" pamphlet printed by The Holy Spirit Association for the Unification of World Christianity, dated 1977. Located in the American Religions Collection, Department of Special Collections, Donald C. Davidson Library, the University of California, Santa Barbara.

[128] Barker.

[129] John T. Biermans, *The Odyssey of New Religious Movements: Persecution, Struggle, Legitimation: A Case Study of the Unification Church* (Lewiston/Queenston: The Edwin Mellen Press, Symposium Series, Volume 19, 1986), 106-107.

[130] Moon, *Divine Principle*, 100.

[131] Moon, *Divine Principle*, 32.

[132] Moon, "Master speaks 'from a brief talk given during a training session led by President Kim." Washington DC, 1972.

[133] Moon, "One God, One World Religion," Lecture given at Goucher College, Towson, Maryland, February 11, 1972.

[134] Moon, *Divine Principle*, 12.

[135] Moon, *Divine Principle*, 12.

[136] Moon, *Divine Principle*, 43.

[137] Walsh, 144.

[138] "Charles," found in Fichter, 32.

[139] Thomas Robbins, Dick Anthony, Madeline Doucas, and Thomas Curtis, in *Science, Sin and Scholarship*, 58.

[140] Beatriz Gonzales, Unification Church brochure entitled "Unification Church: Only if you discover things for yourself." Unification Church, 4 West 43rd Street, NY, NY 10036 (212) 730-5782. Beatriz became a student at Unification Theological Seminary. Located in the American Religions Collection, Department of Special Collections, Donald C. Davidson Library, the University of California, Santa Barbara.

[141] "Andrew" in Fichter, 156.

[142] "Andrew," 166.

[143] James A. Beckford, *Cult Controversies: The Societal Response to the New Religious Movements* (London and NY: Tavistock Publications, 1985), 110.

[144] David G. Bromley, Anson D. Shupe, Jr. and Donna L. Oliver, "Perfect Families: Visions of the Future in a New Religious Movement," in *Cults and the Family*, Florence Kaslow and Marion B. Sussman, eds. (NY: The Haworth Press, 1982), 121.

[145] Grace, vi.

[146] Moon likely was influenced by Confucian ideals about family. Whalen Lai explains that since ancestral sacrifice was tied to the right of inheritance of family land, familial piety was essential for the preservation of the family. Whalen Lai, "Rethinking the Chinese Family: Wandering Ghosts and Eternal Parents," *The Ideal in the World's Religions: Essays on the Person, Family, Society, and Environment*, eds. Robert Carter and Sheldon Isenberg (St. Paul, Minn: Paragon House, 1997), 254.

[147] "Divine Principle" pamphlet (Printed by the Holy Spirit Association for the Unification of World Christianity, 1977), pages 2-3. Located in the American Religions Collection, Department of Special Collections, Donald C. Davidson Library, the University of California, Santa Barbara.

[148] Jonathan Wells, "Marriage and the Family in Unification Theology," in *Dialogue and Alliance*, (Vol. 9, No. 1, Spring/Summer 1995), 68-69.

[149] Reverend and Mrs. Sun Myung Moon, *True Family and World Peace* (NY: Family Federation for World Peace and Unification, dist. HAS Publications, 2000), 4. This book is a collection of speeches given by Moon since 1990. Also in Wells, "Marriage and the Family," 69.

[150] Moon, *True Family and World Peace*, 3.

[151] Frederick Sontag, "Marriage and the Family in Unification Church Theology," in *Update* (6.3, September 1982), 79.

[152] Sontag, "Marriage and the Family," 88.

[153] Ken Sudo, Director of Training. Unification Church Student Manual, Barrytown, NY, 1975. This is taken from a speech recorded in the manual entitled "Family Problems," page 164 and 235. Located in the American Religions Collection, Department of Special Collections, Donald C. Davidson Library, the University of California, Santa Barbara.

[154] Sudo, 235.

[155] Reverend Sun Myung Moon, *True Parents* (DC: Family Federation for World Peace and Unification, International, 1998), 203. These are collected speeches by Moon over the years on the idea of True Parents. Located in the American

Religions Collection, Department of Special Collections, Donald C. Davidson Library, the University of California, Santa Barbara.

[156] Joseph H. Fichter, "Family and Religion Among the Moonies: A Descriptive Analysis," in *Families and Religion: Conflict and Change in Modern Society*, William V. D'Antonio and Joan Aldous, eds. (Beverly Hills, London, New Delhi: Sage Publications, 1983), 289.

[157] Moon, "One God, One World Religion." Lecture given at Goucher College, Towson, Maryland, February 11, 1972. Located in the American Religions Collection, Department of Special Collections, Donald C. Davidson Library, the University of California, Santa Barbara.

[158] Sontag, "Marriage and the Family," 80.

[159] Grace, 5.

[160] Fichter, "Family and Religion," 292.

[161] Sun Myung Moon, "God's Hope for America," text of the speech given at Yankee Stadium on June 1, 1976 printed in the *New York Times*, Thursday, June 3, 1976, C42-43. Located in the American Religions Collection, Department of Special Collections, Donald C. Davidson Library, the University of California, Santa Barbara.

[162] Conversion story in James Fichter, *Autobiographies of Conversion*. Studies in Religion and Society, Vol. 17 (Lewiston/Queenston: The Edwin Mellen Press, 1987), 52.

[163] Ken Sudo, Director of Training at Barrytown Unification Seminary, "The Meaning of Brothers and Sisters," Student Training Manual, 1975, pages 165-166. Located in the American Religions Collection, Department of Special Collections, Donald C. Davidson Library, the University of California, Santa Barbara.

[164] Judi Culbertson, "A New Expression of Hope," *Unified Families, From the Heart of the Co-Creator: A New Philosophy of Love and Truth*, September 18,1968. (Published by Unified Family, 429 S. Virgil, California 90005.)

[165] "Gertrude," in Joseph Fichter's *Autobiographies of Conversion*, Studies in Religion and Society, Vol. 17 (Lewiston/Queenston: The Edwin Mellen Press, 1987), 102-103.

[166] Grace, 265.

[167] Sun Myung Moon, "The Search for Absolute Values: Harmony Among the Sciences." Founders Address, 5th International Conference on the Unity of the Sciences, November 26, 1976, Washington D.C. Printed in *Science, Sin, and Scholarship: The Politics of Reverend Moon and the Unification Church*, edited by Irving Louis Horowitz (Cambridge, MA and London: The MIT Press, 1978), 18.

[168] Sontag, 1977:156-157 quoted in Joseph H. Fichter's "Family and Religion Among the Moonies: A Descriptive Analysis," *Families and Religion: Conflict and Change in Modern Society*, William V. D'Antonio and Joan Aldous (Beverly Hills, London, New Delhi: Sage Publications, 1983), 303.

[169] Tom Walsh, "Celibacy, Virtue and the Practice of True Family in the Unification Church," in *The Family and the Unification Church*, Gene G. James, ed. (Barrytown, NY: Unification Theological Seminary, 1983), 143.

[170] Grace, 217.

[171] Bromley, Shupe and Oliver, 122.

[172] Walsh, 144.

[173] Fichter, "Family and Religion," 299.

[174] Reprinted in Sontag, "Marriage and the Family," 81. It is from the official program of the Unification Church Holy Wedding, New York City, July 1st, 1982.

[175] Grace, 220.

[176] Mrs. Shin Wook Kim interview, "Baby Dedications," in The Blessing Monthly Newsletter of the American Blessed Families Association, Vol. 1, #3, July-August, 1974. Located in the American Religions Collection, Department of Special Collections, Donald C. Davidson Library, the University of California, Santa Barbara.

[177] Ibid.

[178] John T. Beirmans. *The Odyssey of New Religious Movements: Persecution, Struggle and Legitimation: A Case Study of the Unification Church.* Symposium Series Volume 19. (Lewiston/Queenston: The Edwin Mellen Press, 1986), 72.

[179] Ken Sudo, Director of Training at Barrytown Unification Seminary, speech entitled "Family Problems," Student Training Manual, 1975, page 160. Located in the American Religions Collection, Department of Special Collections, Donald C. Davidson Library, the University of California, Santa Barbara.

[180] Sun Myung Moon, "Master Speaks" from a brief talk given during a training session led by President Kim, Washington D.C., 1972. Located in the American Religions Collection, Department of Special Collections, Donald C. Davidson Library, the University of California, Santa Barbara.

[181] "New Life" lecture pamphlet. Distributed by the Unification Church of America, National Headquarters, Washington D.C., 1611 Upshur Street, NW 20011. n.d. Located in the American Religions Collection, Department of Special Collections, Donald C. Davidson Library, the University of California, Santa Barbara.

[182] Whalen Lai, "Rethinking the Chinese Family: Wandering Ghosts and Eternal Parents," in *The Ideal in the World's Religions: Essays on the Person, Family, Society and Environment*, Robert Carter and Sheldon Isenberg, eds. (St. Paul, MN: Paragon House, 1997), 254.

[183] Bromley, Shupe and Oliver, 125.

[184] "Mary," found in Fichter, 146, 152.

[185] Sun Myung Moon, "America and God's Will," *The Washington Post*, Sunday, September 19, 1976, A10-11. Located in the American Religions Collection, Department of Special Collections, Donald C. Davidson Library, the University of California, Santa Barbara.

[186] Ibid.

[187] Sun Myung Moon, "God's Hope for America."

[188] Moon, "America and God's Will."

[189] Moon, "God's Hope for America."

[190] Ibid.

[191] John Winthrop, "A Modell of Christian Charity," written in 1630, found in Giles Gunn's *Early American Writing* (NY: Penguin Classics, 1994), 112.

[192] Moon, "America and God's Will."

[193] Sun Myung Moon, "America in Crisis: Answer to Watergate—Forgive, Love, Unite," printed in the *New York Times*, Friday, November 30, 1973.

[194] Ibid.

[195] "Lionel," found in Fichter, 87.

[196] Moon, "God's Hope for America."

[197] Neil Albert Salonen, President of the Unification Church of America, "The Truth About the Reverend Sun Myung Moon," *Los Angeles Times*, Sunday, January 25, 1976, 6 part VIII. Located in the American Religions Collection, Department of Special Collections, Donald C. Davidson Library, the University of California, Santa Barbara.

[198] "Walter," in Fichter, 205-206.

[199] Mickler, 141-142.

[200] Mickler, 142.

[201] Mickler, 153.

[202] Beckford, 126-127.

[203] Beckford, 127.

[204] Peter Burke, *Varieties of Cultural History* (Ithaca, NY: Cornell University Press, 1997), 188.

[205] Ntozanke Shenge, from *colored girls who have considered suicide/when the rainbow is enuf* (NY: Macmillan Co., Inc., 1975, 1976, 1977) cited *in The Politics of Women's Spirituality: Essays on the Rise of Spiritual Power within the Feminist Movement*, ed. Charlene Spretnak (NY: Anchor Books, Doubleday, 1982), 3.

[206] Jean and Ruth Mountaingrove, in Margot Adler's *Drawing Down the Moon: Witches, Druids, Goddess-Worshippers, and Other Pagans in America Today* (Boston: Beacon Press, 1979, 1986), 186.

[207] Mark Bahnisch, Queensland University of Technology, TASA 2001 Conference, The University of Sydney, 13-15 December 2001, unpublished paper entitled "Sociology of Religion in Postmodernity: Wicca, Witches and the Neopagan Myth of Foundations," page 2.

[208] Adler, *Drawing Down the Moon: Witches, Druids, Goddess-Worshippers, and Other Pagans in America Today* (Boston: Beacon Press, 1979, 1986), 49-52. She cites Norman Cohn, *Europe's Inner Demons* (New York: Basic Books, 1975), 125.

[209] Adler, 52-54. She cites H. R. Trevor-Roper, "The European Witch-Craze and Social Change," in *Witchcraft and Sorcery*, ed. Max Marwick (Harmondsworth, Eng: Penguin Books, 1970), pp. 121-123, 127-128, 131-132, 136, 140 and 146.

[210] Philip G. Davis, *Goddess Unmasked: the rise of neopagan feminist spirituality* (Dallas, TX: Spence Publ., 1998).

[211] Ronald Hutton, *The Triumph of the Moon: A History of Modern Pagan Witchcraft* (Oxford, NY: Oxford University Press, 1999).

[212] Cynthia Eller. "The Birth of a New Religion," in *Women and World Religions*, Lucinda Joy Peach, ed. (Upper Saddle River, NJ: Prentice Hall, 2002), 354-355. There are several articles discussing the beliefs and practices of neo-paganism in this chapter of Peach's book.

[213] Eller, 355-356.

[214] Eller, 356.

[215] Cynthia Eller, *The Myth of Matriarchal Prehistory: Why an Invented Past Won't Give Women a Future* (Boston: Beacon Press, 2000). Problems with using this myth as a basis for a future, according to Eller, are threefold: 1) origin myths tend to reduce history to timeless archetypes not specific enough to be useful, 2) origin myths such as this tend to create a nostalgia for a non-existent lost past which tend to be escapist thinking rather than functional, and 3) this myth tends to assume that the matriarchy was the "natural" way for humans to live, which implies that the current way of living is unnatural, pages 183-184.

[216] Adler, 54-56. She cites Mircea Eliade, "Some Observations on European Witchcraft," in *Occultism, Witchcraft, and Cultural Fashions* (Chicago: University of Chicago Press, 1976), 71.

[217] Carol P. Christ and Judith Plaskow, eds. *Woman Spirit Rising: A Feminist Reader in Religion* (San Francisco: Harper and Row Publishers, 1979), 3.

[218] Carol P. Christ, *Diving Deep and Surfacing: Women Writers on Spiritual Quest*, 2nd ed. (Boston: Beacon Press, 1980), 10-11.

[219] Cynthia Eller, Cynthia Eller, *The Myth of Matriarchal Prehistory: Why an Invented Past Won't Give Women a Future* (Boston: Beacon Press, 2000), 15.

[220] Lynda L.Warwick, Feminist Wicca: Paths to Empowerment," *Women's Spirituality, Women's Lives* (NY: Haworth Press, 1995), p 121-133. Also see [220] Pearson, Joanne. "Assumed Affinities: Wicca and the New Age," *Nature Religion Today.* (Edinburg: Edinburg University Press, 1998: 45-56).

[221] Rosenberg, Roberta, *The Language of Power: Women and Literature, 1945-Present. Volume 19 of the Writing About Women Feminist Literary Studies Series* (NY: Peter Lang, 1996), 7.

[222] Personal correspondence with Roberta Rosenberg, Feminist literature professor at Christopher Newport University, on July 4, 2006 and discussed in her *The Language of Power: Women and Literature, 1945 to the Present.* (NY: Peter Lang, 1996), 4.

[223] James R. Lewis, *Witchcraft Today: An Encyclopedia of Wiccan and Neopagan Traditions* (Santa Barbara, CA: ABC-CLIO, 1999).

[224] *Neo-Pagan Witchcraft I*, edited by J. Gordon Melton (NY and London: Garland Publishing, 1990).

[225] Adler, 46.

[226] Charles Godfrey Leland, *Aradia, or the Gospel of the Witches* (London: David Nutt, 1899, reprinted NY: Samuel Weisen, 1974). This edition is cited in Adler's *Drawing Down the Moon.*

[227] Adler, 57.

[228] Robert Graves, *The White Goddess*, amended and enlarged edition (New York: Farrar, Straus, and Giroux, 1966). Cited in Margot Adler's *Drawing Down the Moon.*

[229] Adler, 59-60.

[230] Melton, *Handbook*, 324.

[231] Ronald Hutton, *The Triumph of the Moon: A History of Modern Pagan Witchcraft* (Oxford, NY: Oxford University Press, 1999), 206.

[232] Hutton, 206.

[233] Adler, 234-235.

[234] Hutton, 340.

[235] Hutton, 340.

[236] Hutton, 340-341.

[237] Hutton, 341.

[238] Hutton, 341.

[239] Manifesto printed in Robin Morgan's *Sisterhood is Powerful* (NY: Random House, 1970), 539.

[240] Hutton, 341-342.

[241] Heinnich Kramer and Jacob Sprenger: *Malleus Maleficarum* (first published in 1486. London: The Folio Society, 1968).

[242] Roberta Rosenberg, *The Language of Power: Women and Literature, 1945 to the Present,* Volume 19 of the Writing About Women Feminist Literary Studies. (NY: Peter Lang, 1996), 142-143. She cites here Sylvia Plath, *The Collected Poems* (NY: Harper and Row, 1981), 222-223.

[243] Rosenberg, 143. She cites here Jean Temperman, "Witch," in *No More Masks! An Anthology of Poems by Women,* ed. Florence Howe and Ellen Bass (NY: Anchor Books, 1973), 333.

[244] Rosenberg, 146. She cites here Adrienne Rich, "Transcendental Etude," *in The Fact of a Doorframe: Poems Selected and New: 1950-84* (NY: W.W. Norton, 1984), 162-164.

[245] Rosenberg, 142. She cites here Mary Daly from "Witch: Spooking the Patriarchy During the Late Sixties," in *The Politics of Women's Spirituality,* ed. Charlene Spretnak (NY: Anchor Books, 1982), 428-29.

[246] Cynthia Eller, *In the Lap of the Goddess,* 3-4.

[247] Cynthia Eller, *In the Lap of the Goddess,* 41.

[248] Hutton, 355.

[249] Pamela Sue Anderson, *A Feminist Philosophy of Religion* (Oxford, UK, and Malden, MA: Blackwell Publications, Inc., 1998), 7.

[250] Margot Adler, *Drawing Down the Moon: Witches, Druids, Goddess-Worshippers, and Other Pagans in America Toda.* (Boston: Beacon Press, 1979, 1986), 180.

[251] Adler, 180.

[252] Bahnisch, 3.

[253] Sheila D. Collins, "The Personal is Political," in *The Politics of Women's Spirituality: Essays on the Rise of Spiritual Power within the Feminist Movement* (NY: Anchor Books, Doubleday, 1982), 362.

[254] Adler, 181.

[255] Adler, 183.

[256] Leigh Star, "The Politics of Wholeness: Feminism and the New Spirituality," excerpt from unknown Wicca newsletter, pages 36-44, late 1970s. Paper in American Religions Collections, Davidson Library, University of California, Santa Barbara.

[257] Adler, 189-191.

[258] Adler, 192.

[259] Kelley Schara, "A Personal Reconcilliation: Neopaganism and Feminism," (June 1983), 1. Unpublished paper in American Religions Collections, Davidson Library, University of California, Santa Barbara.

[260] Schara, 6.

[261] Mike Nichols, "Reflections on 'Old Guard' Paganism," MIST-ERIES, reprinted in *Womanspirit* with permission from The Faeries Camp, Kansas City, KS, 1988. From the American Religions Collections, Davidson Library, University of California, Santa Barbara.

[262] Ann Forfreedom, "Feminist Wicce Works," A.D.A., 1980. Unpublished paper in American Religions Collections, Davidson Library, University of California, Santa Barbara.

[263] Zsuzsanna Budapest, *The Feminist Book of Lights and Shadows* (Luna Publications, 1976. Copies: The Feminist Wicca: A Matriarchal Spiritual Center, 442 Lincoln Blvd, Venice, CA 90291. 399-3919), 2.

[264] Zsuzsanna Budapest, *The Holy Book of Women's Mysteries: Feminist Witchcraft, Goddess Rituals, Spellcasting, and Other Womanly Arts...* (Oakland: Wingbow Press, 1980, 1986, 1989), xviii.

[265] Budapest, xxiv.

[266] Z. Budapest, *The Feminist Book of Lights and Shadows.* (Luna Publications, 1976. Copies: The Feminist Wicca: A Matriarchal Spiritual Center, 442 Lincoln Blvd, Venice, CA 90291. 399-3919), 1.

[267] Zsuzsana Budapest, publicity flyer, "Zsuzsanna Budapest, President, The Women's Spirituality Forum," contact Melissa Reed, (415) 444-7724, nd. Located in the American Religions Collections, Davidson Library, University of California, Santa Barbara.

[268] Ibid.

[269] Zsuzsanna Budapest, publicity flyer, "Who is Zsuzsanna Budapest?" no contact information or date. Located in the American Religions Collections, Davidson Library, University of California, Santa Barbara.

[270] Zsuzsanna Budapest, rough draft of biography, "Budapest, Z." no contact information or date. Located in the American Religions Collections, Davidson Library, University of California, Santa Barbara.

[271] Starhawk, *The Spiral Dance: A Rebirth of the Ancient Religion of the Great Goddess* (NY, San Francisco: HarperCollins Publishers, 1979, 1989, 1999), 6.

[272] Starhawk, 6.

[273] Starhawk has authored several books, including *Spiraldance* (1979, 1989, 1999), *Dreaming the Dark* (1982, 1988, 1997), *Truth or Dare* (1988), *Webs of Power: Notes from the Global Uprising* (2003), and *The Earth Path* (2004). Starhawk has also been consulted or contributed to the films *Signs Out of Time: The Story of Archaeologist Marija Gimbutas, Goddess Remembered, The Burning Times,* and *Full Circle.*

[274] Starhawk, 9.

[275] Starhawk, 27.

[276] Hutton, 352.

[277] Hutton, 352.

[278] Adler, 295.

[279] Stephen A. Kent, *From Slogans to Mantras: Social Protest and Religious Conversion in the Late Vietnam War Era* (Syracuse, NY: Syracuse University Press, 2001), xiii and 2.

[280] Nancy Whittier, *Feminist Generations: The Persistence of the Radical Women's Movement* (Philadelphia: Temple University Press, 1995), 10-11.

[281] Mary Farrell Bednarowski, *The Religious Imagination of American Women.* (Bloomington and Indianapolis, Indianna University Press, 1999), 4-5.

[282] Mary McCanney Gergen, ed. *Feminist Thought and the Structure of Knowledge.*(NY and London: New York University Press, 1988), ix.

[283] Mary Farrell Bednarowski, *The Religious Imagination of American Women,* 4.

[284] Anne Phillips, ed. *Feminism and Equality* (Washington Square, NY: New York University Press, 1987), 1.

[285] Phillips, 1.

[286] Andrea Nye. *Feminist Theory and the Philosophies of Man* (London, NY, Sydney: Croom Helm, 1988), 2-3.

[287] Nye, 3.

[288] Nye, 3.

[289] Nye, 2.

[290] Whittier, 19.

[291] Cynthia Eller, *Living in the Lap of the Goddess: The Feminist Spirituality Movement in America* (NY: Crossroad, 1993), 43.

[292] Whittier, 19.

[293] Whittier, 55.

[294] Whittier, 245.

[295] Cynthia Eller, *In the Lap of the Goddess,* 45.

[296] Whittier, 23.

[297] Bednarowski, *Religious Imagination of American Women,* 5-6.

[298] Gergen, ed., ix.

[299] Adler, 45-46.

[300] Eller, *The Myth of Matriarchal Prehistory,* 3.

[301] Charlene Spretnak, ed. *The Politics of Women's Spirituality: Essays on the Rise of Spiritual Power within the Feminist Movement* (NY: Anchor Books, Doubleday, 1982), xvii.

[302] Ronald Hutton discusses Marija Gimbutus' influence *in Triumph of the Moon: A History of Modern Pagan Witchcraft,* 356-358. Her most influential text for the feminist movement was *The Gods and Goddesses of Old Europe* (London: Thames and Hudson, 1974).

[303] In addition to Marija Gimbutus, see Merlin Stone's *When God Was a Woman.* 9NY: Barnes and Noble, Doubleday, 1976) and Riane Eisler's *The Chalice and the Blade* (San Francisco: HarperCollins Publishers, 1987) for examples.

[304] Juliette Wood, "The Concept of the Goddess," in Sandra Billington and Miranda Green, eds. *The Concept of the Goddess* (London and NY: Routledge, 1996), 9.

[305] Merlin Stone, "The Great Goddess: Who Was She?" in Charlene Spretnak's *The Politics of Women's Spirituality*, (NY: Anchor Books, Doubleday, 1982), 8.

[306] Stone, "The Great Goddess," 8.

[307] Stone, "The Great Goddess," 9.

[308] Stone, "The Great Goddess," 10.

[309] Cynthia Eller, *The Myth of Matriarchal Prehistory*, 18.

[310] Eller, *Myth of Matriarchal Prehistory*, 15.

[311] Juliette Wood, 9.

[312] Charlene Spretnak, *Lost Goddesses of Early Greece: A Collection of Pre-Hellenic Myths* (Boston: Beacon Press, 1978, 1981, 1992), 97.

[313] Lucinda Joy Peach, *Women in World Religions* (Upper Saddle River, NJ: Prentice Hall, 2002), 350.

[314] Adler, 81, citing Aidan Kelly, "The Rebirth of Witchcraft: Tradition and Creativity in the Gardnarian Reform," (unpublished manuscript, 1977), 4.

[315] Ibid, 82.

[316] Alder, 86 and also personal communication with Isaac Bonewits, April 13, 2005 by email: (ibonewits@neopagan.net).

[317] Isaac Bonewits, personal communication, April 13, 2005 via email: (ibonewits@neopagan.net).

[318] Naomi Goldenberg, "Feminist Witchcraft: Controlling Our Own Inner Space," in Charlene Spretnak's *The Politics of Women's Spirituality*, 213.

[319] Ann Forfreedom, "Feminist Wicce Works," A.D.A., 1980. Unpublished paper located in the American Religions Special Collection, Davidson Library, University California, Santa Barbara, page 3.

[320] Carl Weschcke, in Dave Hill's column entitled, "Witches, Warlocks, Astrologers, Palm Readers and Mystics Converging on the Twin Cities This Week," *The Sun*, Thursday, July 22, 1976 (page 5-6).

[321] Letter from Carl L. Weschcke, editor of Llewellyn Publications, to J. Gordon Melton, dated January 28, 1975. Located in the American Religions Special Collection, Davidson Library, University of California, Santa Barbara.

[322] Charlene Spretnak, *The Politics of Women's Spirituality*, 5.

[323] Gerina Dunwich, 13.

[324] Marcello Truzzi, "Toward a Sociology of the Occult: Notes on Modern Witchcraft," in *Religious Movements in Contemporary America*, ed. Irving Zaretsky and Mark Leone (Princeton: Princeton University Press, 1974), 636. Cited in Adler, 91.

[325] Juliette Wood, 9.

[326] Juliette Wood, 22.

[327] Temma Kaplan, "Forward" to *Who's Afraid of Feminism?* Ann Oakley and Juliet Mitchell, eds. (NY: The New Press, 1997), xiv.

[328] Robert T. Smith, "The Rise of the Occult," *Minneapolis Tribune Picture Magazine*, Sunday, December 17, 1972 (page 14-19).

[329] Don Ahern, "See Craft as Religion: Witches Disown Potboiler Image," *St. Paul Dispatch*, Saturday, September 22, 1973.

[330] Carol Christ, with Judith Plaskow, is the author of *Womanspirit Rising: A Feminist Reader in Religion* (NY: Harper and Row, 1979). She also was one of the organizers of the women's caucus in the American Academy of Religion in 1971. This information comes from Mary Ellen Shaw's dissertation "The Varieties of Goddess Experience: Feminist Pragmatism in the Study of Women's Spirituality," in partial fulfillment of the requirements for the degree of Doctor of Philosophy at the University of Minnesota, May 2001, page 34.

[331] Cynthia Eller, *In the Lap of the Goddess*, 47.

[332] Miller, Casey and Kate Swift, *Words and Women: New Language in New Times* (Garden City, NY: Anchor Books, 1977), 67.

[333] Zsuzsanna Budapest, *The Feminist Book of Lights and Shadows* (Luna Publications, 1976), 2-3.

[334] Charlene Spretnak, *The Politics of Women's Spirituality*, xix.

[335] Carol Christ, "Why Women Need the Goddess," 372.

[336] Starhawk, 237.

[337] Gerina Dunwich, *Candlelight Spells: The Modern Witch's Book of Spellcasting, Feasting, and Natural Healing* (NJ: Citadel Press, 1988), 14.

[338] Zsuzsanna Budapest, *Holy Book of Women's Mysteries*, xxv.

[339] Bahnisch, 4.

[340] Starhawk, *Spiraldance*, 224-225.

[341] Starhawk, *Spiraldance*, 37.

[342] Dennise C. Brown, "Feminist and Witch," *Womanspirit* 6, 21 (Fall 1979), 59.

[343] Cynthia Eller, "The Birth of a New Religion," in Lucinda Joy Peach's *Women and World Religions* (Upper Saddle River, NJ: Prentice Hall, 2002), 359.

[344] Cheri Lesh, "Feminist Spiritual Alternatives," c. early 1980s unpublished paper in American Religions Collections, Davidson Library, University of California, Santa Barbara.

[345] Sally McFague, *Models of God: Theology for an Ecological, Nuclear Age* (Philadelphia: Fortress Press, 1988), 82.

[346] Carol P. Christ, "Why Women Need the Goddess: Phenomenological, Psychological, and Political Reflections," in Lucinda Joy Peach's *Women and World Religions* (Upper Saddle River, NJ: Prentice Hall, 2002), 365.

[347] Christ, 365.

[348] Mary Daly's argument in *Beyond God the Father* cited in Christ, 366.

[349] Zsuzsanna Budapest, *Holy Book of Women's Mysteries: Feminist Witchcraft, Goddess Rituals, Spellcasting and Other Womanly Arts...* (Oakland: Wingbow Press, 1980, 1986, 1989), 283.

[350] Starhawk, *Spiraldance,* 102-103.

[351] Starhawk, *Spiraldance*, 103.

[352] Margaret Andreas, Indiana, Pennsylvania, "The Witch Loves All and Keeps All," *Womanspirit* 6, 21 (Fall 1979), 59.

[353] Denise C. Brown, "Feminist and Witch," *Womanspirit*, 6, 21 (Fall 1979), page 59.

[354] Denise C. Brown, 59.

[355] Seagull Mari, Menlo Park, California, "My Own Witchcraft," in *Womanspirit* 5, 17 (Fall 1978), 21.

[356] Zsuzsanna Budapest, *The Holy Book of Women's Mysteries* (Oakland: Wingbow Press, 1980), 126-128.

[357] Adler, 183-184.

[358] Carol Christ, "Why Women Need the Goddess," 368.

[359] Starhawk, "Reclaiming the Sacred," by Starhawk and Jennifer Conner in Lucinda Joy Peach's, *Women in World Religions* (Upper Saddle River, NJ: Prentice Hall, 2002), 374-375.

[360] Starhawk, "Reclaiming the Sacred," 375.

[361] Carol P. Christ, *Rebirth of the Goddess: Finding Meaning in Feminist Spirituality* (NY and London: Routledge Press, 1997), xiii.

[362] Adler, 20.

[363] Adler, 22-23.

[364] Adler, 22-23.

[365] Adler, 76-77.

[366] Adler, 77.

[367] Max Weber, *Economy and Society: An Outline of Interpretative Sociology.* Guenther Roth and Claus Wittich, eds. (NY: Bedminster Press, 1968), Vol. 3, page 954.

[368] Morgan McFarland, feminist and witch, quoted in Margo Adler's *Drawing Down the Moon*, 181-182.

[369] McFarland, in Adler's *Drawing Down the Moon*, 184.

[370] Zsuzsanna Budapest, *Feminist Book of Lights and Shadows*, 1.

[371] Zsuzsanna Budapest, *Feminist Book of Lights and Shadows*, 1.

[372] Zsuzsanna Budapest, *Feminist Book of Lights and Shadows*, 1.

[373] Zsuzsanna Budapest, *The Holy Book of Women's Mysteries*, 297.

[374] Hutton, 346.

[375] Starhawk, *Spiraldance,* 216-217.

[376] Riane Eisler, *The Chalice and The Blade: Our History, Our Future* (San Francisco: Harper Collins, 1987), 193-194.

[377] Eisler, 198-199.

[378] Hutton, 360.

[379] Zsuzsanna Budapest, *The Holy Book of Women's Mysteries*, 69.

[380] The author of the "Circle Round" chant is unknown.

[381] Hutton, 360.

[382] Member of Ursa Minor coven quoted in Margo Adler's *Drawing Down the Moon*, 196.

[383] Carol Christ, "Why Women Need the Goddess: Phenomenological, Psychological, and Political Reflections," in *Womanspirit Rising*, 286.

[384] Christ cites Clifford Geertz "Religion as a cultural system," in William L. Lessa and Evon V. Vogt, eds. *Reader in Comparative Religion*, 2nd edition. (NY: Harper and Row, 1977), 206-210.

[385] Yahweh ben Yahweh, *Our True History, The World's Best Kept Secret: We are the People of the Old Testament Bible* (Saguin, Texas: PEES Foundationm 1979, 1982, 1992, 1993), 26.

[386] Sydney Freedberg, *Brother Love: Murder, Money and a Messiah* (NY: Pantheon Books, 1994), 85.

[387] Moses, Wilson Jeremiah. *Black Messiahs and Uncle Toms: Social and Literary Manipulations of a Religious Myth.* (University Park, PA: The Pennsylvania State University Press, 1993), 194.

[388] For instance, James Lewis has an entry in his *Encyclopedia of Cults, Sects and New Religious Movements* and Franklin Devon Waddell prepared a paper for a New Religious Movements class at the University of Virginia, which can be found at http://religiousmovements.lib.virginia.edu//nrms/nyah.html. Both of these texts have short entries describing the formation of the movement and their belief system, but do not offer an analysis of the movement.

[389] Sydney P. Freedberg, *Brother Love: Murder, Money and a Messiah* (NY: Pantheon Books, 1994).

[390] Sydney P. Freedberg, *Brother Love,* 38.

[391] Freedberg, *Brother Love,* 46-47.

[392] Freedberg, *Brother Love,* 48-50.

[393] Freedberg, *Brother Love,* 50-53.

[394] Freedberg, *Brother Love,* 54-55.

[395] Freedberg, *Brother Love,* 59-64.

[396] Freedberg, *Brother Love,* 66.

[397] Freedberg, *Brother Love,* 68-73.

[398] Freedberg, *Brother Love,* 77.

[399] Freedberg, *Brother Love,* 78-81.

[400] Freedberg, *Brother Love,* 92-98.

[401] Freedberg, *Brother Love,* 105-124.

[402] Freedberg, *Brother Love,* 138.

[403] Freedberg, *Brother Love,* 181.

[404] Susan Sachs, "Cult's Self-Styled Messiah Inspires Discipline, Fear," *Miami Herald,* December 8, 1985.

[405] Robert Rozier's Testimony Summary, from *United States of America v. Yahweh ben Yahweh, et. al.* 90-CR-868-NCR *(or USA v. Robert Louise Beasley, Jr. et. al).*

[406] United States v. Robert Louis Beasley, aka Dan Israel, et. al. United States Court of Appeals, Eleventh Circuit, No. 92-4773, dated January 5, 1996.

[407] Lloyd Clark Witness Testimony, *USA v. Yahweh ben Yahweh, et. al.*

[408] Robert Rozier's and Lloyd Clark's Trial testimony.

[409] Waddell.

[410] New Dominion Pictures produced a show for the Discovery Channel entitled "Temple of Fear: the FBI Files," which profiled the Nation of Yahweh. It focuses mostly on the murders of the dissidents of the sect. The show aired on the Discovery Channel on October 14, 2001.

[411] Jon Nordheimer, "Violence Brings Sect Under Scrutiny," The New York Times, NY, November 27, 1986.

---

[412] Charles Leerhsen and Peter Katel, "Busting the Prince of Love," *Newsweek*, November 19, 1990.

[413] Larry Rohter, "Sect Leader Convicted On Conspiracy Charge," *The New York Times*, New York, May 28, 1992.

[414] Dan Christensen, "Yahweh Ben Yahweh would be banned from meeting with Spiritual Followers," *Daily Business Review*, July 6, 2001.

[415] Dan Christensen, "Yahweh Ben Yahweh would be banned from meeting with Spiritual Followers," *Daily Business Review*, July 6, 2001.

[416] George Lardner, Jr., "14 Seized in Cult Killings in Florida; FBI Says Nation of Yahwehs Terrorized the Miami Community," *The Washington Post*, Washington, DC, November 8, 1990, page 20.

[417] Amy Driscoll, "Dying Yahweh wants parole lifted," *The Miami Herald*, October 1, 2006.

[418] *The Associated Press*, "US Judge will not interfere in parole process of ex-cult leader," October 16, 2006.

[419] Richard Wright, one of America's great black authors was likely the first to use the phrase "Black Power" in his text *Black Power: A Record of Reactions in a Land of Pathos* (Westport, CT: Greenwood Press, 1954). His other important works were *Native Son* (1941) and *Black Boy* (1945).

[420] Martin Luther King, Jr., "The Birth of the Black Power Slogan," in *The Rhetoric of Black Power*, Robert L. Scott and Wayne Brockried, eds. (NY, Evanston, London: Harper and Row Publishers, 1969), 30.

[421] John T. McCartney, *Black Power Ideologies: An Essay in African American Political Thought* (Philadelphia: Temple University Press, 1992), 120-125.

[422] Manning Marable, *Race, Reform and Rebellion: The Second Reconstruction in Black America 1945-1990*, 2nd edition. (Jackson, Mississippi & London: University Press of Mississippi, 1991), 90.

[423] Marable, 89-90.

[424] Malcolm X, in Marable, 90.

[425] Marable, 90.

[426] Marable, 96.

[427] Johnnie H. Miles, Juanita J. Davis, Sharon E. Ferguson-Roberts, and Rita G. Giles, *Almanac of African American Heritage* (Paramus, NJ: Prentice Hall Press, 2001).

[428] Martin Luther King, Jr., "The Birth of the Black Power Slogan," in Scott and Brockried, 32.

[429] Stokely Carmichael, "Stokely Carmichael Explains Black Power to a Black Audience in Detroit," July 30, 1966, in Scott and Brockriede, 87-94.

[430] Carmichael, in Scott and Brockriede, 116.

[431] Charles V. Hamilton, "An Advocate of Black Power Defines It," in Scott and Brockriede, 181.

[432] Marable, 97.

[433] Marable, 98.

[434] McCartney, 168-169.

[435] Moses, *Black Messiahs and Uncle Toms*, 49.

[436] Yahweh ben Yahweh, *You Are Not A Nigger: Our True History, The World's Best Kept Secret* (Beaconsfield, Quebec, Canada: PEESS Foundation, 1981, 1983, 1985, 1994), 63-64.

[437] Yahweh ben Yahweh, *You Are Not A Nigger*, 64.

[438] Yahweh ben Yahweh, *You Are Not A Nigger*, 64-65.

[439] Yahweh ben Yahweh, *You Are Not A Nigger*, 66.

[440] He cites Psalm 2:5, 10-12, naming himself as the "son" mentioned in the passage that the believers must follow. Yahweh ben Yahweh, *Yahweh Judges America* (Seguin, Texas: PEESS Foundation, 1985), 100.

[441] Yahweh ben Yahweh, *You Are Not A Nigger*, 107.

[442] Carmichael in Scott and Brockried for Carmichael, 94.

[443] Yahweh ben Yahweh, *You Are Not A Nigger*, 118.

[444] Sydney Freedberg, *Brother Love*, 134.

[445] Sydney P. Freedberg and Donna Gehrke, "From Idealists to 'Death Angels,'" *Miami Herald*, December 31, 1990.

[446] Freedberg and Gehrke.

[447] Hamilton, "Advocate," Scott and Brockriede, 181.

[448] Sydney Freedberg, *Brother Love,* 116.

[449] Sydney Freedberg, *Brother Love*, 17.

[450] Elijah Israel (Aston Green) was found beheaded by a machete in a rock quarry. Later, witnesses, who were members of the Circle of Ten, said that he was beaten in the temple and then transported to the quarry, where he was beheaded. Sydney Freedberg, *Brother Love*, Chapter 18. The information came from trial testimony and police witness transcripts.

[451] Lloyd Clark Witness Testimony, *USA v. Yahweh ben Yahweh, et.al.*

[452] Excerpt from newsletter entitled "Open Letter to the World: We Must Support Yahweh ben Yahweh," Presented by The People for Truth, Volume 2, Issue 1, page 2.

[453] Wilson Jeremiah Moses, *Black Messiahs and Uncle Toms: Social and Literary Manipulations of a Religious Myth* (University Park and London: The Pennsylvania State University Press, 1982), 183.

[454] Moses, 194.

[455] Yvonne Chireau and Nathaniel Deutsch, eds. *Black Zion: African-American Religious Encounters with Judaism* (NY and Oxford: Oxford University Press, 2000), 8.

[456] Albert J. Raboteau, "African Americans, Exodus, and the American Israel," in David G. Hacket's *Religion and American Culture*, 2nd ed. (New York and London: Routledge, 2003, page 73-87), 84.

[457] Cain Hope Felder, *Troubling Biblical Waters: Race, Class and Family* (Maryknoll, NY: Orbis Books, 1994), 6.

[458] Vincent L. Wimbush, "The Bible and African Americans" in *Stony the Road We Trod: African American Biblical Interpretation*, Cain Hope Felder, ed. (Minneapolis: Fortress Press, 1991), 89.

[459] Wimbush, 57-58.

---

[460] Singer, Merrill. "Black Judaism in the United States," in *Down by the Riverside: Readings in African American Religion*, Larry G. Murphey, ed. (NY and London: New York University Press, 2000), 226.

[461] Wimbush, 58-59.

[462] Wimbush, 59.

[463] Chireau and Deutsch, 61.

[464] Freedberg, *Brother Love*, 67-69.

[465] Ben Ammi, *Yeshua the Hebrew Messiah or Jesus the Christian Christ?* (Washington D.C.: Communicators Press, 1996), 8.

[466] Ammi, 12.

[467] Sydney Freedberg, *Brother Love*, 5.

[468] Sydney Freedberg, *Brother Love*, 19.

[469] After Yahweh ben Yahweh began denouncing people in the community and making other questionable pronouncements, Yakim Israel became concerned. After his friend Elijah Israel was killed, he and his wife Mildred Banks were approached by police and gave testimony about their fears. They were attacked two days later, and Yakim was killed. According to later trial testimony, the temple members feared disunity and felt that they were enacting God's revenge. Mildred Banks survived and gave testimony at the trial. She had been put into a witness protection program after her recovery. Sydney Freedberg, *Brother Love*, Chapters 1-6, from police transcripts and trial testimony.

[470] This passage is taken from 2 Esdras as found in *The Missing Books of the Bible*, Volume 1 (Owings Mills, MD: Halo Press, 1996), 120. These are books found in the Apocrypha.

[471] Nation of Yahweh website: http://yahwehbenyahweh.com/beliefs.htm

[472] Nation of Yahweh website

[473] Yahweh ben Yahweh, *You Are Not a Nigger,* 41.

[474] James R. Lewis. "Nation of Yahweh" entry. *The Encyclopedia of Cults, Sects, and New Religions.* (Amherst, NY: Prometheus Books, 1998), 356.

[475] Yahweh ben Yahweh, *You Are Not A Nigger*, 36.

[476] Franklin Devon Waddell, prepared for a New Religious Movements class. "Nation of Yahweh," found at http://religiousmovements.lib.virginia.edu//nrms /nyah.html. They had acquired a building and named it "The Temple of Love."

[477] Yahweh ben Yahweh, *You Are Not A Nigger*, 6.

[478] Yahweh ben Yahweh, *You Are Not A Nigger*, 6-7.

[479] Yahweh ben Yahweh, *You Are Not A Nigger*, 22.

[480] Yahweh ben Yahweh, *You Are Not A Nigger*, 23-24.

[481] Yahweh ben Yahweh, *You Are Not A Nigger*, 25.

[482] Yahweh ben Yahweh, *You Are Not A Nigger*, 93.

[483] The sermons from each night of the 1991 Feast of Tabernacles have been published by the PEESS Foundation. Night #6 is entitled "Ye Are Gods and You are Children of the Most High." Night #7 is entitled "Yahweh ben Yahweh is Building the Kingdom that Will Never Be Destroyed."

[484] Lloyd Clark Witness Testimony, *USA v. Yahweh ben Yahweh, et. al.*

[485] Yahweh ben Yahweh, *Yahweh Judges America,* 33.

[486] Yahweh ben Yahweh, *Yahweh Judges America*, 65.

[487] Yahweh ben Yahweh, *Yahweh Judges America*, 72.

[488] Freedberg, *Brother Love*, 66-67.

[489] Freedberg, *Brother Love*, 69.

[490] Freedberg, *Brother Love*, 69.

[491] Yahweh ben Yahweh, *You Are Not A Nigger*, 157 and Susan Sachs, "Cult's Self-Styled Messiah Inspires Discipline, Fear, *Miami Herald*, December 8, 1985.

[492] Yahweh ben Yahweh, *You Are Not A Nigger*, 159.

[493] Yahweh ben Yahweh, *You Are Not A Nigger*, 157.

[494] Freedberg, *Brother Love*, 83.

[495] Yahweh ben Yahweh, *Yahweh Judges America*, 153.

[496] No author listed, "FBI Arrests Members of Black Sect in 14 Slayings," *The New York Times*, NY, November 8, 1990, page A29.

[497] Sydney Freedberg, *Brother Love*, 116.

[498] Yahweh ben Yahweh, *Adam's 6,000-Year Deep Sleep* (Seguin, TX: PEESS Foundation, 1993, 1994), 21.

[499] Yahweh ben Yahweh, *Our True History*, 2.

[500] Yahweh ben Yahweh, *Our True History*, 5.

[501] Sydney Freedberg, *Brother Love*, 156.

[502] Freedberg and Gehrke.

[503] Freedberg and Gehrke.

[504] Freedberg and Gehrke.

[505] Sydney P. Freedberg and Donna Gehrke, "From Idealists to 'Death Angels,' *Miami Herald*, December 31, 1990.

[506] Freedberg and Gehrke.

[507] Yahweh ben Yahweh, *You Are Not A Nigger, 7.*

[508] Yahweh ben Yahweh, *You Are Not A Nigger*, 41.

[509] Yahweh ben Yahweh, *You Are Not A Nigger*, 41.

[510] Yahweh ben Yahweh, *You Are Not A Nigger*, 46-48.

[511] Yahweh ben Yahweh, *You Are Not A Nigger*, 49.

[512] Yahweh ben Yahweh, *You Are Not A Nigger*, 49.

[513] Yahweh ben Yahweh, *You Are Not A Nigger*, 50-51.

[514] Yahweh ben Yahweh, *Yahweh Judges America*, 24-25.

[515] Yahweh ben Yahweh, *Yahweh Judges America*, 27.

[516] Yahweh ben Yahweh, *Yahweh Judges America*, 76.

[517] Sydney Freedberg, *Brother Love*, 141.

[518] Emilia Askari, "Singer Changes His Tune for Yahwehs," *Miami Herald*, August 13, 1987.

[519] Patricia Andrews, "South Broward Sect's Message: Whites are Evil. Hebrew Israelite Temple Puts Faith in Racial Pride," *Miami Herald*, October 16, 1983.

[520] Sydney Freedberg, *Brother Love*, 149.

[521] Freedberg and Gehrke.

[522] Freedberg and Gehrke.

[523] Freedberg and Gehrke.

[524] Freedberg and Gehrke.

[525] Lloyed Clark Witness Testimony, *USA v. Yahweh ben Yahweh, et. al.*

[526] Max Weber, Basic *Concepts in Sociology*, trans. By H. P. Secher. (NY: Citadel Press, 1968), 82.

[527] Richard T. Hughes. *Myths America Lives By* (Urbana and Chicago: University of Illinois Press, 2003), 85.

[528] Jim Lewis, *Legitimating New Religions*, 233.

[529] J. Gordon Melton, "Perspective: Toward a Definition of 'New Religion," *Nova Religio* (July 2004, Vol. 8, No. 1), 73-87.

[530] Robert A. LeVine, "Properties of Culture: An Ethnographic View," in *Culture Theory: Essays on Mind, Self and Emotion*, Richard A. Shweder and Robert A. LeVine, eds. (NY and Cambridge, UK: Cambridge University Press, 1984), 77.

BIBLIOGRAPHY

Adler, Margot. *Drawing Down the Moon: Witches, Druids, Goddess-Worshippers, and Other Pagans in America Today.* Boston: Beacon Press, 1986 revised and expanded edition.

Albanese, Catherine. *Nature Religions in America: From Algonquin Indians to the New Age.* Chicago and London: University of Chicago Press, 1990.

Ammi, Ben. *Yeshua the Hebrew Messiah or Jesus the Christian Christ?* Washington D.C.: Communicators Press, 1996.

Anderson, Pamela Sue. *A Feminist Philosophy of Religion.* Oxford, UK, and Malden, MA: Blackwell Publications, Inc., 1998.

Andrews, Patricia. "South Broward Sect's Message: Whites are Evil. Hebrew Israelite Temple Puts Faith in Racial Pride, *Miami Herald*, October 16, 1983.

Askari, Emilia. "Singer Changes His Tune for Yahwehs," *Miami Herald*, August 13, 1987.

Bahnisch, Mark. "Sociology of Religion in Postmodernity: Wicca, Witches and the Neopagan Myth of Foundations," Queensland University of Technology, TASA 2001 Conference, The University of Sydney, 13-15 December 2001, unpublished paper.

Bainbridge, William Sims. *The Sociology of New religious movements.* NY: Routledge, 1997.

Bal, Mieke, Jonathan Crewe, and Leo Spitzer, eds. *Acts of Memory: Cultural Recall in the Present.* Hanover and London: Dartmouth College, 1999.

Banta, Martha. *Imaging American Women: Idea and Ideals in Cultural History.* NY: Columbia University Press, 1987.

Barker, Eileen. *The Making of a Moonie: Choice or Brainwashing?* NY, Oxford: Blackwell, 1984.

Barnett, H.G. *Innovation: The Basis of Cultural Change.* NY, Toronto, London: McGraw-Hill Book Company, Inc., 1953.

Beckford, James A. *Cult Controversies: The Societal Response to the New Religious Movements.* London and NY: Tavistock Publications, 1985.

Beckford, James, ed. *New religious movements and Rapid Social Change.* Research Committee 22 of the International Sociological Association. London, Beverly Hills, CA: Sage Publications, 1986.

Bednarowski, Mary Farrel. *New Religions and the Theological Imagination in America*. Bloominton and Indianapolis: Indiana State University Press, 1989.

—. *The Religious Imagination of American Women*. Bloomington and Indianapolis, Indianna University Press, 1999.

Berman, William C. *America's Right Turn: from Nixon to Bush*. Baltimore, MD: John Hopkins University Press, 1994.

Biermans, John T. *The Odyssey of New Religious Movements: persecution, struggle, legitimation: A Case Study of the Unification Church*. Lewiston, NY: E. Mellen Press, 1986.

Binder, Louis Richard. *Modern Religious Cults and Society: A Sociological Interpretation of a Modern Religious Phenomenon*. NY: AMS Press, 1970.

Bloch, Jon P. *New Spirituality, Self and Belonging: How New Agers and Neo-Pagans Talk About Themselves*. Westport, CT: Praeger Publishing, 1998.

Bloom, Alexander. *Long Time Gone: 60s America Then and Now*. Oxford, NY: Oxford University Press, 2001.

Brick, Howard. *The Age of Contradiction: American Thought and Culture in the 1960s*. NY: Twayne Publishers, 1998.

Bromley, David, Bruce C. Busching, and Anson D. Shupe, Jr. "The Unification Church and the American Family: Strain, Conflict and Control," in *New Religious Movements: A Perspective for Understanding Society*, ed. Eileen Barker. NY and Toronto: Edwin Mellen Press, 1982.

Bromley, David G. Anson D. Shupe, Jr. and Donna L. Oliver, "Perfect Families: Visions of the Future in a New Religious Movement," in *Cults and the Family*, Florence Kaslow and Marion B. Sussman, eds. NY: The Haworth Press, 1982.

Brown, Dennise C. "Feminist and Witch," *Womanspirit* 6, 21 (Fall 1979).

Budapest, Zsuzsanna. *The Feminist Book of Lights and Shadows*. Luna Publications, 1976. Copies: The Feminist Wicca: A Matriarchal Spiritual Center, 442 Lincoln Blvd, Venice, CA 90291. 399-3919.

—. *The Holy Book of Women's Mysteries: Feminist Witchcraft, Goddess Rituals, Spellcasting, and Other Womanly Arts*. Oakland: Wingbow Press, 1980, 1986, 1989.

Burke, Peter. *Varieties of Cultural History*. Ithaca, NY: Cornell University Press, 1997.

Burlein, Ann. "Counter-memory on the Right: The Case of Focus on the Family," in *Acts of Memory: Cultural Recall in the Present*, Mieke

Bal, Jonathan Crewe, and Leo Spitzer, eds. Hanover and London: Dartmouth College, 1999.

Burner, David. *Making Peace with the 60s.* Princeton, NJ: Princeton University Press, 1996.

Carmichael, Stokely. "Stokely Carmichael Explains Black Power to a Black Audience in Detroit," July 30, 1966, in Scott and Brockriede, 87-94.

Cavallo, Dominick. *A Fiction of the Past: the 60s in American History.* NY: St. Martin's Press, 1999.

Chartier, Roger. *Cultural History: Between Practices and Representations.* Ithaca, NY: Cornell University Press, 1988.

Chireau, Yvonne and Nathaniel Deutsch, eds. *Black Zion: African-American Religious Encounters with Judaism.* NY and Oxford: Oxford University Press, 2000.

Christ, Carol P. *Diving Deep and Surfacing: Women Writers on Spiritual Quest*, 2nd ed. Boston: Beacon Press, 1980.

—. "Why Women Need the Goddess: Phenomenological, Psychological, and Political Reflections," in *Womanspirit Rising*, 286.

Christ, Carol P. and Judith Plaskow, eds. *Woman Spirit Rising: A Feminist Reader in Religion.* San Francisco: Harper and Row Publishers, 1979.

Christensen, Dan. "Yahweh Ben Yahweh would be banned from meeting with Spiritual Followers," *Daily Business Review,* July 6, 2001.

Collins, Sheila D. "The Personal is Political," in *The Politics of Women's Spirituality: Essays on the Rise of Spiritual Power within the Feminist Movement.* NY: Anchor Books, Doubleday, 1982.

Chryssides, George D. *The Advent of Sun Myung Moon: The Origins, Beliefs and Practices of the Unification Church.* New York: St. Martin's Press, 1991.

—. *Historical Dictionary of New religious movements.* Lanham, MD: Scarecrow Press, 2001.

Culbertson, Judi. "A New Expression of Hope," *Unified Families, From the Heart of the Co-Creator: A New Philosophy of Love and Truth,* September 18,1968. (Published by Unified Family, 429 S. Virgil, California 90005.)

Cunningham, Agnes J., Robert Nelson, William L. Hendricks, and Jorge Lara-Braud, "Critique of the Theology of the Unification Church as Set Forth in Divine Principle," in Horowitz, Irving Louis. *Science, Sin, and Scholarship: The Politics of Reverend Moon and the Unification Church.* Cambridge: MIT Press, c1978.

Davis, Philip G. *Goddess Unmasked: the rise of neopagan feminist spirituality.* Dallas, TX: Spence Publishing, 1998.

Dawson, Lorne L. *Comprehending Cults: The Sociology of New religious movements* Oxford, NY: Oxford University Press, 1998.

Dean, Roger Allen. *Moonies: A Psychological Analysis of the Unification Church*. Cults and Nonconventional Religious Groups: A Collection of Outstanding Dissertations. New York: Garland, 1992.

Driscoll, Amy "Dying Yahweh wants parole lifted," *The Miami Herald*, October 1, 2006.

Dunwich, Gerina. *Candlelight Spells: The Modern Witch's Book of Spellcasting, Feasting, and Natural Healing*. NJ: Citadel Press, 1988.

Eisler, Riane. *The Chalice and The Blade: Our History, Our Future*. San Francisco: Harper Collins, 1987.

Eller, Cynthia. *Living in the Lap of the Goddess: The Feminist Spirituality Movement in America.* NY: Crossroad, 1993.

—. "The Birth of a New Religion," in *Women and World Religions*, Lucinda Joy Peach, ed. Upper Saddle River, NJ: Prentice Hall, 2002.

—. *The Myth of Matriarchal Prehistory: Why an Invented Past Won't Give Women a Future*. Boston: Beacon Press, 2000.

Ellwood, Robert S. *Alternative Altars: Unconventional and Eastern Spirituality in America*. Chicago: University of Chicago Press, 1979.

—. *Religious and Spiritual Groups in Modern America*. Englewood Cliffs, NJ: Prentice Hall, 1973.

Enroth, Ronald ed. *A Guide to New Religious Movements*. Downers Grove, Ill: InterVarsity Press, 2005.

Farber, David. *The Age of Great Dreams: America in the 1960s*. NY: Hill and Wang, 1994.

—. *From Memory to History*. Chapel Hill, NC: University of North Carolina Press, 1994.

Farber, David, and Jeff Roche, eds. *The Conservative Sixties*. NY: Peter Lang, 2003.

Felder, Cain Hope. *Troubling Biblical Waters: Race, Class and Family*. Maryknoll, NY: Orbis Books, 1994.

Fichter, Joseph H. *Autobiographies of Conversion*. Lewiston, NY: Edwin Mellon Press, 1987.

—. "Family and Religion Among the Moonies: A Descriptive Analysis," in *Families and Religion: Conflict and Change in Modern Society*. Eds William V. D'Antonio and Joan Aldous. Beverly Hills, London, New Delhi: Sage Publications, 1983.

Freedberg, Sydney P. *Brother Love: Murder, Money, and a Messiah*. NY: Pantheon Books, 1994.

Freedberg, Sydney P. and Donna Gehrke, "From Idealists to 'Death Angels,' *Miami Herald*, December 31, 1990.

Geertz, Clifford. "Religion as a Cultural System," *The Interpretation of Cultures*. NY: Basic Books, 1973.

Gergen, Mary McCanney ed. *Feminist Thought and the Structure of Knowledge*. NY and London: New York University Press, 1988.

Gitlin, Todd. *The Sixties: Years of Hope, Days of Rage*. Toronto, NY: Bantam Books, 1987.

Goldenberg, Naomi. "Feminist Witchcraft: Controlling Our Own Inner Space," in Charlene Spretnak's *The Politics of Women's Spirituality: Essays on the Rise of Spiritual Power within the Feminist Movement*. NY: Anchor Books, Doubleday, 1982.

Gonzales, Beatriz. Unification Church brochure entitled "Unification Church: Only if you discover things for yourself." Unification Church, 4 West 43rd Street, NY, NY 10036 (212) 730-5782.

Grace, James H. *Sex and Marriage in the Unification Movement: A Sociological Study*. Studies in Religion and Society, Vol 13. New York: Edwin Mellen Press, c1985.

Graves, Robert. *The White Goddess*, amended and enlarged edition. New York: Farrar, Straus, and Giroux, 1966.

Greene, Jack P. *Imperatives, Behaviors, and Identities: Essays in Early American Cultural History*. Charlottesville and London: University Press of Virginia, 1992.

Griffin, Wendy. "Goddess Spirituality and Wicca," *Her Voice, Her Faith*. Boulder, CO: Westview Press, 2003.

Hirshman, Charles. "America's Melting Pot Reconsidered, *Annual Review of Sociology*, 1983. Volume 9, 397-423.

Horowitz, Irving Louis. *Science, Sin, and Scholarship: The Politics of Reverend Moon and the Unification Church*. Cambridge: MIT Press, c1978.

Howell, Martha and Walter Prevenier. *From Reliable Sources: An Introduction to Historical Methods*. Ithaca and London: Cornell University Press, 2001.

Hughes, Richard T. *Myths America Lives By*. Urbana and Chicago: University of Illinois Press, 2003.

Hunt, Stephen. *Alternative Religions: A Sociological Introduction*. Aldershot, Hampshire, England; Burlington, VT: Ashgate, 2003.

Hunter, James Davidson. *Culture Wars: The Struggle to Define America*. New York: Basic Books, Harper Collins Publishers, 1991.

Hutton, Ronald. *The Triumph of the Moon: A History of Modern Pagan Witchcraft*. Oxford, NY: Oxford University Press, 1999.

Introvigne, Massimo. *The Unification Church: Studies in Contemporary Religion.* Salt Lake City, UT: Signature Books; Torino, Italy : CESNUR, c2000.

Jenkins, Philip. *Mystics and Messiahs: Cults and New Religions in American History.* Oxford, NY: Oxford University Press, 2000.

Kaplan, Jeffrey and Helene Loon, eds. *The Cultic Milieu: Oppositional Subcultures in an age of Globalization.* Walnut Creek: AltaMisa Press, 2002.

Kaplan, Temma. "Forward" to *Who's Afraid of Feminism?* Ann Oakley and Juliet Mitchell, eds. NY: The New Press, 1997), xiv

Kent, Stephen A. *From Slogans to Mantras: Social Protest and Religious Conversion in the Late Vietnam War Era.* Syracuse, NY: Syracuse University Press, 2001.

Kim, Mrs. Shin Wook. "Baby Dedications," in *The Blessing Monthly* Newsletter of the American Blessed Families Association, Vol. 1, #3, July-August, 1974.

King, Martin Luther Jr. "The Birth of the Black Power Slogan," in *The Rhetoric of Black Power,* Robert L. Scott and Wayne Brockried, eds. NY, Evanston, London: Harper and Row Publishers, 1969.

Klein, Anne Carolyn. *Meeting the Great Bliss Queen: Buddhists, Feminists, and the Art of the Self.* Boston: Beacon Press, 1995.

Kramer, Heinnich and Jacob Sprenger: *Malleus Maleficarum,* first published in 1486. London: The Folio Society, 1968.

Lai, Whalen. "Rethinking the Chinese Family: Wandering Ghosts and Eternal Parents," in *The Ideal in the World's Religions: Essays on the Person, Family, Society and Environment.* Eds. Robert Carter and Sheldon Isenberg. St. Paul, Minn: Paragon House, 1997.

Lardner, George Jr. "14 Seized in Cult Killings in Florida; FBI Says Nation of Yahwehs Terrorized the Miami Community," *The Washington Post,* Washington, DC, November 8, 1990.

Leerhsen, Charles and Peter Katel, "Busting the Prince of Love," *Newsweek,* November 19, 1990.

Leland, Charles Godfrey. *Aradia, or the Gospel of the Witches.* London: David Nutt, 1899, reprinted NY: Samuel Weisen.

LeVine, Robert A. "Properties of Culture: An Ethnographic View," in *Culture Theory: Essays on Mind, Self and Emotion,* Richard A. Shweder and Robert A. LeVine, eds. NY and Cambridge, UK: Cambridge University Press, 1984.

Lewis, James R. *Witchcraft Today: An Encyclopedia of Wiccan and Neopagan Traditions.* Santa Barbara, CA: ABC-CLIO, 1999.

—. *Cults in America: A Reference Handbook*. Santa Barbara, CA: ABC-CLIO, 1998.

—. *The Encyclopedia of Cults, Sects, and New Religions*. Amherst, NY: Prometheus Books, 1998.

—. *The Oxford Handbook of New religious movements*. Oxford University Press, 2003.

—. "The Scholarship of 'Cults' and the 'Cult' of Scholarship," *Journal of Dharma*, 12 Ap-Je, 1987, p. 96-107.

Lewis, Sarah. "The Family Federation for World Peace and Unification," in Christopher Partridge's *New Religions: A Guide*. NY: Oxford University Press, 2004.

Lofland, John and Rodney Stark, "Becoming a World-Saver: A Theory of Conversion to a Deviant Perspective," in *American Sociological Review*. Vol. 30, No. 6, December, 1965, 862-875.

Lowney, Kathleen S. *Passport to Heaven: Gender Roles in the Unification Church*. Cults and Nonconventional Religious Groups. New York : Garland, 1992.

Lucas, Phillip Charles and Thomas Robbins, eds. *New religious movements in the Twenty-First Century: Legal, Political and Social Challenges in Global Perspective*, NY: Routledge Press, 2004.

Marable, Manning. *Race, Reform and Rebellion: The Second Reconstruction in Black America 1945-1990*, 2nd edition. Jackson, Mississippi & London: University Press of Mississippi, 1991.

McCartney, John T. *Black Power Ideologies: An Essay in African American Political Thought*. Philadelphia: Temple University Press, 1992.

McFague, Sally. *Models of God: Theology for an Ecological, Nuclear Age*. Philadelphia: Fortress Press, 1988.

Melton, J. Gordon. *Encyclopedic Handbook of Cults in America*. NY: Garland Publishing, 1986.

—. ed. *Neo-Pagan Witchcraft I and II*. NY and London: Garland Publishing, 1990.

—. "Perspective: Toward a Definition of 'New Religion," *Nova Religio*, July 2004, Vol. 8, No. 1, 73-87.

—. *New Age Encyclopedia: A Guide to the Beliefs, Concepts, Terms, People and Organizations that Make Up the New Global Movement Toward Spiritual Development, Health and Healing, Higher Consciousness, and Related Subjects*. Detroit, MI: Gale Research, 1990.

Mickler, Michael L. *A History of the Unification Church in America 1959-1974: Emergence of a National Movement.* Cults and Nonconventional Religious Groups. New York : Garland, 1993.

Miles, Johnnie H., Juanita J. Davis, Sharon E. Ferguson-Roberts, and Rita G. Giles, *Almanac of African American Heritage.* Paramus, NJ: Prentice Hall Press, 2001.

Miller, Casey and Kate Swift, *Words and Women: New Language in New Times.* Garden City, NY: Anchor Books, 1977.

Moon, Sun Myung. *The Divine Principle*, published by The Holy Spirit Association for the Unification of World Christianity, NY, 1973.

—. "November 12th Could Be Your Re-Birthday," speech given by Moon on October 21, 1973 and reprinted in the *Chicago Tribune*, Thursday, November 7, 1974, Section 3, 21.

—. translated by Mrs. Won Pok Choi. "The True Pattern of Family Life," Barrytown, NY, March 7, 1975. Located in the American Religions Collection, Department of Special Collections, Donald C. Davidson Library, the University of California, Santa Barbara. Moon also explains filial piety in the *Divine Principle*, 49.

—. "New Hope for America: Christianity in Crisis." Excerpts from "New Hope: 12 Talks by Sun Myung Moon," 1973. Located in the American Religions Collection, Department of Special Collections, Donald C. Davidson Library, the University of California, Santa Barbara.

—. "God's Hope for America," speech given at Yankee Stadium on June 1, 1976 printed in the *New York Times*, Thursday, June 3, 1976, C42-43.

—. "One God, One World Religion," Lecture given at Goucher College, Towson, Maryland, February 11, 1972.

Moon, Sun Myung and Mrs. Sun Myung Moon. *True Family and World Peace.* NY: Family Federation for World Peace and Unification, dist. HAS Publications, 2000.

Moon, Sun Myung. *True Parents.* DC: Family Federation for World Peace and Unification, International, 1998.

Moore, R. Laurence. *Religious Outsiders and the Making of Americans.* NY and Oxford: Oxford University Press, 1986.

Mosely, James G. *A Cultural History of Religion in America.* Westport, CT and London, England: Greenwood Press, 1981.

Moses, Wilson Jeremiah. *Black Messiahs and Uncle Toms: Social and Literary Manipulations of a Religious Myth.* University Park, PA: The Pennsylvania State University Press, 1993.

Nation of Yahweh website: http://yahwehbenyahweh.com/beliefs.htm

"New Life" lecture pamphlet. Distributed by the Unification Church of America, National Headquarters, Washington D.C., 1611 Upshur Street, NW 20011, n.d.

Nordheimer, Jon. "Violence Brings Sect Under Scrutiny," The New York Times, NY, Novermber 27, 1986.

Nye, Andrea. *Feminist Theory and the Philosophies of Man.* London, NY, Sydney: Croom Helm, 1988.

Partridge, Christopher, ed. New Religions, *A Guide: New religious movements, Sects, and Alternative Spiritualities.* NY: Oxford Press, 2004.

Peach, Lucinda Joy. *Women in World Religions.* Upper Saddle River, NJ: Prentice Hall, 2002.

Pearson, Joanne. "Assumed Affinities: Wicca and the New Age," *Nature Religion Today.* Edinburg: Edinburg University Press, 1998: 45-56.

Phillips, Anne, ed. *Feminism and Equality.* Washington Square, NY: New York University Press, 1987.

Raboteau, Albert J. "African Americans, Exodus, and the American Israel," in David G. Hacket's *Religion and American Culture*, 2nd ed. New York and London: Routledge, 2003, page 73-87.

Rohter, Larry. "Sect Leader Convicted On Conspiracy Charge," *The New York Times*, New York, May 28, 1992.

Rosenberg, Roberta, *The Language of Power: Women and Literature, 1945-Present. Volume 19 of the Writing About Women Feminist Literary Studies Series.* NY: Peter Lang, 1996.

Sachs, Susan. "Cult's Self-Styled Messiah Inspires Discipline, Fear," *Miami Herald,* December 8, 1985.

Saliba, John A. *Understanding New religious movements*, 2nd ed. Walnut Creek, CA: AltaMira Press, 2003.

Salonen, Neil Albert, President of the Unification Church of America. "The Truth About the Reverend Sun Myung Moon," *Los Angeles Times*, Sunday, January 25, 1976, 6 Part VIII.

Schneider, Gregory L. *Conservatism in America Since 1930: A Reader.* NY, London: New York University Press, 2003.

Shaw, Mary Ellen. "The Varieties of Goddess Experience: Feminist Pragmatism in the Study of Women's Spirituality," in partial fulfillment of the requirements for the degree of Doctor of Philosophy at the University of Minnesota, May 2001.

Shenge, Ntozanke. *colored girls who have considered suicide/when the rainbow is enuf* NY: Macmillan Co., Inc., 1975, 1976, 1977.

Shweder, Richard A. and Robert A. LeVine, *Culture Theory: Essays on Mind, Self and Emotion.* Cambridge, U.K.: Cambridge University Press, 1984.

Siegler, Elijah. *New Religious Movements,* Religions of the World Series. Upper Saddle River, NJ: Prentice Hall, 2007.

Singer, Merrill. "Black Judaism in the United States," in *Down by the Riverside: Readings in African American Religion,* Larry G. Murphey, ed. NY and London: New York University Press, 2000.

Sontag, Frederick. "Marriage and the Family in Unification Church Theology," in *Update,* 6:3, September 1962.

—. "Sun Myung Moon and the Unification Church: Charges and Responses," *in Science, Sin and Scholarship: The Politics of Reverend Moon and the Unification Church,* edited by Irving Louis Horowitz. (Cambridge, MA and London: The MIT Press, 1978), 35.

Spretnak, Charlene, ed. *The Politics of Women's Spirituality: Essays on the Rise of Spiritual Power within the Feminist Movement.* NY: Anchor Books, Doubleday, 1982.

Star, Leigh. "The Politics of Wholeness: Feminism and the New Spirituality," Unpublished paper in American Religions Collections, Davidson Library, University of California, Santa Barbara.

Starhawk, *The Spiral Dance: A Rebirth of the Ancient Religion of the Great Goddess.* NY, San Francisco: HarperCollins Publishers, 1979, 1989, 1999.

—. "Reclaiming the Sacred," by Starhawk and Jennifer Conner in Lucinda Joy Peach's, *Women in World Religions.* Upper Saddle River, NJ: Prentice Hall, 2002.

Stone, Merlin. "The Great Goddess: Who Was She?" in Charlene Spretnak's *The Politics of Women's Spirituality,* 8.

Sudo, Ken, Director of Training at Barrytown Unification Seminary. "The Meaning of Brothers and Sisters," Student Training Manual, 1975, page 164.

Thompson, Ross. "Immanence Unknown: Graham Ward and the Neo-Pagans," *Theology,* 95 Ja-F 1992, p 18-26.

Truzzi, Marcello. "Toward a Sociology of the Occult: Notes on Modern Witchcraft," in *Religious Movements in Contemporary America,* ed. Irving Zaretsky and Mark Leone. Princeton: Princeton University Press, 1974.

Waddell, Franklin Devon. "Nation of Yahweh," unpublished paper found at http://religiousmovements.lib.virginia.edu//nrms/nyah.html.

Walsh, Tom. "Celibacy, Virtue, and the Practice of True Family in the Unification Church," in *The Family and the Unification Church,* ed.

Gene G. James. Barrytown, NY: Unification Theological Seminary, 1983.

Warwick, Lynda L. "Feminist Wicca: Paths to Empowerment," *Women's Spirituality, Women's Lives*. NY: Haworth Press, 1995, 121-133.

Weber, Max. *Economy and Society: An Outline of Interpretative Sociology*. Guenther Roth and Claus Wittich, eds. NY: Bedminster Press, 1968.

—. *Basic Concepts in Sociology*, translation by H. P. Secher. NY: Citadel Press, 1968.

Welch, Robert. "Americanism versus Amorality," in Robert A. Rosestone's *Protest from the Right*. Beverly Hills, Glencoe Press, 1968.

Wells, Jonathan. "Marriage and the Family in Unification Theology," in *Dialogue and Alliance*, Vol. 9, No. 1, Spring/Summer 1995.

Whittier, Nancy. *Feminist Generations: The Persistence of the Radical Women's Movement*. Philadelphia: Temple University Press, 1995.

Williams, Rhys H. "Religion as Political Resource: Culture or Ideology?" *Journal for the Scientific Study of Religion*, Vol. 35, No. 4 (December, 996), pages 368-378.

Wilson, Brian and Jamie Cresswell, eds. *New religious movements: Challenge and Response*. London and NY: Routledge, 1999.

Wimbush, Vincent L. "The Bible and African Americans" in *Stony the Road We Trod: African American Biblical Interpretation*, Cain Hope Felder, ed. Minneapolis: Fortress Press, 1991.

Winthrop, John. "A Modell of Christian Charity," written in 1630, in Giles Gunn's *Early American Writing*. NY: Penguin Classics, 1994, 112.

Wood, Juliette. "The Concept of the Goddess," in Sandra Billington and Miranda Green, eds. *The Concept of the Goddess*. London and NY: Routledge, 1996.

Wright, Richard. *Black Power: A Record of Reactions in a Land of Pathos*. Westport, CT: Greenwood Press, 1954.

Yahweh ben Yahweh, *You Are Not A Nigger! Our True History, the World's Best Kept Secret: Yahweh God of Gods*. Pees Foundation, nd.

Zablocki, Benjamin and Thomas Robbins, eds. *Misunderstanding Cults: Searching for Objectivity in a Controversial Field*. Toronto, Buffalo, London: University of Toronto Press, 2001.

BIOGRAPHICAL SKETCH

Dr. Dawn L. Hutchinson is an Assistant Professor of Philosophy and Religious Studies for Christopher Newport University in Newport News, Virginia